**Praise for *The Secrets of Successful Adoptive Parenting***

'By far one of the best all-around adoption books I have ever read. I can feel the real-life, in the trenches experience of the author come through with deep wisdom and understanding. If there were an adoption parenting road map for establishing love and relationship in a home this is it. Please read and reread. Books at this level of true applicability and parenting guidance are rare.'

*– Bryan Post, www.postinstitute.com*

'Sophie Ashton has added to the rich literature by adopters for adopters. We know at Adoption UK how valuable the advice of experienced adopters is. Adoption transforms children's lives because adopters provide parenting that goes beyond what most parents have to deal with. Many adopted children and their families need and receive the support of professionals, what all benefit from is the wisdom and knowledge of those who have been there. Sophie's contribution is a valuable one and I can fully recommend this book.'

*– Hugh Thornbery, Chief Executive, Adoption UK*

'This is an essential book to prepare and accompany adoptive families and the professionals that support them for both pre and post adoption. The book offers a down to earth approach to managing the inevitable challenges and often trying situations that impact adoptive families. It is a well thought, well written and comprehensive 'adoption survival guide'. A highly recommended read.'

*– Inbar Sagiv, Integrative Child Psychotherapist (MA) and Social Worker (BA)*

'This is the most honest, sensitive and hands-on practical book I have ever read on how to successfully navigate the emotional challenges of adopting a child. This is not advice based on theory, it is an experiential account of what works. Not just in terms of preparation, but right through the long, long period of ups and downs, angst, fear, frustration, tears, love and adjustment to the dawning of a happy family unit. Sophie Ashton handles raw emotional and psychological issues involving the dynamics of the whole family head on. Her focus on building self-esteem and nurturing through the senses to develop the brain are crucial. Do not read The Secrets of Successful Parenting if you want a Disney perspective, this is a real book that, I believe, will become a reference book for many people wanting to adopt or have adopted a child.'

*– Dr Lynda Shaw, Cognitive Neuroscientist,*
*Fellow of the Royal Society of Medicine*

'This is a must-have guide of tried and tested success strategies that adoptive parents can continually refer to when experiencing overwhelming challenges and emotions. This book offers practical support and structure for facing inevitable (but often taboo) difficulties, helping adoptive parents to integrate their adoptive child in crucial aspects of development such as self-esteem and attachment. The real-life examples reassured me that, through effective communication and self-care, I could manage and face any difficulty. I was also reassured that my own responses to our adopted child were natural and encouraged to carry on in a well informed and positive way. This book is engaging, inspiring and relevant.'

*– Adoptive Mother, Buckinghamshire*

'Sophie has managed to do something unique: to simultaneously show the realities of adopting a child, and also give us lots of good ideas on how to make this happen successfully. As a potential gay adopter, I found the suggested games and activities very inspiring. Sophie obviously has lots of hands-on experience in this area, and does not approach the topic from a purely theoretical angle. This makes her book feel human, and the suggestions immediately applicable. Potential adoptive parents, as well as those for-ever parents who need some practical advice, would really benefit from reading this book.'

– *Mariano Tufro, Potential Adoptive Parent*

'I read this book whilst going through the adoption process myself, and it was the only one of many I read that gave practical solutions to real-life problem situations we might encounter with any adopted child. It is also the most candid about the feelings of frustration and bewilderment you may feel when dealing with your adopted child. The fact that it is written by somebody speaking from experience adds credibility to the advice being given. The book should serve as a source of inspiration and hope for those who are really struggling with their child and is proof that you can work through any difficulties and have your own happy ending. The emotional side of things is coupled with tried-and-tested methods for coping as adoptive parents, whilst also dealing with difficult children. If we are lucky to have a child placed with us I will definitely be using this book as an invaluable reference point, and I highly recommend it to anybody either going through the process or who has adopted already and is struggling with challenging situations.'

– *Lal Lister, Potential Adoptive Parent*

*of related interest*

**Parenting Adopted Teenagers**
**Advice for the Adolescent Years**
*Rachel Staff*
*Foreword by Hugh Thornbery*
ISBN 978 1 84905 604 5
eISBN 978 1 78450 069 6

**Keeping Your Adoptive Family Strong**
**Strategies for Success**
*Gregory C. Keck and L. Gianforte*
*Foreword by Rita L. Soronen*
ISBN 978 1 84905 784 4
eISBN 978 1 78450 028 3

**The Unofficial Guide to Adoptive Parenting**
**The Small Stuff, The Big Stuff and The Stuff In Between**
*Sally Donovan*
*Forewords by Dr Vivien Norris and Jim Clifford OBE and Sue Clifford*
ISBN 978 1 84905 536 9
eISBN 978 0 85700 959 3

**No Matter What**
**An Adoptive Family's Story of Hope, Love and Healing**
*Sally Donovan*
ISBN 978 1 84905 431 7
eISBN 978 0 85700 781 0

**Attaching Through Love, Hugs and Play**
**Simple Strategies to Help Build Connections with Your Child**
*Deborah D. Gray*
ISBN 978 1 84905 939 8
eISBN 978 0 85700 753 7

**Why Can't My Child Behave?**
**Empathic Parenting Strategies that Work for Adoptive and Foster Families**
*Dr Amber Elliott*
*Foreword by Kim S. Golding*
ISBN 978 1 84905 339 6
eISBN 978 0 85700 671 4

**Preparing for Adoption**
**Everything Adopting Parents Need to Know About Preparations, Introductions and the First Few Weeks**
*Julia Davis*
*Foreword by Hugh Thornbery*
ISBN 978 1 84905 456 0
eISBN 978 0 85700 831 2

# THE SECRETS OF SUCCESSFUL ADOPTIVE PARENTING

*Practical Advice and Strategies to Help with Emotional and Behavioural Challenges*

Sophie Ashton

Foreword by Bryan Post

Jessica Kingsley *Publishers*
London and Philadelphia

First published in 2016
by Jessica Kingsley Publishers
73 Collier Street
London N1 9BE, UK
and
400 Market Street, Suite 400
Philadelphia, PA 19106, USA

*www.jkp.com*



**Library of Congress Cataloging in Publication Data**
Names: Ashton, Sophie, 1966- author.
Title: The secrets of successful adoptive parenting : practical advice and strategies to help with emotional and behavioural challenges / Sophie Ashton.
Description: London ; Philadelphia : Jessica Kingsley Publishers, 2016.
Identifiers: LCCN 2016003863 | ISBN 9781785920783 (alk. paper)
Subjects: LCSH: Adoptive parents. | Parenting. | Adopted children.
Classification: LCC HV875 .A75 2016 | DDC 649/.145--dc23 LC record available at
http://lccn.loc.gov/2016003863

**British Library Cataloguing in Publication Data**
A CIP catalogue record for this book is available from the British Library

ISBN 978 1 78592 078 3
eISBN 978 1 78450 340 6

Printed and bound in the United States

*To all adoptive parents in the world.*
*Thank you for giving children a*
*second chance at a happy childhood.*

# CONTENTS

FOREWORD BY BRYAN POST 15
ACKNOWLEDGEMENTS 17
DISCLAIMER 19
A NOTE FROM THE AUTHOR 21
PREFACE 23

**Part One: Prepare for the Emotional Journey 31**

1. **Anticipate the Emotional Journey 33**
   You may not be as prepared as you think 34
   You may feel overwhelmed with mixed emotions 35
   Your emotions may be more intense if you have a birth child 37
   Feeling overwhelmed is natural 39
   Be reassured – you can tame the overwhelming feelings! 40
   It's natural to have initial regrets 42
   Let's break the taboo 43
   Create space for additional stress in your life 45
   Ask for help 47
   Summary 50

2. **Anticipate What May Cause You Frustration 53**
   Values drive behaviours 54
   Unacceptable behaviour in your eyes may be appropriate in your child's! 55
   Growing tension and frustration can lead to disruption of a placement 57
   Understand the root cause of challenging behaviours 58
   Don't get cross – get curious 63

Help your child learn new behaviours 65
Managing your frustration 67
Forgive yourself and move on 69
Summary 71

**Part Two: Parent with Empathy** **73**

**3. Understand Your Child** **75**
Learn about the triggers to your child's emotional state 76
Interpret behaviour with care 79
Acknowledge insecurities and fears 81
Learn through observation, interaction and discussion 88
Observe the clues 91
Assemble the clues 95
Follow the cues 97
Summary 100
References 101

**4. Facilitate Your Child's Memories and Emotions** **102**
Pace your child and help them move forwards 102
Put yourself in your child's shoes 104
Reinforce the permanence of their new situation 106
Narrative and metaphor will help your child process their life story 108
Your child's memory may be clear and confused 112
Validate and acknowledge your child's memories 114
Summary 117

**5. Support Your Child Through Their Grieving Process** **119**
The five stages of grief 120
'Denial' is the first stage of grief 121
'Anger' is the second stage of grief 123
'Bargaining' is the third stage of grief 125
'Depression' is the fourth stage of grief 127
'Acceptance' is the fifth stage of grief 131
Grief is not sequential 131
First foster carer visit 132
Summary 135
References 136

Part Three: Nurture with Compassion 137

6. Pay Back the Nurture Debt 139
Ensure the basic building blocks of nurture are in place 139
Don't underestimate the importance of paying back the nurture debt 151
Summary 152

7. Nurture Through the Senses for Brain Development 154
Brain development is influenced by early experiences 155
Develop your child through their sense of sight 157
Develop your child through their sense of hearing 159
Develop your child through their sense of touch 162
Develop your child through their sense of smell 164
Develop your child through their sense of taste 166
Summary 169
References 170

8. Build Your Child's Self-esteem and Facilitate Their Attachment 171
Delight in your child 172
Help your children experience the feeling of pride 173
Create the virtuous circle of delight 174
Emotionally connect with your child 176
Facilitate your child's attachment 179
Anticipate an uneven attachment 180
Beware the vicious circle of rejection 183
Summary 185

Part Four: Communicate Thoughtfully 187

9. Help Your Child Feel Listened To 189
Practise empathic listening 190
Improve your empathic listening skills 191
Listen to your child before expecting them to listen to you 194
Ground rules for helping your child feel 'listened to' 195
Summary 196
References 197

10. **Communicate with the Outcome in Mind** 198
Learn from your child's response and level of understanding 200
Manage your mood when communicating 201
Actively manage escalating emotions 204
Pause and ponder 206
Focus on the key words 210
Focus on what you want, not what you don't want 211
Forgive and move on 214
Reinforce your message with your style of delivery 216
Choose the best vehicle for the communication 218
Anticipate and communicate 221
When you say 'no' – mean it! 222
Summary 223

**Part Five: Enable Your Child's Development** 227

11. **Provide Structure and Consistency** 229
Introduce boundaries to guide behaviour 230
Sensible boundaries are made from a calm state 231
Develop routines to help your child feel secure 237
Combine boundaries and routine to provide structure 238
Reinforce the boundaries 245
Prepare for boundaries to be tested 249
Be consistent 252
Explain don't blame 254
Notice and encourage good behaviour 255
Motivate your child with appropriate rewards 258
Summary 262

12. **Close the Development Gap** 264
Help your child to develop through play 266
Develop your child through conversation 269
Enable a healthy body and a healthy mind 270
Summary 271

Part Six: Prepare Carefully for Your New Arrival 273

13. Involve Family and Friends 275
Prepare other children for the new arrival 275
Involve existing children in the practical preparation 278
Educate and involve significant people 279
Influence your friends and family just in case! 284
Summary 285
References 286

14. Plan for the Introductions and the Transition 287
The introductions can be emotionally challenging 288
Be prepared for any greeting 289
Have ideas of what to do with your child during the introductions 292
Anticipate the arrival of your child's belongings 293
Carefully manage your child's transition from their current home to yours 295
Plan your first few days 298
Summary 299

15. Carefully Integrate Your Child into Your Life 301
Help existing children manage the reality of a new sibling 302
Make time for existing children 302
Support your other children's emotional needs 304
Communicate, communicate, communicate! 308
Anticipate your child's support needs 308
Create opportunities for your child 311
Help the teachers to help your child 313
Instigate a home/school communication book 316
Anticipate potentially challenging topics at school 318
Remember to live your life! 319
Summary 322

FINAL WORDS 325
GLOSSARY 329
BIBLIOGRAPHY 333

# FOREWORD

The secrets are out and you've got them right in the palm of your hands!

But wait, they may not be quite what you imagine. Have you ever wondered how or why something becomes a secret? Usually what is being shared can be quite powerful – and this book is no exception.

Sophie Ashton learned the secrets to successful adoptive parenting the hard way and realised that though they weren't easy, they could provide the most honest and predictable path to true adoptive parenting success – and these secrets equally apply to foster and biological parenting.

Every social worker has an internal struggle when they meet a new potential foster or adoptive parent. The struggle is whether or not to reveal the true challenges that come along with fostering and adopting. Whether or not to disclose the emotional turmoil that the parents are likely to experience triggered by the sheer weight of a traumatised child's emotional demands. They hesitate to share this truth for fear that it may scare away the future adoptive parents, but it's the failure to share which creates the challenges that we later see.

Not sharing this truth results in potential parents buying into the fantasy of having a new child. Much the same as a child dreams of having a new puppy. They are permitted to go merrily down the yellow brick road towards the Oz of parenting. It sparkles and it gleams, for it is after all golden.

Future parents are allowed to believe that though these children have most likely come from 'difficult' early circumstances, a fair bit of tender loving care will be just what the doctor ordered to help soothe their sad souls. To help with their preparation the future parents attend classes and meetings and jump through hoops. They are offered basic parenting tools and ideas about how to care for such children. Such proffered tools, the same as have been offered for years, are woefully and predictably inadequate and simply not sufficient.

The outcome of not sharing the truth?

Frequent disruptions, broken homes, and both parents and children left devastated. This same devastation is equally shared in the U.S. where I reside. Two countries and both doing the same thing and expecting a different result. Yet, the outcomes remain the same, more placements than you would expect end in disruption than permanency.

And yet, there is hope.

This book speaks the hard truth while offering guidelines and new approaches to support parents themselves as well as the children as they transition through the challenges to become a stable and happy family unit.

Not only will the contents of this book prove life changing for adoptive parents but they can equally be utilised for improving adoption readiness programs and redefining some of the many myths we hold about what to and not to share with future adopters.

The secrets held within this book can still be elusive. Secrets are usually whispers so they are quiet. They are not loud, so listen my friend. Read with quiet intent and listen closely to that still small voice within you because the secrets held within this book can change your life and give you exactly what both you and your child have been needing.

Choose Love,
Bryan Post
www.postinstitute.com

# ACKNOWLEDGEMENTS

To my husband for his unfailing support over the 15 years it took us to build our family. Our road to parenthood was complex and challenging; I will love you forever for your belief in me, your patience during some very challenging times and for being a wonderful father and husband.

To both my children, who give me so much joy and whom I love beyond measure. You keep me grounded and remind me of what is important in life.

To my parents for your continued support, love, nurturing and encouragement. I love you.

Thank you to the social workers and child psychologists from social services and Child and Adolescent Mental Health Services (CAMHS) who reassured us in our parenting approach and gave us confidence to continue.

To my family for fanning the flame of my idea to write this book, for their continued interest, reviews, suggestions and to my brother and sister-in-law for their challenge in the form of a deadline for me to be brave enough to contact a publisher – without such a challenge I might still be polishing the draft version of this book.

To the adoptive families that shared their stories with me, thank you for sharing so openly, may you continue to go from strength to strength.

To the people who took time to review my draft and give me such insightful feedback and wonderful encouragement to help me on my way: AJ, AG, C and R, IS, LA, LL, LS, MT, PM and VJ.

To our social worker, who supported us throughout our journey. Thank you.

To my oldest and most treasured friend, JC, who always listens so well and finds a way to make me laugh. Thank you.

To AR, my friend, coach and counsel, thank you for your friendship, being there to listen and for giving me a good talking to whenever I need it.

And to my many other friends who support me and my family in so many ways – thank you all.

Finally, thank you to the authors who have made time to share their wisdom and insights so that we can all continue to learn and strive to be the best parents that we can be.

# DISCLAIMER

All the stories presented in this book are true. As promised to the parents, all names have been changed and some experiences have been mixed between children to protect their identities.

# A NOTE FROM THE AUTHOR

Hello, I am Sophie. I am a mother of two wonderful children, a birth son and an adopted daughter.

When our birth son was three years old, following years of heartache caused by infertility, my husband and I decided to expand our family through adoption. Four years later we had a little girl placed with us for adoption and it wasn't long until the challenges of integrating this little girl into our family started to hit home. At this time, I found that much of what I had learned in the course of my career combined with my experience of being a mother and the knowledge gleaned from an ever-growing pile of parenting and adoption-related books, guided us as we helped this little girl manage the transition from a challenging child to a much-cherished daughter.

Professionally I have spent 25 years working as a management consultant and an executive coach. I work with individuals and teams, helping people better understand themselves and each other and the impact they can and do unknowingly have on each other. By helping people improve their listening and communication skills, gain broader perspectives and interact in a more thoughtful way I am able to help people dissipate tension, resolve conflict, build effective relationships and ultimately help them achieve the successes that they desire. Over the years I have also worked as a volunteer with disadvantaged children through schools and through the criminal justice system, helping raise children's self-esteem and fill their time with productive activities that encourage them away from a path of delinquency.

If after reading this book, you would like more help and information please go to www.sophieashtonadoption.co.uk

# PREFACE

Becoming a parent is to start on an exciting and emotional journey. There are many ways to become a parent and each can have its challenges, but arguably one of the most challenging is becoming a parent through adoption of children who have been removed from their birth parents and placed into the care system.

As you have chosen to read this book, there is a high chance that you are somewhere on the journey to becoming an adoptive parent or are involved with adoptive parents in some capacity.

The primary purpose of this book is to alert adoptive parents to the emotional turmoil that may lie in store for them following placement of their child, to reassure them that this is a normal part of the process and to provide strategies to help them cope. As an adoptive parent, once you are able to understand and effectively manage your emotions you will be better able to parent a traumatised and potentially challenging child therapeutically, consistently and with love.

The secondary purpose of this book is to share parenting strategies and approaches that have helped others and may also help you as you support your child and help them make progress towards becoming a cherished family member able to achieve their potential.

As an adoptive parent, one of the challenges you may experience is managing your own potentially overwhelming emotions while at the same time striving to implement parenting strategies that help your child develop, feel secure and attach to you.

This is not a 'touchy-feely' book. It is a practical hands-on guide that offers tools and approaches to help you confidently take control of the emotional rollercoaster as well as your child's development until the highs and lows even out and you enter the realm of a happy, fulfilled and settled life with the new addition to your family firmly ensconced.

Unfortunately, some adoption placements do not work out as successfully as hoped, and either the parents struggle on with conflicting emotions, making little headway with integrating their child into their family, or in extreme cases, the child is handed back into care. When a child is handed back into care, this is called disruption of a placement. Adoption placements disrupt for many reasons including mismanaged expectations, undisclosed or unknown medical conditions and behavioural issues, to name a few. But there are also situations that look like a perfect match where it seems straightforward and the prospective parents appear well prepared, but due to the overwhelming and conflicting emotions that can accompany an adoptive placement, the adoptive parents feel debilitated to the point where disruption of the placement seems the only option.

This book is here to support all adoptive parents as they navigate the challenges of assimilating a 'looked after child' into their family to become one of their own. I hope this book will help prevent those instances where the adoption placement should work out but doesn't.

Through conscious anticipation you will, I hope, be better equipped to deal with the unexpected and powerful emotions that can accompany an adoption placement. By preparing more fully for these emotions, you will be better placed to support your child as they grieve for lost relationships and adapt to new expectations while beginning to feel secure, with an emerging sense of trust and self-worth, which can pave the way for secure attachments.

---

## Our story

Following eight years of unsuccessful fertility treatment, with everyone around us seemingly able to make babies with no effort, I finally fell pregnant with our son. After having our son, we tried unsuccessfully for a further three years of fertility treatment to conceive another child.

After 11 years focused on trying to have a baby, we decided to get off the fertility treadmill and be happy as a family of three. As content as we were, there was a gap. Both my husband and I wanted another child and our son spoke of wanting a little sister. We decided to look into adoption and we were all excited by the prospect.

After four long years in the adoption process anticipating, dreaming and longing for a daughter for us, a sister for our son and to be a 'forever family' to a little girl who needed a new family, a little girl was placed with us for adoption.

It had been an emotionally exhausting adoption journey for us, yet we were excited, upbeat and ready. Our daughter Lucy was coming; our family would be complete. We had read many adoption-related books and attended numerous courses, we felt totally prepared for Lucy's arrival. Indeed, we were told that we were the best prepared couple the adoption matching panel had ever seen. Life was great and was about to get better!

Within the first few days of Lucy moving in with us, it became apparent that assimilating her into our family was going to be much more challenging than we had anticipated. We had read Lucy's background information through rose-tinted glasses, from a position of optimism, hope and excitement. In reality Lucy's challenges and behaviours were more severe than indicated in her information and the impact on our previously serene life was much bigger than we had anticipated.

We experienced a maelstrom of unanticipated emotions, which in the short term felt threatening, debilitating and caused us some panic. We soon found ourselves feeling overwhelmed and understanding – *really* understanding – why some children placed into families with a view to adoption actually get handed back before the adoption order is made.

The theory we had gleaned from experts through books and courses helped us understand Lucy but hadn't helped us anticipate the conflicting and overwhelming emotions we were experiencing that were so challenging. If we couldn't manage our emotions, putting in place any parenting theory didn't seem possible!

Our challenges with Lucy were significant. Taming our emotions, managing our mind-set and being consistent in our approach with Lucy supported us through the rough patches, to a place of stability where we now find ourselves a happy and settled family. Lucy is settled, our family is settled. Lucy completes our family, we all love her and cannot imagine life without her. Life before Lucy was great – but life now, with Lucy is better.

---

Following our experience, we learned of many families that experienced anguish in those first few lonely months following the placement of their child. Some of those families pushed through the emotional pain and frustration and are now happily settled as a new family unit with their adopted child well integrated into their family; others, however, ended up with disruption of the placement and handing the child back to the authorities.

Whatever wisdom and advice this book offers has been learned the hard way. When we made mistakes we reflected on what we could have done differently and we adapted. Our biggest lesson is that being an effective parent involves more than just the capacity to 'love'. There are skills that we each can learn to help us become better parents and to become more emotionally resilient. Parenting is part intuition and gut feel, but there are definite skills and approaches that can be learnt to help you manage situations that you probably can't even imagine at this point. Remember though, there is no such thing as a perfect parent, and it is very easy for us to feel guilty that we could and should be doing better. The fact that you are reading this book already sets you apart as a parent who is willing to consider other ideas and to learn from the experience of others.

I believe that if you consciously parent in a way that helps your child develop the fundamental feelings of trust, attachment, security and self-esteem, you will pave the way for their successful development and so will enable them to have the best chance to become all that they can be.

So whether you are an adoptive parent or a potential adoptive parent, or whether you support the adoption process, children or parents in some other capacity, you may take useful thoughts from this book. I hope to help you better understand the emotional challenges that accompany adoption and to develop some approaches to help you deal with situations you may face.

## Meet the children

Over the years, I have spoken with many adoptive parents who have shared some of their adoption related experiences with me. Some of their experiences were really challenging, others much less so. In addition to our daughter Lucy, I have purposely used experiences from five of the families who had the most challenges, to help illustrate some of my thoughts. In all cases, I have changed the names of the children and mixed up some of their experiences, to protect their identity.

**Bethany** was the youngest of five siblings all taken into care. Her elder siblings were placed in pairs with other foster families. Bethany witnessed and experienced violent behaviour in her birth family and was mistreated by her elder siblings. Bethany was placed in foster care with different siblings, but none of the combinations worked out, resulting in her moving between foster families a few times. She was eventually placed for adoption without her siblings. Bethany was placed into foster care when she was three years old and arrived at her permanent adoptive placement when she was almost five years old.

**Donna** experienced serious neglect and malnourishment with her birth family. As she was the first child born to her birth parents, the family was not known to social services, and as a consequence the neglect went undetected until she was two and a half years old, at which point she was removed from their care and placed with a foster family. The birth parents contested the removal and went to parenting classes, determined that Donna should be returned to them. Donna was briefly returned to her birth parents but they were unable to sustain appropriate levels of care for her, so she was returned to foster care with the longer-term plan for adoption. Donna was four and a half when she was placed into an adoptive family.

**Jayden** was found wandering along the side of a relatively busy road in the countryside. Jayden's family was found to be from a travelling community who were passing through the area. Jayden's parents said that he had wandered off without them noticing. Jayden insists he was made to get out of the car by his daddy. Either way, the events led him to be taken into care. Jayden spent a total of 18 months in foster care with three different foster families. He was placed with his foster family just after his fourth birthday.

**Connor and Ben** are brothers who were removed from their birth mother at ages three and almost two, respectively. The mother had been known to the authorities since Connor was born as she was struggling to care for him. Once Ben came along she struggled even more and, despite all the help and support offered to her by the authorities, she was not able to provide a clean and safe home environment for the boys.

**Grace** was removed from her birth parents at the age of two and a half due to the inability of her parents to recognise the risk to their daughter of leaving her in the care of their extended family. On both sides of the family were uncles and grandparents who had convictions for sexual offences against minors. Both parents had been sexually abused during their childhood by their relatives, were developmentally delayed and unable to recognise the dangers involved with allowing their extended family to look after their daughter. Grace moved into her adoptive home when she was three and a half years old.

## How to use this book

This book is split into six parts that will help you anticipate and prepare both emotionally and practically for your new arrival. Each section has a number of chapters, the content of which builds on information previously discussed, so the logical way to read this book is to work your way through from front to back. Each chapter concludes with a summary presented in bulletpoint format with the key messages from the chapter. If you are limited for time, you may choose to read the chapter summaries, and then dip into those chapters that address your immediate need; however, you may miss out on the richness of the content if you use this approach.

If you are in the throes of being matched with a child and the introduction period or arrival of your child is imminent, go straight to Part Six, where there is practical advice on how to actively manage the introductions and the transition of your child into your home and family. Once you have read this section, put aside time as soon as you can to then read through Parts One to Five.

At the end of the book, there is a section on suggestions for further reading and a glossary that explains some of the terms common in the world of adoption, which if you are new to the process may be unfamiliar to you. Any direct references in the text are given in detail at the end of each chapter.

Please note: the term 'parent' can refer to birth parent, foster parent or indeed adoptive parent. As the adoptive parent is the focus of this book, and will most probably be the most active parent in the life of an adopted child, for the purposes of this book if I ever use the term 'parent' as a standalone noun, I am referring to the adoptive parent.

PART ONE

# Prepare for the Emotional Journey

*Without conscious consideration, it is unlikely you will be prepared to handle the quantity and the variety of emotions that may accompany the placement of your child. Some emotions will challenge you and take you to depths you have not imagined, and there will be others that delight you and give you feelings of unimagined fulfilment. Your adopted child will be experiencing a cocktail of emotions as well. While you are juggling and managing your emotions, you have to find a way to help your child to process theirs while encouraging them to develop feelings of attachment for you. The first few weeks and months may well be the most emotional for all concerned.*

CHAPTER 1

# Anticipate the Emotional Journey

***WARNING: this chapter is brutally honest about what you may feel when your adopted child is placed with you. Please do not be put off by this chapter. The rest of the book will empower you to get through this phase, should you experience it, and into a much happier place.***

Having gone through the journey of becoming an adoptive parent, and having spoken to many others, some of whom have succeeded and some who have not, I have come to realise that the enormity of the emotional challenge that accompanies such an undertaking is often underestimated.

My intent with this chapter is to help you become fully aware of the emotional challenges that may lie in wait for you and to help you prepare. I don't want you to be caught unawares as we were, and as a result, stray from one of the most potentially rewarding endeavours of your life.

'Forewarned is forearmed.' With some conscious emotional preparation you will be much better placed to survive the waves of emotion and focus on helping your child settle into your family, so achieving the vision of your family for the future.

## You may not be as prepared as you think

The adoption approval process involves a kaleidoscope of emotions and somewhere in the mix, as you attend your matching panel, will be relief that you have finally got this far, excitement about meeting your child, along with some apprehension about the unknown. The predominant feeling that results, however, is generally more positive than negative – which makes sense, otherwise we probably wouldn't continue!

Most first-time adopters don't have children and, therefore, will probably not have had the experience of caring for a child 24/7. Adopters with birth children may assume that their parenting experience will help them parent an adopted child, and in some ways it will. However, parenting an adopted child can be very different to parenting a birth child when dealing with all of the complexities involved, not to mention the additional emotional dynamics that will be present in those families with birth children.

As part of the adoption approval process, you will be asked to anticipate various situations and describe what you might feel or how you might handle these situations. At best, without having experienced the situations before, you can only guess. As long as seemingly well-considered answers are given to the probing questions, the adoption process will swiftly move on. You can answer the question as a theoretical situation without actually having any sense of what it will be like to experience the emotions that go along with the situation. Also, it is human nature to be optimistic and confident and not want to focus too much on the negative feelings for fear that they might make you reconsider your decision to adopt.

It is very easy to get swept up in the practical aspects of the adoption process: the various training courses, the social worker assessment, the initial panel meeting; searching for and finding your child, the matching panel and then planning for the arrival of your child. You will be thinking about the immediate hurdles, and asking yourself: 'What questions might we get asked at panel?', 'How should we respond?', 'What does the panel want to hear?', 'How can we demonstrate the amount of preparation we have done?', 'Which child will suit us best?', 'What can we learn about the potential challenges our child may face?'

We experienced the adoption approval process to be very thorough in vetting us as suitable parents, but in hindsight it was quite light-touch on helping us prepare for the onslaught of emotions that was waiting for us once our daughter was placed. We had not considered that we may experience challenging, overwhelming and debilitating emotions following the placement of our child. In speaking to many other adoptive families since, I realise we are not alone in our lack of emotional preparation, or the feelings we had once our child arrived.

Keeping busy with the practical demands and the intellectual side of the approval process can leave little space to engage with the potential emotional aspects. Being engulfed in an emotion caused by a situation may bring about different reactions from those you had anticipated when you were simply thinking about what your emotions may be, from the comfort of a detached perspective.

## You may feel overwhelmed with mixed emotions

In reality, despite their best efforts, there is no way that social workers can help adoptive parents to anticipate the exact emotions they will feel in response to the placement of their child. What may help, however, is helping potential adopters realise that it is impossible to fully anticipate what life will be like with an adopted child and to appreciate that it is *normal* to experience intense conflicting emotions that may challenge their motivation to continue down the adoption path they have chosen.

## Prepare for emotional free-fall

My husband and I considered ourselves thoroughly prepared for the placement of a little girl. We had read lots of books, been on many training courses and, already having a son, we felt confident in our parenting. We felt more than ready. Yet only two weeks into the placement we had never felt so unready for anything in our entire lives! We started drowning in a sea of emotions that we just had not anticipated. We had thought through just about every scenario we might face and had planned how to handle all of them – in that regard we were very prepared. However, we were taken by surprise by the potency of the cocktail of emotions that accompanied handling the situations about which we had only theorised.

We felt a scramble of emotions in the weeks after our daughter arrived, in which we flipped between positive and negative, resourceful and unresourceful, fulfilled and depressed. The emotions could change from hour to hour or day to day. My husband and I could experience the same emotion at the same time, in which case the impact was magnified, or we could be at completely different ends of the emotional spectrum, which caused tension. My husband, our son and I all experienced our daughter differently and, therefore, had different associated feelings generated by our responses. We also experienced emotions as a response to each other's reactions to our daughter. So there were layers upon layers of emotions that we had not anticipated and so many feelings flying around that it was exhausting.

While feeling hopeful for, and protective of Lucy, we were at the same time hugely protective of and worried for our son and the huge impact that the situation was having on his life. We felt angry with the care system that had allowed her to languish in foster care for far too long and angry at her birth family for subjecting her to awful early life experiences, the results of which we were now seeing on a daily basis.

At night after we had managed to settle our daughter to bed, waves of panic would engulf us as we realised the enormity of the challenge we had taken on, not to mention the potential impact of the decision we had made, on us, our son and our family as a whole.

We had spent so many years preparing for adoption intellectually and progressing steadily through the adoption approval process, that at some level we had expected our family to expand and absorb a new member with minimal pain. When speaking with friends and family we had been excited and upbeat and they had been excited for us. We had dwelled only on the positives, so when the challenges came, although we had discussed them hypothetically, the reality of the emotional onslaught that accompanied them was almost overwhelming and we felt isolated and lonely.

None of the adoptive parents that we had spoken to during our preparation had ever mentioned experiencing the challenging emotions that were so prevalent for us. We were very confused. We felt that we were alone in experiencing these emotions and that maybe the adoption placement wasn't progressing as it should. We realise now that it is not uncommon to feel overwhelmed by the onslaught of emotions following the placement of a child. Had we realised this at the time, we would have been more prepared and reassured that this overwhelming state was only temporary.

---

## Your emotions may be more intense if you have a birth child

Not everyone feels overwhelmed but there is an increased chance that you will do if you already have birth children and are planning to adopt a child from the care system. The natural instinct is to protect your family unit, especially existing children, from negative influences and harm. If the child you choose to adopt is particularly challenging in the early weeks, you may feel an overwhelming urge to protect your existing family unit.

Your first experience of having a child may have been uncomplicated, you may have fallen in love with your child at first sight, and from the moment you met them you would have gladly laid down your life for them. This may not be so for your adopted child.

---

### Our emotions almost got the better of us

We had an expectation that we would fall in love with our adopted daughter at first sight, and that we would feel the same intensity of love for her that we did for our son. In hindsight this seems completely unrealistic and naive, but none of the adoption preparation modules led us to think about what we might feel for our adopted daughter when we first met, so we had assumed it would be love at first sight, which it wasn't. Added to all of the other challenging emotions, we felt guilty for not loving this little girl straight away, we were convinced she deserved better.

Add into this mix our little boy, seven years old, who was thrust into the middle of a tornado of emotions and challenging behaviours. In hindsight he was coping excellently, far better than my husband and I, but in the early weeks we wanted to make his life simple and calm again.

At times, we felt depressed, isolated with our emotions, guilty for having negative feelings and ashamed that although we thought we were thoroughly prepared, in reality we weren't coping emotionally. Lucy was four years old when she arrived at our home. She was confused and missed her foster carers so much that we also felt guilty for having taken her away from them.

We almost managed to convince ourselves that our daughter would be happier back with her foster family than being adopted by us!

---

## Feeling overwhelmed is natural

In the midst of our emotional turmoil, we reached out to the adoptive parents with whom we had spoken during our adoption preparation, especially those with birth children. We were hugely reassured to hear that many of them had experienced all the overwhelming feelings that we were experiencing! The panic, the confusion, the guilt – all of it! Apparently it is a natural part of the process that some people experience – but no one had thought to mention it to us.

We wish we had known. I believe we would have felt much better prepared for the reality if we had known such feelings were a possibility. We would have taken reassurance from knowing that what we were experiencing was a normal part of the process and it would have removed an element of the feeling of panic that we found so debilitating, not to mention exhausting.

We understood intellectually that our family would have to stretch and grow to accommodate another child. What we hadn't fully appreciated was the discomfort that we would have to endure as our family unit adapted to include another child. Stretching your emotions to absorb another human being into your life and family, especially a child rather than a baby, and especially if you already have children, is a huge undertaking. Like childbirth, the process can hurt, but it is absolutely worth it!

## Be reassured – you can tame the overwhelming feelings!

We recognised that we were feeling stressed, overwhelmed and panicked, and while feeling those emotions we were not able to think clearly. We knew we had to tame our emotions, and so we consciously took control of our mind and emotions in four ways.

1. When we felt frustrated, we consciously accessed compassion instead. We reminded ourselves that at the centre of this turmoil was a little girl who had asked for none of this; she just had the misfortune to be born to a family ill-prepared to meet her needs, where she remained far longer than she should have done, and then was moved to live with foster carers who loved her and looked after her, but had not provided structure or encouraged her development. Our daughter was very much the product of her experiences to date and presented as a four-year-old toddler when she was placed with us. We realised that any frustration we felt in response to this little girl's behaviour was not originally of her making and this enabled us to feel compassionate towards her, rather than frustrated in response to her.
2. When we felt overwhelmed we imagined a future where we had given up and handed this little girl back to the care system. We imagined how we would feel, what our son would think and feel. We anticipated we would feel forever sad and regretful of the events and of the negative impact that we would have had on an already blighted life. We also realised that from that future perspective the current experiences we were finding so challenging and overwhelming wouldn't seem so bad. We realised that being in the 'thick of it' was awful, but getting some perspective and looking in on it from the outside – momentarily it didn't seem quite as bad.

These brief emotional respites were like a miracle tonic and gave us the energy to dig deep and carry on.

3. When the future looked bleak, we consciously created a strong, positive, fulfilling, inspiring and engaging vison about how great our life would be when we had succeeded. We mentally painted our vision of the future of our happy family, with our daughter well settled, all relationships positive and how fulfilling and rewarding our lives would be when we were all settled. We discussed it, shared it and allowed this to create new and more resourceful feelings that inspired us to continue.
4. When we questioned what we were doing, we reminded ourselves of the reasons we wanted to adopt a little girl. We reflected on what we hoped to achieve for her, for our son and for ourselves. We found that checking in regularly with the motivation behind our decisions re-energised us, filled us with hope and gave us the determination to continue.

These four conscious interventions helped us regain control of our emotions and gave us the strength and fortitude to continue. They may also help you. We referred to these four steps frequently.

---

### Making progress and growing together

So we continued day by day, hour by hour and sometimes interaction by interaction. Progress was slow at first, with any semblance of normal family life seeming an ever-moving target. But little by little, together we made progress as we all learned to live together and to love each other. Our daughter changed a lot as she grew to trust us and to attach to us, and as a family unit we changed as well, as we integrated our daughter and became a family unit of four.

Now, three years on, our life is as rewarding and as fulfilling as we hoped it would be. We adore our daughter, she completes our family and we cannot imagine life without her. It scares us to think that had we not been so resilient and determined to succeed, the negative feelings that overwhelmed us *may* have caused us to give up and hand our daughter back to the care system.

---

We are in the position now of fully understanding that all of the challenging emotions and feelings of panic we had in the early weeks and months were a normal part of the process, and that the approach we took in helping our daughter settle and progress worked for us.

## It's natural to have initial regrets

Having been through the adoption process and run the gamut of emotions from beginning to end, going in as a happy family of three and coming out as a fabulous family of four, and having spoken to many adoptive parents who have also gone through the emotional turmoil and emerged at the other side more positive, I have some reassuring news for you. To feel these challenging mixed emotions is to be human. It is completely natural and normal to:

- question the sanity of your decision to adopt
- wish at times that you hadn't entered into the adoption process
- yearn for your old uncomplicated life
- feel panicked and overwhelmed
- worry that you may never love your child.

Many more positive emotions are waiting for you once you weather the initial emotional storm, as is a hugely rewarding and immensely enjoyable life with your adopted child. Feelings of amusement, fondness, caring, worry, admiration, respect, awe and love, as well as many other positive and rewarding emotions will come with time.

## Let's break the taboo

As it is so normal to feel the emotional overwhelm, I am confused as to why it is such a taboo subject. The more we can talk about it as being normal, the more we could offer support to those people in the midst of overwhelming feelings, and the more those people would feel supported as they navigated successfully through the challenges to the other side.

As adoptive parents, we strive for many years to achieve our goal of having a child placed with us for adoption. We have been enthusiastic and upbeat to our friends who have supported us through the process. We have been diligent and strong to prove to the social workers that we are fit parents to handle the complications of parenting a child from the care system. To then admit to feeling overwhelmed, panicked and fearful may feel like admitting a huge weakness and admitting that we feel like a failure.

It would help break the taboo if anyone involved in the preparation and support of adoptive families could encourage the discussion of feelings more openly. This might make it easier for adoptive families to share their true feelings. If it were naturally part of the discussion regarding what they may expect, adoptive parents would know that whatever they are feeling is probably appropriate and that the only way is forwards. Once adoptive families share their true feelings, it would be easier to help them find the support they need. They may just need someone to talk to, who can reassure them that what they are feeling is natural.

## Disruption due to overwhelming emotions

One couple I spoke to had a six-year-old birth daughter and had a three-year-old boy placed with them for adoption. This little boy had no significant issues, was meeting all of his milestones and had come from a supportive foster care family. All was set to go smoothly.

However, the sense of doubt and panic started during the introduction process and persisted into the first week of the little boy moving in. Their birth daughter and the little boy seemed to get on very well, but the adoptive mother felt resentment of the time her husband got to spend with their daughter while she was playing with and taking care of the little boy. Soon both the adoptive mum and her husband were feeling an intense mixture of confusing emotions that they were struggling to sort out. They felt guilty as they didn't instantly love the little boy, and couldn't ever imagine loving him in the same way they loved their birth daughter. They didn't know what they wanted, didn't understand what they were feeling and couldn't see an end to feeling overwhelmed.

When the little boy had been with them for almost two weeks, they were in the thick of the emotional overload, didn't feel able to think straight, couldn't sort out the negative emotions that had taken them by surprise and they asked for the little boy to be taken back into care.

Months later the mother was still reeling from the experience, and was wondering what had gone wrong. In hindsight she couldn't remember the intensity of the overwhelming emotions, and questions whether they made the correct decision in handing the little boy back. She feels that as a family they could have persevered, sought help and worked through the emotions.

The whole situation above is regretful and damaging both to the adoptive family and to the little boy, who may now be harder to place as he has one failed placement behind him.

## Create space for additional stress in your life

Adoption is a life-changing experience, for you as well as your adopted child, and it is not going to be 'stress free'. Anticipate that there will be some stress introduced into your life by your new bundle of joy! As human beings, we can cope with quite a lot of stress but not infinite levels. Listen to your social workers when they advise you to minimise the other stressors that you have in your life at the time of placement and for the next few months. Create some capacity in your life for some extra stress.

Also be aware that you never know what is round the corner! When our daughter was placed with us, I was due to take a year off work and be a stay-at-home mum until she started school. However, two months after she arrived, my husband's work situation changed and, as a consequence, I went back to work part-time. You never know when your personal situation will change or a loved one may get sick; life is full of surprises good and bad.

One adoptive mum I spoke to had the tragic situation of her own father being diagnosed with cancer two days after a sibling group was placed with her. She and her family then had to cope with her father's rapid decline and death six weeks after her children moved in.

It really is important to pay attention to the stressors in your life and to minimise and control what you can, so that you have bags of extra capacity for your new arrival and any unforeseen circumstances that may crop up.

---

**Disruption due to escalating stress**

I spoke to another couple who had two school age birth children and had a two-year-old girl placed with them for adoption. They explained that as they had little control over the timing of the arrival of the little girl, and against the advice of their social worker, they felt they had no choice but to continue with their house renovation, which started soon after she moved in.

The mother was also juggling part-time work, school runs, after school clubs and homework of their birth children. The father was managing a stressful job as well as continuing with other commitments that took him out of the house a few evenings a week. Much of the stress of managing the little girl fell to the adoptive mum.

The relationship became strained between the husband and wife and eventually there was too much stress to cope with, the placement disrupted and the little girl was handed back into care after 10 months with the family, never having been officially adopted. A year on and the adopted mum still regretted the whole chain of events and, in hindsight, acknowledged that they didn't create the necessary space to accommodate the addition of another person to their family by reducing their other stressors.

---

In order that you are able to give the levels of physical and emotional energy to meet the needs of your adopted child in the early months you do need to find ways to reduce the other stressors in your life and recharge your own batteries. Don't feel selfish, put time aside for you. Go out with your friends occasionally, build in time to go for a run or a walk, or whatever it is that is just for you. Identify whatever it is that continues to make you feel normal and be sure to build it into your life. You may consider it a challenge to achieve this, but you may find life more of a challenge if you don't.

The adopters with whom I spoke all mentioned how important they consider it to have some respite in terms of time to go the gym, for a run/walk or to visit with friends. Not all managed to achieve it, but all felt it was extremely important. Some suggested getting a trusted babysitter early on that can step in and help out to give you real time off. All these activities were considered essential in managing stress, emotions and helping build reserves of patience. Not all of the adopters with whom I spoke did get precious respite time, but those who didn't, wished in hindsight that they'd planned for it.

## Ask for help

There may be times of the day after your child has moved in when you feel your energy and your patience are at their lowest, you feel at your least resourceful and you may wish you had some extra help. If this is the case, ask for it. It may be that your emotions are bubbling out of control and you simply need some help in the form of someone to talk to. Ask your friends and family to listen. You may just need a couple of hours' break to take a walk, do some exercise or simply have a cup of tea. Ask your friends and family to be with your child to give you a break. You will have identified people to be in your support network for a reason; you'll need their help, ask them; they'll want to help, let them.

---

### My low-energy time

I quickly became aware of my 'times of low energy', soon after my husband returned to work following his two-week adoption leave. With my husband at work and my son at school I was alone all day with Lucy, managing her behaviour, anticipating and meeting her needs and helping her to learn to trust me. After parenting Lucy all day on my own, and having done the school runs, after school clubs and homework with our son, by the time the children's bedtime came around I was wrung out emotionally and physically.

Bedtime was initially a tricky time for Lucy, she didn't like being left alone and she missed the familiarity of her foster carers. I quickly became aware that I didn't have the necessary energy reserves at that time of day to meet her needs in the way that she desperately needed and deserved. After some fraught evenings of challenging behaviour and tears – mine as well as hers – my husband managed to rearrange his work commitments to get home in time for the bath and bedtime routine and attend to our daughter's needs with energy reserves that I just didn't have left at that time of the day.

For us this worked really well, and over a period of a few weeks my husband managed to bring down Lucy's angst around bedtime to levels that I could cope with given the energy reserves I had left at the end of the day. At the same time, the structure and nurturing I was providing during the day resulted in the days being less demanding, and so I was able to parent effectively throughout the day from dawn until dusk and still have enough energy left for our son after Lucy had gone to bed.

---

If you don't have the additional support immediately to hand, for example, if you are a single adopter, then make sure you prepare your support network to lend a hand or be at the end of the phone when you need it. It is essential to have some form of physical and/or emotional support to help you cope during that portion of the day when you have less energy, less patience and are feeling emotionally drained. Don't wait until you can't cope before you ask for help – enlist the help before it gets that far. Don't wait until you are exhausted to sit down and take a break. Force yourself to sit down when you can for a few minutes here and there to let your batteries recharge. Sometimes you may not need practical support, you may just need a friendly ear to offload to.

---

### Ten friendly ears

Once every couple of months five friends and I try to meet up for dinner. The scheduled day for our next dinner happened to be two weeks to the day after Lucy had moved in. I was determined to go, despite the whirlwind occurring in our home. I was a little late as I wanted to know that Lucy was settled in bed before I left. When I arrived to the restaurant my five friends were deep in discussion and enjoying catching up with each other.

When they saw me arrive all conversation stopped as they waited eagerly to hear my news. They had heard nothing from me since the day of the matching panel and they knew that Lucy had moved in two weeks ago and they were eager to hear how it was going. I was struck by the normality of the scene: my five friends and I, having a regular and fun catch up. But it wasn't the same – my world had changed in a major way – my life was so different now from the way it had been just a few weeks before. I had walked into a pocket of normality and I wanted to hang on to it for a little bit longer, and so I encouraged them to continue with their conversations and I just sat at the edge of the discussions and observed.

Soon though, their current conversations had run their course and all eyes turned to me. I knew what they wanted to hear: that it was wonderful, all was going well and smoothly, that we adored Lucy, we felt blessed, it was easy, life was great – but I couldn't. When one of my friends finally asked me how it was going, I could find no words and so I simply burst into tears.

Once I'd sobbed for a minute or two, I explained how overwhelmed I was feeling, how I had no time for my son, how my emotions were all mixed up and how Lucy was such hard work, and how exhausted I was. My friends listened, and they listened some more. Finally, when I had run out of things to say, they shared their own stories about how overwhelmed they felt when they had their first and then second, sometimes third and fourth child. How emotional, how conflicted, sometimes resentful they felt, and of how hard it was for them too. I knew that their challenges were different to mine but they were still challenges, exhausting emotional challenges, and having them all listen to me and then share their stories really helped.

After I had given vent to my feelings of exhaustion and conflicting emotions I found myself talking about Lucy, how brave she was, how much she had been through in her short life, what this change of family must be like for her, her little quirks, and how she had on occasion made us laugh, and actually some of the positive changes we had already seen in her behaviour. I found myself taking a different perspective and feeling protective and compassionate and proud of this new little girl who had turned our life upside down.

For a few hours that evening I'd stepped back into normality, reconnected with some friends, managed to broaden my perspective and got strength to continue. That evening was like a tonic, I returned home feeling less isolated, more balanced and knowing that I was not the only person to feel challenging emotions in response to the arrival of a child, no matter where they had come from!

---

## Summary

★ Although it is not much talked about, welcoming another child with challenges into your home will create a whirlwind of emotions that it is almost impossible to predict. Although the adoption preparation process will have helped prepare you a little, it is easy to pay lip service to the emotional preparation, to think you are prepared and only realise you are unprepared when the onslaught of challenging emotions hits you after your child has moved in.

★ Some people ride the wave of challenging emotions until they enter calmer waters, other people consider that it is abnormal and take it as a sign that the adoption placement is not meant to be, and so wheels are put in motion that can lead to disruption of the placement. In all cases, better emotional anticipation and expectation will help prepare you for situations that you will then be better able to handle.

★ Feeling overwhelmed by the reality of assimilating another child into your life is completely normal. Even more so, when the child in question has had negative life experiences and has not been fully nurtured. Expecting to feel overwhelmed, and having plans in place with how to cope with this, would help reduce the feelings of frustration, and ease the journey through the overwhelming emotions into stability.

★ Strive to access compassion rather than frustration. Imagine how you will feel in the future if you do give up. When you look back to now from the future, will it really seem as bad as it seems now? Develop a bright and compelling vision of your family's future, which includes your adopted child. Cling onto this vision and the belief that it can happen. Remind yourselves of the reasons you wanted to adopt originally. Feel the desire to adopt. Don't allow your original motivations to be obliterated by the current maelstrom of emotions.

★ Creating space in your life for additional stress; recognising that these feelings of panic and overwhelm are quite normal; and getting support from family and friends, social services and other people that have been through similar experiences will help you get through the rough emotional waters and into the calm.

★ Realise that you may have less energy and patience than needed at certain times to meet the demands of parenting your adopted child. Build in some respite or some support to help you cope with these times.

★ Don't isolate yourself in your home for the months after your child arrives, make time in the early weeks to reconnect with normal situations outside your home and with friends – you will draw strength from reconnecting with the outside world.

CHAPTER 2

# Anticipate What May Cause You Frustration

To prepare yourself more thoroughly for the emotions that could overwhelm you upon arrival of your child into your home, it is useful to go back to basics and consider your fundamental beliefs regarding what is important to you in family life. Many people have never taken the time to do this. One of the areas in which you may be able to prepare more fully is to better understand yourself and what may cause you stress and frustration when your child gets placed with you. One common facet of being human is that we all have values. Our values may differ, but we all have values that when offended can cause us feelings of frustration.

Values can be a nebulous topic and I didn't find them discussed much, if at all, in the adoption books I read when we were going through the adoption approval process. For me, however, values are right up there. The more we can understand about our values, what is important to us and non-negotiable in family life, the more we can understand ourselves and anticipate what our feelings might be in response to certain situations. The more we observe the behaviours of our adopted children, the more we can learn about the values they have learnt in early life. One of the great causes of frustration is when we experience a clash of values with another person. This frustration can be huge if the clash of values is with our child.

My intent with this chapter is to help pique your interest in the importance of values, to help you anticipate your emotions in response to certain situations and to make plans for how to manage those emotions. I'd like you to consider that your child's behaviour is an expression of their values, which have evolved as a result of their early experiences. I believe that your child's values and behaviours can change to be more in line with the norms of your family in response to demonstrative, thoughtful and well-considered parenting by you.

## Values drive behaviours

Values are principles or qualities that at some level we consider to be important. We can experience shame or frustration with ourselves if we behave in ways that go against our own values, and we can get impatient and frustrated with others if they act in a way that disregards or offends those values that are important to us.

Our values and beliefs develop over time from a very early age as we observe the behaviours and decisions made by those close to us. As we grow up in different families with unique influences and experiences, the values that we develop and the resulting behaviours that we exhibit may also vary.

People from different walks of life, different extended family groupings and different cultures may live their lives in line with different values and therefore might demonstrate some behaviours which, although acceptable to them, are considered unacceptable by others.

Many children taken into care are born into families that raise their children in line with values that are considered acceptable and appropriate within their family group, but inappropriate and unacceptable in wider society. I realise this is a sensitive topic and that some children are taken into care through no fault of their parents, however, to illustrate what I mean, families that have had children removed may, for example:

- allow young children out late at night unsupervised and open to negative influences
- provide a poor diet or no diet at all
- leave children on their own at a very young age for long periods of time, unsupervised
- groom children for sex
- act in physically, mentally or sexually abusive ways towards their children
- expose their vulnerable children to harmful situations, substances or people.

Parents who behave in this way are not observing the same values that seem normal in our society. Many of these parents were themselves parented in this way, which led them to develop the values held and behaviours demonstrated by their parents.

## Unacceptable behaviour in your eyes may be appropriate in your child's!

When you observe your child exhibit a behaviour you do not favour, or that offends your sense of what is appropriate or not, i.e. your values, don't assume they are being naughty, or wilfully misbehaving – it is more likely that they are exhibiting a behaviour that was considered normal or acceptable in a former part of their life. Understanding this may help reduce some of the disappointment, frustration or anger you experience in response to your child's behaviour.

The following story is the first story about Bethany. Please refer back to the 'Meet the children' section in the Preface to understand more about Bethany's start in life.

---

### Spitting when angry

Bethany would spit on people when she was angry and frustrated with them. She found it hard to express her frustration verbally and easier just to spit! She would get even crosser when told off for spitting. It wasn't until she was settled in her adoptive home that she shared that her birth parents and older siblings used to spit on her when they were cross or annoyed with her. It seemed to makes sense that she therefore learned this behaviour from them. In her birth family this is how she was taught to show anger and frustration. When the adoptive family realised this, the frustration they had been experiencing as a result of her spitting behaviour immediately dissolved and they felt compassion for her. The adoptive parents helped Bethany learn new ways of showing that she was angry. To start with, the easiest way was simply for her to yell 'I'M ANGRY WITH YOU!', which was much easier to handle and respond to calmly compared with being spat at.

---

This story reminded me of an incident I observed one chilly Saturday morning as I dropped my then six-year-old son at his football team training. I was shocked to observe one boy shrinking at the edge of the car park as his parents were screaming at each other in a very heated argument. The shouting ended with the boy's mother spitting in the most shocking manner on the man I assume was his father, before storming off, dragging the boy to his football practice. It was hardly surprising that later in the football training this young boy was asked to sit out for a time when he spat on a team mate for not passing him the ball. Although this was very bad behaviour, actually the blame lies with those people who, acting as his role models, were teaching him that you spit on those with whom you are angry! I am sure that this young boy, like Bethany in the story above, could easily learn different, more socially acceptable ways of showing his displeasure and annoyance, if he had some different role models.

## Growing tension and frustration can lead to disruption of a placement

The reality is that your child may well have an undesirable set of learnt behaviours that stem from what they observed in their early life. Do not underestimate the tension that can grow between various members of your immediate family as a direct result of your child's challenging behaviour.

This growing tension may lead to you feeling increased emotional pain alongside a decreased sense of control and hope, all of which can fuel your feelings of frustration towards your child. This can ultimately result in an unfair wave of negative feeling and blame being aimed at your newly placed child. It is 'unfair', as your child is only trying to live life in line with the behaviours they have observed and been taught while growing up; they don't know any different.

The most immediate way to soothe emotional pain is to remove the root cause. Unfortunately, the root cause is sometimes seen to be the child rather than the child's behaviours and so, on occasion, the child is handed back to the authorities and the placement disrupts. This disruption can happen before or after the adoption order is made.

I spoke with one adoptive mother for whom this had happened. Within a couple of weeks of the placement disruption as she reflected back on the situation, she realised that it was her own frustration in response to the child's behaviour that needed to be managed not just the child's behaviour. She regretted letting her frustrations get the better of her as, in hindsight, she felt she had different options to manage and interact with the child that she couldn't see at the time as she was blinded by frustration.

Early recognition and resolution of any tension- and frustration-causing behaviours is essential for the long-term success of the adoption placement.

## Understand the root cause of challenging behaviours

Depending on the age of your child when they join your family, they may well come with a range of behaviours that, quite frankly, you wish they didn't have. You may not like these behaviours for any number of reasons: they frustrate you or dishonour your values; they are dangerous for your child or others; they embarrass you; and you don't want others seeing the behaviour and, without knowing the history of your family, wrongly attributing it to your style of parenting. Whatever the reason, if you have a child placed with you who has had negative influences in their lives that have shaped their behaviours, there will be some, if not many, behaviours that you would prefer they change.

As adoptive parents, the more we can realise that it is the child's behaviours that are causing us the emotional pain and not the child themselves, the less frustration we will feel. If we look behind the behaviours to understand where they stem from and how they served the child positively in the past, we may be able to understand why the child developed the behaviour in the first place.

In certain situations, some children may exhibit behaviours involving scavenging, over-familiarity with strangers, self-harming, spitting, general aggression, complete withdrawal or something else entirely. If unprepared it would be easy to react negatively to these behaviours, which would immediately impact your child's feeling of self-worth as well as challenging their ingrained behaviours borne out of an instinct to survive. Inadvertently, by reacting negatively you may trigger their undesirable behaviours even more.

These survival behaviours may persist until your child feels secure, safe, loved and nurtured. Eventually, when your child has no need for those behaviours anymore, you may see the behaviours diminish and stop altogether. At least that was our experience. Thinking behind your child's challenging behaviours to the root cause and positive intent can help you cope while helping your child's behaviour change.

The following is the first story about Donna. Please refer back to the 'Meet the children' section in the Preface to understand more about Donna's start in life.

---

### Always in search of food

Donna seemed programmed to seek out food. It was the one thing she was driven to do all of the time. Her adoptive family gave her plenty of food at regular intervals so they felt sure that there wasn't time in between meals and snacks for her actually to get hungry. However, she did seem to feel that she was hungry all the time. Donna often grabbed food from the kitchen worktop regardless of what it was. On one occasion she actually grabbed an onion that had been peeled ready to chop and took a big bite out of it.

The biggest challenge for the adoptive mum was when she took Donna out of the home. If they went to a coffee shop, Donna would grab the leftover scraps from tables that hadn't been cleared as she walked past them. She would pick up anything from the floor that looked like she could eat it and either hide it or eat it before it could be taken away from her. The most embarrassing incidents for the mum involved Donna rummaging through the baskets under other children's buggies looking for snacks and biscuits, and approaching strangers in the street, pointing to what they were eating and simply saying loudly, 'I have that'.

Donna's mum recalled how once at a soft play area, Donna came out of the play area and made a beeline for a table of strangers and started eating the snacks at their table rather than returning to her mum and the snacks she had ready for Donna.

Each time Donna took or demanded food from another adult she succeeded in eating something. The adults involved were quite bewildered by Donna's behaviour but in most cases would happily share their food with her, which only served to reinforce Donna's food-seeking behaviours.

Donna's mother found Donna's behaviour around food challenging to cope with, and spent most of her time when she was out with Donna feeling embarrassed and fearful of what she would do next to try to get food. She coped by trying to distance herself from Donna's behaviour, explaining that Donna wasn't really hers, and that she'd only recently been placed with her for adoption.

Donna's mum felt awful about disowning Donna in this way, but was so shocked by these unexpected behaviours it was the only way she could find in the short term to cope with the situations that presented.

As these behaviours weren't mentioned by the foster carers, it was thought that Donna's earlier anxieties around food were triggered by her move from the foster carers' home, where she had felt settled, to her adoptive placement.

Once the adoptive family understood that Donna's behaviour was driven by a basic survival instinct to get food wherever she could, they instantly felt more compassion and less frustration in response to the behaviours. They realised that this little tot of a girl had developed ways to keep herself fed when her parents should have been doing that for her. The adoptive parents felt better able to be patient and to parent with empathy when they understood the ingrained drivers behind Donna's behaviour.

Through many months of patient reassurance and regular food routines, Donna lost her anxieties around food and stopped the scavenging behaviours that the adoptive family had found so hard to cope with.

---

The following story is the first story about Jayden. Please refer back to the 'Meet the children' section in the Preface to understand more about Jayden's start in life.

---

## Over-familiarity

Jayden presented as a happy boy, who interacted in a friendly and familiar way with everyone from the first instant he met them. People instantly liked Jayden, but in the early days this over-familiarity with people he didn't know caused a lot of frustration for his adoptive family. Jayden always wanted to hold hands and be picked up for a cuddle. It seemed that he preferred anyone, even strangers, to his new adoptive family. He always made a beeline for the newcomer to a group and would want to sit on their knee for a cuddle, whether he knew them or not.

Initially this was very hard for the parents as they wanted to be the special people in Jayden's life. They felt frustrated and hurt that Jayden seemed to prefer to be with people he had only just met rather than to be with them. 'Stranger danger' was, however, their biggest concern, as Jayden seemed to trust anyone and everyone, and would follow them anywhere if they showed him some kindness.

Jayden's adoptive parents knew that, while living with his birth family, he was frequently left for extended periods with people he didn't know well, if at all. They also knew that Jayden's journey through the care system had not been smooth, which had resulted in him spending time with many officials, social workers and four different foster families, all of whom were initially strangers to him.

Jayden's adoptive parents had read about attachment disorders and felt sure that he had some challenges with attachment that had not been highlighted to them previously.

Everyone was friendly towards Jayden and most people probably seemed more fun to Jayden than his new parents as they were trying to introduce boundaries into his life, which he probably considered no fun at all.

As Jayden was so friendly and confident, most people reciprocated his familiarity and friendliness, and unwittingly reinforced his beliefs that all strangers are safe and friendly and more fun than his new mum and dad!

Once Jayden's parents realised that his behaviours had evolved as a result of his life experiences it did help them think differently about how to help him. They felt less frustrated and, rather than feeling annoyed with Jayden and trying to get him to change his behaviour, they took control, explained the situation to the people around them and asked for their support in helping Jayden develop attachment to them, his new adoptive family. They simply asked people not to be so familiar with Jayden and to encourage him towards his new family for care and affection.

Jayden's adoptive family found that people were relieved to have some guidelines about how to interact with Jayden, as his over-familiarity and demands for affection had made them feel a little awkward, but they hadn't wanted to cause offence by pushing him away.

As a result of this intervention the adoptive parents had more opportunity to demonstrate physical affection for Jayden, who in turn started to seek more connection from them, so little by little they started to grow towards each other.

Jayden is now eight, is very attached to his adoptive family, is appropriately wary of strangers and doesn't seek affection from random people.

---

The frustration felt by Donna and Jayden's families in response to their behaviours dissipated when they understood the root cause of the children's challenging behaviours. The adoptive families were able to access compassion instead of frustration, which provided a better mood from which they could think and parent effectively.

## Don't get cross – get curious

When I feel cross, angry, frustrated, disappointed or any number of other negative emotions, I have learned to get curious about what it is that is causing that feeling. I ask myself: 'What is it about this situation that is making me cross?' or 'What is it about that behaviour that really offends me?'

As parents, the more we are able to shift our focus away from feeling cross and frustrated and onto the reasons behind our feelings, the more we can start to understand ourselves and regain control of our emotions. We can then endeavour to model new values, and build structure into our child's life to encourage more appropriate behaviours in line with the values of our family.

To support a positive behaviour change process, you can develop patterns of communicating that acknowledge the positive intent behind your child's challenging behaviour and remind them of the love and support they have around them now, and how their needs can be met in other ways. You may need to repeat these messages many, many times, as the root cause behind the behaviour may be heavily ingrained. Eventually, however, hand in hand with their growing attachment and feeling of being nurtured, it is highly likely that your messages will start to register and your child's behaviour will start to change. Relationship building, reinforcement and repetition of messages are key.

## Recoding hungry

In the early weeks following placement with her adoptive family, Donna would claim that she was hungry every five minutes without fail and she would request food from anybody that was in the vicinity, known or unknown to her.

Alongside making sure that Donna had healthy meals and plenty of snacks, her adoptive parents used conscious communications consistently in the belief that it would help her change.

They were consistent and persistent. It took many months but it did work, completely. Each time Donna told them she was hungry and asked them or anyone for food, they would use the same formula in their response. They would:

- empathise and acknowledge that they believed her when she said she was hungry
- remind her of when she last ate, what she last ate and how recently it was
- tell her when the next meal or snack time would be, and they would show her the time on the clock, where the hands had to be
- remind her that in her new family she would always have more than enough food
- help her understand what else she might actually be feeling that she was interpreting as hunger.

It might be that she needed to go to the toilet, or that she was bored, or that she missed her foster carers, or even that something about her was uncomfortable. In the early months, any uncomfortable sensation on the outside or inside of her body seemed to be interpreted by Donna as hunger.

Through gentle repetition many, many times every day, Donna's behaviour slowly changed and, after 18 months, she did not continually ask for food and instead presented as a regular balanced child around food and was appropriately aware of when she was hungry.

If on occasion Donna starts to feel dysregulated and can't figure out what is wrong, she does sometimes start pestering constantly for food again.

---

## Help your child learn new behaviours

It has been shown by many people that children can change their behaviours in response to good parenting. Parenting with empathy and compassion, combined with bags of patience, skilful communication, structure and consistency, can help your child feel safe and secure, and develop trust, attachment and healthy self-esteem. As a parent, you will be a valued role model in your child's life and they will naturally start to be influenced by you in terms of their values and ultimately their behaviour.

For each challenging behaviour, seek to understand:

- the situation(s) that trigger the behaviour
- what your child may be thinking and feeling
- what your child is trying to achieve for themselves
- the consequences of their behaviour for your child and for you.

When you are able to think behind the behaviour in a rational rather than emotional way you will be better placed to:

- anticipate and minimise the triggers to your child's undesirable behaviour
- empathise and communicate effectively
- help your child learn different ways in which they can get their needs met

- provide structure, with rewards and consequences that support your child as they learn which behaviours are acceptable and which are not.

Many parents have found this simple approach, when applied consistently over many months, can really work. As your child's behaviours align more with your values, any negative feelings and frustrations will reduce, your hopes will increase and you will start enjoying life with your adopted child more.

---

### From 'tolerance' to 'love'

Bethany was almost five when she moved in with her adoptive parents, who were both in their early 40s. Having not had children before, their only experience of parenting had been through spending time with friends' children, nephews, nieces and a growing number of godchildren.

Even after formally adopting her, Bethany's parents admitted to sometimes feeling disgusted and embarrassed by Bethany's behaviour, particularly her spitting and violence in the early weeks and months, but took the approach that 'we've made our bed – we'll lie in it'. They could never imagine loving Bethany as they had grown to love their nephews, nieces and godchildren. They were filled with sadness rather than joy in response to their daughter; they 'tolerated' rather than 'loved' her.

After six months of tolerating Bethany's behaviour, they started reading books and attending courses, more than they had done in preparation for the adoption. They implemented what they learnt and they started seeing changes. Once the changes started, they came thick and fast and Bethany adapted to new ways of being, and responded well to the feelings of warmth and love that started to come her way.

After a year, Bethany had made great progress and both her parents now felt love for her that was growing every day. It was no longer a case of 'we've made our bed – we'll lie in it'; it was very definitely 'this is our daughter Bethany whom we love, we are proud of and we could not imagine our life without her'.

---

## Managing your frustration

Some parents reported feeling a slowly escalating sense of frustration towards their child without being able to pinpoint the exact reasons why.

If you feel a growing sense of frustration towards your child, it might help to ask yourself:

- In which situations do I experience this frustration?
- What is my child doing or not doing that may be causing this growing sense of frustration I am experiencing towards them?
- How does my child's behaviour need to change to ease my frustration?
- How can I learn more about my child and the behaviours they are exhibiting that frustrate me?
- Given everything going on for my child at this time, how can I manage my expectations regarding their behaviour?
- On reflection, what behaviours do I need to help my child change and/or how can I realign my expectations to be more reasonable given the current situation?

When you are able to think around the situation it may be easier to regain control of your emotions and make a plan for how to deal with your child's behaviour and your resulting frustration.

---

### Walking safely and calmly

Getting out of the house for walks, shopping, meeting friends or going on family outings was really important for Jayden's adoptive family. His parents soon noticed, however, that holding their hand and walking anywhere in a relatively calm manner was a real challenge and almost impossible for Jayden. He would point blank refuse to hold a hand and instead would run wildly around, banging on anything he could find, including shop windows and front doors, climbing on whatever was available, zig-zagging across the pavement, running randomly into shops and grabbing whatever he liked the look of. Jayden's behaviour when out was exhausting for the parents – not to mention dangerous – and began to cause high levels of frustration and anxiety every time they thought about taking Jayden out.

The adoptive parents realised that this behaviour was not Jayden's fault. He had not been exposed to these situations before, everything seemed new and he had not really had the opportunity to learn appropriate behaviours when walking down a street, or indeed out anywhere.

Jayden's parents quickly realised that most trips out of the house would at some point involve the need to 'walk nicely' without the chaotic behaviour he had been demonstrating. As 'walking nicely' was a component part of so many other activities, they focused on helping Jayden learn how to do it! Taking him out initially for a five-minute walk, they would start at one end of a short street and would walk to the other end. Many times on different trips, these outings had the sole purpose of practising walking safely and calmly in busy areas.

This repetition for Jayden worked. Their outings progressed to longer streets for more minutes. Soon taking Jayden anywhere that involved walking would start out well, so by the time they got to the main purpose of the trip they were all still refreshed and relaxed and not frustrated and frazzled.

Helping Jayden learn to walk calmly and safely was an important part of helping integrate Jayden into his adoptive parents' life. They realised early on that this was a challenge for Jayden and they were also aware of the frustration they both felt in response to his chaotic behaviour when out of the house, so this was something they found they focused on and resolved early in their relationship.

---

Be prepared that your child might demonstrate some behaviours that cause you a low lying level of frustration, which may pass under your radar to start with, but if not addressed, may build over time. Spot these behaviours early and address them before the frustration levels build.

## Forgive yourself and move on

It's practically impossible to react in a correct and planned way each and every time your child demonstrates a behaviour that you perceive to be inappropriate, especially if they are repeating the same behaviour countless times. Repetition of approach from you is so important, but so is forgiving yourself when you don't act in the way that with hindsight you wish you had.

As parents, there may well be times when our frustration levels feel so acute that we have a knee-jerk response to a situation and act in a way that we are not too proud of. I know it has happened to me, and it may well happen to you, and that is okay; we are humans not machines.

---

## I am only human

My morning routine with Lucy before school is the same each day. The last thing we do before leaving for school is for me to brush Lucy's hair and plait it. However, one day I needed to leave for work early, so I had to plait Lucy's hair earlier than normal in the morning's routine. I didn't warn Lucy of this change, as I had forgotten until that morning that I would need to leave early to make my work commitment.

So when the realisation dawned that I needed to leave the house in 10 minutes to catch my train, I asked Lucy to stop what she was doing so that I could brush and plait her hair. Lucy resisted strongly, began to get quite upset by this unexpected change to her routine and wouldn't come. I wasn't as patient with my explanation to Lucy as I could have been and in response she became even more defiant. The minutes had soon flown by and I was faced with the prospect of missing my train. In desperation I shouted at Lucy, pulled her up from her sitting position and hurriedly brushed and plaited her hair. Lucy was screaming and crying, I was furiously brushing and plaiting, it was not the normal calm start to our morning!

As I left the house that morning, Lucy was still upset and resisted my attempts at a goodbye hug and kiss. By the time I got to the train station I'd had time to reflect on what had happened. I was cross with myself for the way I had acted, and I hated having left Lucy in an upset state for my husband to deal with and calm down before taking her to school.

In hindsight, I know I should have anticipated the change to routine, patiently explained the change to Lucy the night before, reminded her in the morning when she woke up and left more time for the brushing and plaiting. Alternatively, once I sensed it was all going wrong, I could have chosen to leave her to get on with what she was doing, let my husband do her hair or, as a last resort, let her go to school with scruffy hair for one day. It wouldn't have been the end of the world.

Hindsight is a wonderful thing, and I felt like the worst mother in the world. I swapped some texts with my husband, who reminded me that I was only human, Lucy was fine and to get on with my day. But I will never forget that morning, it reinforced what I already knew but didn't practise: anticipate, plan and communicate thoughtfully.

---

I strive to do my best all of the time, but I am only human – as are you. We will all make mistakes, possibly lots of them. There may be times when you act in a way that you wish you hadn't. There are plenty of times when I have acted in a way that I wish I hadn't. The secret is to reflect on those instances, learn from them, forgive yourself and move forwards, always with the intent to do your best. You can't ask any more from yourself than that.

## Summary

- ★ Understanding your values around home and family life will help you anticipate what you may feel in response to certain behaviours your child may demonstrate.
- ★ Your child's behaviours may be driven by a set of values learned from people significant in your child's earlier life who operated from a set of values different to yours.
- ★ Through patient parenting, your child's values and resulting behaviours can evolve to be more in line with your hopes and expectations.
- ★ Your child may exhibit behaviours that cause you frustration, but remember that it is just their learned behaviours – not the child – that are causing you the frustration. It is important to attribute any feelings of frustration just to the behaviour and not to your child.

★ Some adoption placements disrupt before the adoption order is made, which results in the child being handed back into care, only for the potential adoptive parents to regret the path of events and to wish they had better managed their frustrations. This hindsight comes all too late for them and for the child who was handed back into care.

★ The more you can identify your values around family life and parenting and anticipate behaviours and responses to certain situations, the more you will feel in control and unphased by undesirable situations and behaviours that may occur.

★ Get curious about what is driving your child's undesirable behaviours and proactively help them learn more desirable ones that are more in line with the values of your family.

★ You are only human and there will be times when, in hindsight, you wish you had acted in a different way. Forgive yourself and move on. You are doing your best.

PART TWO

# Parent with Empathy

*Empathic parenting is a style of parenting much talked about in many parenting and adoption-related books. To parent with empathy means to actively parent in the moment, in a way that allows your child to know that you understand what they are feeling and that you are responding to what they need. Parenting with empathy will demonstrate your non-judgemental acceptance of your child and will continue to pave the way for their growing sense of trust in you.*

CHAPTER 3

# Understand Your Child

The intent of this chapter is to help you better understand and appreciate what may be going on for your child at any point in time, as this will help expand your awareness, and consider different parenting options in response to situations in which you may find yourself.

It will help you to understand more about your child, if you:

- listen to what your child is saying and not saying
- notice what their body language is telling you
- imagine what they might be feeling given their past experiences
- anticipate what they might feel in response to a certain situation.

For your child to feel your empathy they need to believe that you understand what they are feeling and experiencing. When you respond to them in a way that demonstrates compassion and understanding, when they hear you talk in terms of what they are thinking and feeling, then they can believe that you understand what they are feeling and experiencing.

If you let your child know that you value them, their thoughts and opinions, that you are interested in what they have to say and that you love them for who they are, they will feel better when they are around you as you will positively influence their feeling of self-worth.

Even if you don‘t agree with what they are saying, feeling or doing, you can still acknowledge that you understand why they are saying, feeling and behaving in the ways that they are. I believe that once our children feel truly accepted by us they will start to emotionally connect with us. Acknowledging your child's behaviour doesn't mean that you need to accept it and put up with it, you can still help them find more appropriate ways of expressing their feelings.

Once your child has learned to trust you to understand them and to meet their needs emotionally as well as practically, a true relationship is possible. When your child trusts you, they will also entrust you with helping them understand themselves better. If you see they are struggling with an emotion, and they experience you as someone who is empathic, they will trust you to help interpret their emotion for them and help them make sense of it.

## Learn about the triggers to your child's emotional state

Some children are not able to manage their emotions. This is true of many children who have not been nurtured in their early years, as well as children who have not benefitted from effective role models to demonstrate self-regulation of emotions. The term 'emotional dysregulation' describes a spectrum of behaviour that results when a child (or adult!) is no longer in control of their emotions or reactions and is acting in ways that are unpredictable and can lead to them spinning out of control emotionally.

Being in a dysregulated state is an uncomfortable feeling for your child, and may even be scary for them and damaging to their progress. Different children will have different situations that trigger their dysregulation and will exhibit varying degrees of emotional instability when they are feeling overly emotional or out of control. Some will become hyperactive and unpredictable, others may become very calm and withdrawn. You will soon get to know more about your child's emotional state and what may nudge them towards dysregulation however it manifests for them.

Try to notice what was happening for your child just before they became emotionally dysregulated, and look to learn more about what triggers this state for them. Once you understand more about the situations that may lead to dysregulation for your child, you can seek to avoid situations or minimise the impact of the triggers. You can't control everything, however, and there will be times when your child's state is dysregulated and there is nothing you could have done to prevent it. In these times you can use empathic listening and thoughtful communication (see Part Four) to help them through their dysregulation and back to feeling safe and regulated again.

Look for indicators that your child is starting to become dysregulated. As you get to know your child you will know what to look for. Indicators that precede dysregulation for some of the children in this book include:

- shifting eyes, not able to hold eye contact
- increased level of fidgeting
- scratching
- increase in verbal and/or physical energy
- jumping at people like an excited puppy
- irrational responses
- increased breathing rate
- random disjointed talking
- bursting into tears
- self-harming
- zoning out and going into a trance-like state
- making grunting and squeaking sounds.

## Managing dysregulation

Jayden was an unsettled child, who presented as dysregulated much of the time early in his adoptive placement. His adoptive parents quickly became aware that there were many triggers for his dysregulation.

- *Situational*: including any break in his routines, unexpected visitors, meeting new people or simple rules being broken by other people.
- *Physiological*: including him being hungry, tired or excited.
- *Diet*: including any junk food, sugary food and sweets, some additives.

Being dysregulated is exhausting for Jayden and his adoptive parents, as his behaviour becomes unpredictable and can be very hyperactive, wilfully naughty and/or overly emotional.

Jayden's adoptive parents strive to help him regain his emotional stability so that he can feel regulated. They do this by empathising and interacting with Jayden as though he is much younger than his five years, continual calm talking, letting him know that they understand he is upset/excited/frustrated or whatever emotion they sense that he is feeling and telling him that they know it is all very confusing for him. They try to get him to a point where they can distract him with a favourite toy and focus his attention elsewhere. They have even found that giving him something to suck on can help to calm him down.

Occasionally there is nothing his adoptive parents feel they can do to help Jayden regulate, and occasionally, once he has started on a path towards dysregulation, it is a one-way street and he can't get calm until his dysregulation has peaked. When this happens they make sure not to get pulled into the swirl of escalating emotions. They remain calm for Jayden, make sure he is safe and can't hurt himself and this seems to help him peak and calm relatively quickly (20 minutes or so) rather than the hours that it took him in his early months with them.

## Interpret behaviour with care

Brain imaging research in children and adults now suggests that the brains of children who have suffered neglect and trauma in their formative years develop differently to the brains of children brought up in a nurturing environment (McCrory 2012). Messages passing around the brain appear to be routed and processed differently. It may be that when your adopted child is spoken to in a certain way, they are incapable of processing what is being said the way you might expect. The conversation may trigger certain emotions that cause their brain to process the emotions and input received in a different way. Some children may perceive different conversations as threatening and go straight to a fight, flight or freeze response.

Normally you can tell how a child is feeling by watching their predominant behaviours and how they interact with their immediate environment. With an adopted child, however, observing behaviours is not necessarily a good indicator of what they are feeling. Often through extreme neglect, lack of stimulation or overexposure to certain negative environmental situations, the capacity of the child to experience certain emotions will have been impaired, or the child may have learned through consequences not to display certain emotions. It may be that your child displays behaviours that you wouldn't expect in certain situations. For instance, a state of excitement may be shown as disruptive behaviour; the unfamiliar feeling of pride may also result in disruptive behaviour, which in turn leads to them being told off. This can result in them feeling shameful, which may be a more normal familiar feeling for them. A feeling of insecurity and fear may manifest as overconfidence.

In order, therefore, to best support your adopted child and to parent with empathy, it is important to interpret the behaviour you observe in the context within which you are observing it. This will provide you with additional insight as to how best to support your child in the moment.

---

## Misleading behaviour

After living with us for eight months, our daughter's foster carers visited us for the first time since her placement. The meeting went very well and our daughter benefitted hugely from the visit.

That evening, however, on her way to bed, she had a *huge* tantrum at bath time and was crying, screaming and yelling at me: 'Get away Mummy, go away, go downstairs, I don't want you, I don't want you here, I hate you, leave me alone!' All the while sobbing, uncontrollably. If I had listened to her words and been guided by her behaviour and her obvious distress, I would have gone downstairs. That certainly was the easier option!

However, putting myself in her position, I could clearly feel her grief. She had been with us for about eight months and was getting settled. The visit from the foster carers was necessary to help her progress through the grieving process, but it had brought up such a sense of loss for her, as she had loved them and she was clearly struggling with the reminder of the losses she had experienced in her life. Although she was yelling at me to go, I knew she was testing me and really wanted me to stay.

I calmly told her that I couldn't go downstairs as I was her mummy and I loved her, and I wanted to look after her, and I needed to stay to make sure that the bath water wasn't too hot or too cold, and to make sure that she had all the toys that she wanted to play with, and to get her towel ready to wrap her up when she got out of the bath and I was getting ready to give her a great big warm loving cuddle when she got out of the bath. I went on to tell her that I would always be there for her, and that I would always love her and that she would never have to leave our home as we would be her family forever. I told her that I could imagine how sad she was feeling and that it was natural to miss her foster carers as she had loved them very much, and that seeing them must have been very exciting for her but very hard to see them go, and that she probably had a 'big' feeling inside her right now that was making her feel confused and upset.

I explained to her that as her mummy I wanted to stay with her and make sure that she was okay, and so that was why I didn't want to go downstairs and why I would be staying put in the bathroom right with her. I talked for a few minutes repeating similar phrases, and finally she stopped yelling and started listening, and then simply asked me to pass her a few toys, engaged me in her game and calmed right down.

I know that if I had have done as she asked and gone downstairs, respecting her wishes and leaving her alone, she would not have been able to manage her feelings of confusion and the tantrum would have escalated. It could well have been days before we got her back to being fully settled again. As it was, the whole episode escalated and she calmed down to her settled state within about 15 minutes.

---

## Acknowledge insecurities and fears

Your child may have a fear that appears to be irrational as far as you, a stable adult, are concerned, but from your child's perspective, based on their experience, their fear may be very real to them.

Parenting with empathy means listening to your child's insecurities and fears, however irrational they may seem to you, and interpreting these insecurities and fears through your child's experiences. Demonstrating to your child that you have listened and that you acknowledge their fears will help them on the path towards developing trust.

## Being patient with physical interaction

Bethany wanted physical contact from her adoptive family only when she initiated it. She enjoyed cuddles and sitting on their knees for stories or sitting close to them when watching television, but only when she wanted to. It was very confusing for her adoptive parents in the early weeks, as any form of physical contact initiated by them was repelled and interpreted as a 'hurt' by Bethany. They felt that to avoid causing Bethany upset and to gain her trust, they should only give her physical interaction when she sought it, and refrain from initiating cuddles when she didn't.

In the process of caring for Bethany's daily needs, however, a certain amount of physical contact was necessary. Getting her in and out of the bath, helping her use the toilet, cleaning her teeth, cutting her fingernails and toenails, and brushing her hair all presented a challenge. Initially it really was difficult as the adoptive parents were trying their best to provide the basic physical care that Bethany needed and were faced with her crying and screaming that they were hurting her. They felt awful, and frustrated, as they were being as gentle as possible, but they could tell that she really thought they were hurting her.

Bethany's adopted parents couldn't figure out whether Bethany was expecting them to hurt her, and that is why she interpreted every touch as a hurt, or whether her senses were a little muddled so she really *was* feeling that their physical care giving hurt. Either way, regardless of the root cause of her reaction, their physical interaction with her was causing anxiety and upset both for Bethany and for her adoptive parents. The adoptive parents soon learned that trying to rationalise with Bethany was futile and that empathising with her and what she was feeling instead, helped more. They rationalised 'If Bethany thinks she feels something that hurts her, who are we to tell her that she isn't feeling that?' They knew they had to gain her trust.

Instead of enduring the tension and frustrations that would have existed had they forced Bethany into letting them cut her nails and brush her hair, they made up and played games with her that allowed them to gain her trust. The games involved simply touching Bethany's fingers, toes and hair. The games took Bethany's focus away from what was actually going on and soon she started to trust their touch. After only a few days, Bethany would happily sit on the adoptive mum's knees and let her play with her fingers, toes and hair. This soon progressed to Bethany allowing her hands and feet to be massaged and eventually her nails to be filed and finally cut. All of this was still done under the guise of a game.

The adoptive parents approached brushing hair and teeth in a similar way to the nail cutting, by playing games over a number of days that encouraged Bethany to trust them to approach her with the brushes.

From those early months onwards, the adoptive parents report that there has not been a single problem with nail cutting, hair or teeth brushing. Bethany no longer interprets their touch as a hurt. Though if she is dysregulated for some reason, they will occasionally get 'you hurt me' thrown at them for no apparent reason!

Reflecting back, the adoptive parents shared the depth of the tension that this unanticipated reaction to physical touch caused in the placement. When they *knew* they were being as gentle as possible, to see her so convinced that she felt pain in response to their touch caused them confusion and increasing frustration. It was only when they acknowledged the possibility of what she was feeling and changed their goal from effective and efficient care giving to building trust in areas where Bethany felt vulnerable, that they were able to resolve the situation and move forwards.

## Scary walls

When Lucy moved in she became really unsettled at bedtimes, not wanting to be left alone in her room. Lucy told us many times that all walls at night time made loud and scary noises. Because she believed this so strongly, she was terrified of being left alone in her bedroom and she didn't want to be on her own when her bedroom walls started making scary noises. Every bedtime was fraught with tears and anxiety.

We tried to tell her that walls couldn't make noises, and that the walls in this house were safe, but she wouldn't believe us. No matter how we tried to convince her, Lucy wouldn't believe us and the more we tried to convince her, the more she seemed to hang on to her belief. Even when we did manage to convince her to stay in her room she was hypervigilant and called out every time she heard a noise in the house after we had turned her light off. She wanted to know exactly what had caused the noise she had heard: a door opening or closing, a flushing toilet, the television, etc. We took to creeping round the house, after her light went out, sitting still in a room and not moving, willing her to sleep.

It got to the point where we all dreaded the bedtime routine. At the end of the day, my husband and I were exhausted anyway, and found it hard to be as patient as we would have liked. Lucy's seemingly irrational fears of 'scary walls' did begin to cause us frustration. The only time we got to ourselves to do normal household chores and relax was when Lucy was asleep and, as she wouldn't fall asleep until almost our bedtime anyway, we found we couldn't get anything done!

The turning point for us came when we stopped and thought about Lucy's early life experiences.

We realised that the environment in which she lived with her birth family may well have had nights full of loud and scary noises. Lucy will have heard these through the walls of her bedroom and as she experienced this from being a baby to being a small child she was too young to attribute the noises to anything but the walls themselves. Hence she developed a belief that all walls made scary noises at bedtime.

We realised that no amount of logic was going to shift Lucy's belief and so we played a game with her to help her learn the sounds in our house. While one of us sat in her bedroom with her someone else went around the house making different noises and Lucy had to help guess what the noise was. Then the game shifted so she could give instructions about what noises she wanted made, so that she could hear those as well. This resulted in a few nights of her shouting out the noises that she was hearing after her light had gone out.

It seems that Lucy had moved from being afraid of the walls, but still was hypervigilant and sensitive to any noise, however small, that she could hear, and therefore struggled to fall asleep.

Eventually we bought a lullaby CD with her name repeated in the songs, and played the CD in her room as soon as her light was turned off. Lucy enjoyed listening to the songs and listening out for her name. This soon took her mind off the other noises in the house and calmed her down from her hypervigilant state. She was soon able to fall asleep quickly with the CD without worrying about all the other noises.

After she'd lived with us about eight months, one night as I was tucking her into bed, Lucy said, 'Mummy, these walls not scary; just the other home, not this home. This home has friendly walls'.

Going to bed was never a problem for Lucy after that day. Normal household noises no longer bother her, and she falls asleep happy.

---

No amount of rationalising with children (or adults!) or trying to convince them with logic will make them change deeply held beliefs. If we empathise, and help them have other experiences that make new beliefs possible, this can help children (and adults) change their beliefs.

Following is the first story about Connor and Ben. Please refer back to the 'Meet the children' section in the Preface to understand more about their start in life.

---

## Swarms of flies

Connor and Ben moved in with their adoptive family when they were four and three years old, respectively. They were a bit of a handful to start with but responded well to boundaries and settled quickly. The one ongoing challenge, however, was when either of them woke up at night, it was a real challenge to get them settled again. Connor in particular used to get very distressed, and seemed to have a recurrent nightmare, although he appeared to be awake while having it.

If Connor woke up in the night, he would cry and panic and be afraid to be anywhere as he was convinced there were flies everywhere. It was worse if he needed to go to the toilet as the bathroom was the room that panicked him most; he would scream at his adoptive parents that all toilets and bathrooms had flies in them. He then wouldn't want to stay in his bedroom as he was convinced flies were in there as well. He would be beside himself, most distraught, crying and screaming, running from room to room to try to escape the flies. He seemed to be awake, which confused his adoptive parents as there clearly weren't any flies, yet they could tell that he really believed there were.

Sometimes during the day if Connor saw a fly in the house, he would dissolve into tears and panic as well. This was frustrating, as Ben, who didn't seem concerned by flies initially, started to copy his brother's behaviour.

On probing the boys' background further with their social worker, the adoptive parents found out that when Connor and Ben were removed, age three and one, there had been animal faeces in different places in the flat where they lived, and the birth family had been using the bath as the toilet, as their actual toilet was blocked. Apparently there were many flies in the flat. It was evident through Connor's dreams that at some level Connor remembered this, though he never actually spoke about it directly.

Connor's adoptive parents didn't really know how to address his fear of flies, and hoped he would grow out of it as his memories faded. In the meantime, however, they started naming any flies they found in the house, and made up stories about the fly and its family. They'd say how pleased they were to have the odd little fly in the house, as that type only lived in happy houses, and they started pointing out the differences between normal little flies and the flies that you would see on animal faeces.

They didn't mention anything specific about Connor's previous experiences or about what they had learned from the social worker as they didn't know whether he consciously remembered it. Also they made sure Connor saw them cleaning the bathrooms and the toilets and talking about how important it is to keep everything nice and clean.

It wasn't long before Connor was naming and talking to the house flies himself, as well as asking about their families and wanting to know if they were happy in the house. After a couple of months the 'waking fly nightmares' stopped and Conner started sleeping through undisturbed by bad dreams.

---

Trying to convince Connor that there were no flies in his bedroom or bathroom would have been pointless. Calming him through his distress, seeking to understand him through his experiences and helping him create new associations, new experiences and new ways of being seemed to be the right approach for him.

Acknowledge your child's insecurities and fears no matter how silly they seem to you. To try to tell them not to be silly, that their fear isn't real, will not help them develop trust in you. In their world, their fears are very real and if you are expecting them to trust you then be prepared to let them know that you believe what they are telling you is real from their perspective, and then seek to understand how they might have arrived at that belief.

## Learn through observation, interaction and discussion

The more you know about your child's likes and dislikes, fears and insecurities, behaviours and experiences as well as about their immediate and extended family, the more you will sense how to best help them attach, trust, feel secure and build their self-esteem.

When you first meet your child it is likely that everything you know about them will have been gleaned through your child's social workers and foster carers, and even through meetings with their birth parents. Yet there will still be lots of information that you don't know, and some of what you think you know may be inaccurate!

From your child's perspective, there will be information that they know about themselves because they have been told, or because they can remember it directly. There will also be information and knowledge that they don't have, because they have not been told, they have forgotten or suppressed memories or just because they are not aware of what values and beliefs they have that are driving their behaviours.

The two dimensions of what you, the parent, 'know' and 'don't know' about your child can be combined with what your child 'knows' and 'doesn't know' about themselves. Inspired by a business communication model by Luft and Ingham (1955) called the Johari Window[1] (see Luft 1984), I have called the resulting model the 'Matrix of Shared Understanding', which illustrates my understanding regarding the availability of the knowledge it is possible for you to have about your child (see Figure 3.1).

| | Known by Your Child | *Not* Known by Your Child |
|---|---|---|
| Known by You | **Shared Knowledge** | **Area of Innocence** |
| *Not* Known by You | **Area of Privacy** | **Subconscious** |

**Figure 3.1** Matrix of Shared Understanding

*Shared knowledge* is that knowledge about your child and their heritage that is possessed by both you and your child. It is an area of shared knowledge within which you can interact with your child regarding experiences, behaviours, fears, insecurities, hopes and aspirations. You can help them reflect, take different perspectives and learn. It is the area in which relationships can be formed, self-esteem built and your child can learn to feel secure.

*Area of innocence* is that knowledge about your child and their heritage that you possess but they don't, either because

1 Johari Window is a technique created in 1955 by two American psychologists, Joseph Luft (1916–2014) and Harrington Ingham (1914–1995), used to help people better understand their relationship with self and others. It is used primarily in self-help groups and corporate settings as a communication tool to help people develop more productive relationships.

they have never been told, or they have forgotten. This is knowledge that may help you understand their behaviours and ways of being, and that they may remember over time, or you may choose to share with them when they are older and the time is right. It is that knowledge of which, for the time being, they are innocent.

*Area of privacy* is that knowledge that your child possesses but that no one in social services has (or they did know and they didn't tell you) and your child has not shared, so it has remained private to them. The more your child develops trust in you and starts to feel attached, the more of this knowledge they may feel inclined to share. Your child may hint at this knowledge or they may share it overtly.

*Subconscious* is that knowledge that is not possessed by you and not consciously held by your child. There may be certain situations that trigger instinctive behaviours or memories which they may or may not understand. The more your child feels a sense of security, attachment and trust in their new family and environment, the more they may become aware of elements currently in their subconscious. If they choose to share them with you, these elements transition and become *shared knowledge*; if they choose to keep the knowledge to themselves, it transitions into the *area of privacy* for them to share at a later date if and when they feel ready.

When you first meet your child you will know less about them than you ever will going forwards as, from that moment onwards, you will consistently learn more about them through observation, interaction, discussion and disclosure. Over time, the shared knowledge area will grow as your child shares more of their experiences and information with you, and as you help them understand different aspects about themselves.

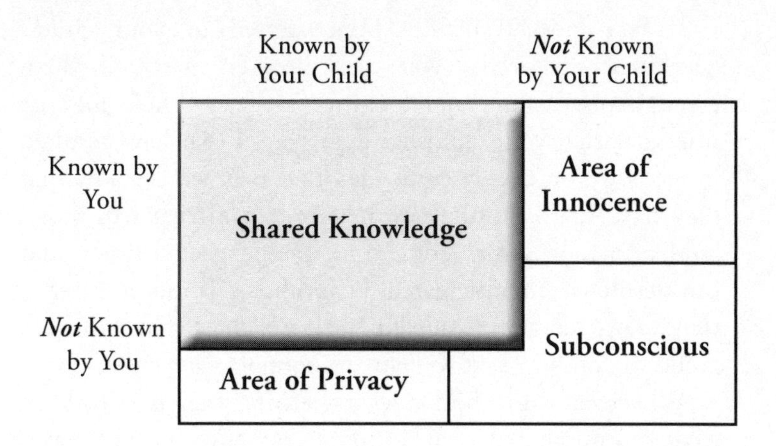


**Figure 3.2** Matrix of Shared Understanding – expanded shared knowledge

There will come a time when the shared knowledge area has grown through your child sharing their memories and self-knowledge with you, and you sharing your observations and knowledge with them. As the shared knowledge area grows you will better understand your child and have the awareness to parent them in a way that works for them and you, and in return your child may start to feel more attached and secure (see Figure 3.2). This state is likely to take many months, and sometimes years, rather than days and weeks.

## Observe the clues

Infants, toddlers and children of different ages have different needs that must be met in order for them to grow into balanced human beings, able to be all that they can be. If your child has missed out on any of the basic steps, they may have needs that must be fulfilled before they can move on. These needs may manifest in them exhibiting much younger, older, inappropriate or challenging behaviour in certain situations.

If you haven't already been alerted to your child's developmental needs, you can discover many of them through observation and looking for clues. There may be situations that your child has experienced that have resulted in memories so deeply embedded that they won't know that they have them, until those memories are triggered. These hidden memories may come back at unexpected times, and can result in unanticipated behaviours. Through careful, mindful observation you will pick up clues that will help guide you on how best to help and support your child.

Whenever your child does something that is outside of what you might expect as normal behaviour, consider that it could be a clue, a little link to a part of your child that they have not shared yet. Rather than just taking the behaviour at face value and reacting to it, take time to think behind the behaviour, give the matter some consideration to see what you may learn about your child.

Following is the first story about Grace. Please refer back to the 'Meet the children' section in Preface to understand more about Grace's start in life.

---

### A goodnight slap!

Grace had been with her adoptive family for over a year when they went on a family holiday where they all shared a hotel room. One night in the hotel room, the adoptive father went to kiss Grace goodnight as she lay in her hotel bed, as he had done recently every night at home, and as he had done for the first few nights in the hotel. So far every night he had received a hug and a kiss in return at bedtime.

This time, however, before he managed to give Grace a goodnight hug and kiss, he received a powerful whack to the side of his head, as she hit him! He admits to being so shocked at her whack, that his initial reaction was to yell loudly at Grace, which he realised in hindsight wasn't the best reaction. Grace was distraught and almost inconsolable in response to both her action and her father's yelling. She clearly hadn't planned to hit her father and had no idea why she had done so at all. She was crying at what she had done and crying because she had been yelled at. What had been the calm end to a lovely day had turned into a screaming nightmare!

Amid the chaos, Grace's parents had the presence of mind to realise there was something deeper at play, as this was most out of character for the Grace they knew now, and was more similar to the behaviour that Grace presented when she first moved in. Once they had calmed the situation down, and helped Grace to settle, they had a chance to reflect on what had happened.

They realised that at home Grace's bed was in the corner of the room, meaning that they approached Grace from the right side of the bed to kiss her goodnight. In the hotel, the orientation of Grace's bed meant it had access from both sides. Up to that night the father had approached her from the right side of her bed to kiss her goodnight, the same as he would at home. But this particular evening, he closed the curtains and then walked to her bed, meaning he approached from the left side, which he had never done before.

The parents could only assume that having a large figure approach her bed from the left side had triggered some deep-seated memories for Grace that had resulted in her lashing out to protect herself. Unfortunately, the possibility of sexual abuse had been strongly suggested in Grace's background information, but had never been confirmed.

---

In this story, Grace gave a clear clue about a current situation in which she felt vulnerable, as well as a clue about possible scenarios that may have resulted in unpleasant experiences for her. The adoptive parents could have become cross with Grace and reacted only to her actions, but in observing the clue that they were given they gleaned some additional information.

Gleaning new knowledge and information will help anticipate situations and reinforce key messages, thereby helping your child feel even more secure and protected. This in turn will help your child develop trust and attach even more to you.

There will be so much to learn in the first few weeks and months after your child moves in. You will be absorbing all kinds of new information. Do be mindful and curious about what you are observing. You will notice many clues that may help you more quickly understand your new child and the challenges that they may face.

---

### Unfortunate accidents

Jayden was placed with his adoptive family just after his fourth birthday and they noticed from the first day that he never said he needed to go to the toilet until he was obviously desperate, and by then it was usually too late and he had an accident.

Initially, the adoptive parents felt sure that Jayden simply couldn't be bothered to stop what he was doing until it was too late. They tried all sorts of incentives from stickers to treats but none made any difference. Sometimes, in an effort to get the treat Jayden would say he needed to go to the toilet, and when he got there, disappointingly for all, had absolutely nothing to offer!

Because Jayden had been left in nappies until after he was four years old the adoptive parents assumed he had never learnt when he needed the toilet and that, over time, he would just learn. It was months before they realised that he wasn't getting any better, and at that point they started exploring other reasons. At about the same time they also realised that he wasn't able to tell when he was hungry or full, or hot or cold, and they realised that recognising the urge to urinate was just another sensation that he was failing to distinguish from other internal stimuli.

The adoptive parents finally sought some help from their local doctor. Jayden was referred in the first instance to a paediatric occupational therapy department as the presenting symptoms seemed to be indicative of a form of sensory processing disorder. Further investigation suggested a problem with his internal sensors that provide feedback regarding what his internal organs feel as a result of the physiological and physical condition of his body. Jayden is now undergoing some therapeutic interventions with that department, and is making progress – I don't know the details of his treatment but he is beginning to interpret internal sensations more accurately now and the prognosis is that this will eventually become second nature to him, as it is with other children.

On reflection, the parents wish they'd paid more attention to his frequent accidents, as they may have made some quicker connections and got him the support he needed a little earlier.

---

## Assemble the clues

In the absence of much information about your child, if you are attentive to their behaviour you will be able to form the semblance of a picture that may give you an idea about some of their history and experiences and you may, therefore, be more prepared in how to help them.

---

### Gleaning more history

The background information provided about Grace by social services was really thin, nothing really to note at all. The adoptive parents could almost conclude that her care had been fine, and that the only reason she was removed from the birth family was due to the risk of sexual abuse if she stayed. The adoptive parents, therefore, didn't anticipate many issues.

In the early months, though, Grace gave her new parents clue after clue about her early experience and the neglect she most likely had experienced.

In the early weeks following placement, Grace called all ladies 'Mum' or 'Mummy'. She clearly thought it was another name for 'lady'. *Possible interpretation: Grace hadn't had a close and meaningful relationship with her birth mum. She didn't understand that a mummy was a special relationship between a child and one lady, who could be relied upon to meet all of her needs.*

Grace appeared instantly comfortable in unfamiliar environments with people she didn't know, and never tried to follow either of her parents if they looked like they were getting ready to leave. *Possible interpretation: Grace was very used to being dropped off and left with complete strangers in unfamiliar places.*

If the adoptive parents were getting ready to go out and started to get her ready she looked positively surprised that she would be coming along too and often would put up a fight wanting to wait at home watching the television. *Possible interpretation: Grace was used to being left on her own.*

Grace would often try to muscle in on interactions between other parents and their children. When visiting the library, if she saw a mother reading a book to her child, she would squeeze in between them. At the park, if a mother was playing with her child, she would rush over and demand that mother's attention. On holiday, she would get between any parent and their child in the swimming pool and start playing with the adult as though that person was her parent. At the park, she would shout past her adoptive parents to any other adults nearby shouting, 'Hey lady, oi man, watch me! Don't watch that girl/boy – look at me!' *Possible interpretation: Grace had been starved of parental attention and was programmed to seek attention from wherever she could.*

These are just some of the many clues that Grace gave to her past experiences. Individually these clues can be overlooked as individual incidents and dealt with separately. However, when the adoptive parents pieced the clues together, the picture they got was of a little girl starved of attention, left to her own devices and not having formed any close connection with a primary carer. It gave them a completely different picture and helped them understand the importance of addressing the roots of these behaviours and offering a thorough nurturing approach to their parenting. They gleaned far more information from the clues that Grace gave them than they did from the background information with which they had been provided.

---

## Follow the cues

While 'observing the clues' may allow you to form a better picture and understanding of your child's background and possible experiences, the 'cues' your child may give offer you a steer on how best to support your child to help repair the harm, process their emotions and move forwards.

I sometimes find myself in situations with Lucy where I just don't know how to respond to best help her. I have learnt in those moments to let go of what I think and to follow her lead. I believe that as long as my response supports her in building the important foundation stones of trust, attachment, security and self-esteem, I have done okay. So there are times when, in the absence of knowing what to do, I simply follow her cues. These situations can feel uncomfortable for me, and I rarely feel confident that I am doing the right thing. However, I have learned to trust in myself that I will respond in the way that she needs in that moment.

Here is one example of many of where I followed a cue from Lucy.

## Following a cue

One day in her bedroom, after Lucy had been with us about eight months, Lucy asked me if I would be her birth mum in a game.

Lucy: 'You be my first mummy.'

Me: *(not feeling comfortable with this role play)* 'No I don't want to play this game, what else can we play?'

Lucy: *(much more insistent)* 'Yes Mummy, you be my first mummy.'

Me: *(really not knowing what to do, and not knowing how to play this game)* 'No, I'd rather not. Let's play something else.'

Lucy: *(very insistent)* 'I want to play this game. You be my first mummy.'

Me: *(finally picking up on the cue and deciding to go with the flow, though not knowing what to expect)* 'Okay, I'll be your first mummy. How do we play?'

Lucy: *(not giving me any indication of how to play, simply asked me a question)* 'Mummy, will you be my mummy?'

Me: *(as birth mum)* 'No. I love you very much but I don't know how to look after you properly. I don't know how to keep you safe and I keep forgetting how to be a good parent.'

Lucy: *(after a simple acknowledging nod)* 'Mummy-Beth *[her foster carer]*, will you be my mummy?'

Me: *(as Mummy-Beth)* 'No. I love you, but my job as a foster carer is to keep you safe, and look after you really well, giving you everything you need to help you grow, until a very special family is found that will be your family forever, with a new mummy and new daddy. When you leave me to go and live with them, I will miss you and I will think about you often, but I will be pleased for you that you will have a home where you will be happy and will stay forever.'

Lucy: *(after another acknowledging nod)* 'Mummy-Sophie, will you be my mummy?'

Me: *(as me)* 'Yes! I will be your mummy and I will love you and look after you. I will keep you safe and warm and happy. We will be your family forever, and we all love you and we are so pleased that you joined our family.'

And with that I reached out and pulled Lucy in close for a big hug. She responded with a big smile and a reciprocating hug and then pulled away from me.

Lucy: *(very insistent)* 'Let's play again. You be my first mummy. Mummy, will you be my mummy?'

And so the exact conversation was repeated three times, entirely led by Lucy, with me playing the parts of each of her significant mummies. Finally after the third round, she gave me a huge hug and asked, 'Can we have lunch now?' and to this day, she has never repeated that game again.

At the time of this conversation, once I realised I was being given a cue, I didn't know what to do. I did however believe that, given Lucy's insistence on playing the game, whatever it was would be significant for her. On reflection I realise what she needed at that point was key chunks of her life putting in place for her with some basic explanations as to why she couldn't stay with each mummy. I believe she needed to know that she was loved by each mummy and that it wasn't her fault that she had to move on. She was trying to make sense of all her mummies' roles, especially mine.

---

I wonder if all children instinctively give cues as to what they need. If only we consciously tuned in and listened more attentively.

I believe that if you watch for the cues, in some instances you will be guided by your child. Use these precious opportunities to reinforce the messages that are important for your child to hear. There may be significant opportunities presented to you by your child for you to really help them process what is emerging for them. This is all part of the 'life-story work' that you can do with your child. You won't know when these moments are going to happen, but they will happen. Be aware, be sensitive and be led by your child. Trust yourself and go with the flow. If you are unsure what to do in the moment, think about your options and decide on the one that would help your child trust you more, attach to you, feel secure and help build their self-esteem. In that interaction, put yourself in your child's shoes and anticipate what they need for you to demonstrate, confirm or validate and in as simple a way as possible – do that for them.

## Summary

- ★ Empathic parenting means seeking to understand what your child is thinking and feeling in a situation and responding in a way that helps them feel understood, while at the same time moving them forwards in their emotional healing and development. Once your child feels that you really understand them, they will start to trust in you and then a real relationship is possible.
- ★ Empathic parenting enables you to access compassion rather than frustration in response to undesirable behaviours by looking behind the behaviour and understanding the root cause and the intention of your child. Accessing compassion gives rise to different, more positive and supportive reactions in response to the situation, which will continue to build and strengthen your relationship with your child.
- ★ Children who have experienced neglect and other undesirable forms of parenting are less easy to interpret through their behaviours. It is important to look at the

context within which your child's behaviour is occurring to get additional insights into what they may be feeling. In these instances, reacting to the root cause of their behaviour rather than the manifestation of the behaviour itself may be the more effective way to resolve a situation.

★ Your child's age, experiences and perspective on life are very different to yours and so what frightens them and what causes them to feel insecure may seem irrational from your perspective. Letting your child feel that you understand and acknowledge their fears may help them start to open up and trust you.

★ Through observation, interaction and discussion, your knowledge and understanding of your child will grow beyond what you have initially read and been told. The way your child acts and behaves can give you many clues about their previous experiences, as well as cues for what they need from you in terms of parenting, reassurances and support to help them move forwards and process their emotions. At times you may feel unsure about how to respond to your child, but if you respond in a way that increases their trust for you, their attachment to you and their feelings of security, and does not harm their self-esteem, you will have responded well.

## References

Luft, J. (1984) *Group Processes: An Introduction to Group Dynamics.* Houston, TX: Mayfield Publishing Co. (original work published in 1963).

McCrory, E. (2012) 'The link between child abuse and psychopathology: A review of neurobiological and genetic research.' *Journal of the Royal Society of Medicine 105*, 4, 151–156.

CHAPTER 4

# Facilitate Your Child's Memories and Emotions

After many months and sometimes years of assessments and preparation, the day will come when you collect your adopted child, bring them home, close the door on the outside world and start your life as a new family. Your world and the world of your child will merge, and in some cases will collide.

The intent of this chapter is to help you anticipate how you can help your newly placed child feel not only that you understand them, but also that you believe them and their memories and feel compassion towards them. If you achieve this, any collision will be softer and the merging of your two worlds will be easier, paving the way for the creation of a rewarding relationship.

## Pace your child and help them move forwards

It is likely that the emotional age of your child will not match their age in years and months. Depending on their emotional maturity, your child may have an understanding of your significance in their lives or not. They may demonstrate excitement or apprehension when meeting you and this will give you no guidance as to their level of understanding about who you are. Even if they are able to explain who you are, it may be that they have just learnt what to say by listening and repeating, but still have no idea about the significance of you in their lives, or they may fully understand!

---

**Preparation doesn't always lead to understanding**

The first day we met Lucy, we were hugely excited to meet her and she seemed equally as excited to meet us. We were thrilled and overwhelmed by her openness, warmth and acceptance of us. It soon became very clear, however, that although she had clearly seen and interacted with all of the introductory information we had prepared and sent to her via the social workers, she didn't actually have the first idea about our significance in her life. Lucy liked playing with the audio photo album in which we introduced ourselves to her and she also enjoyed watching the video of us playing hide-and-seek around our house; however, the significance of the contents clearly had not registered with Lucy.

During the introduction period it slowly dawned on us that actually Lucy didn't have a clue about who we were or what was going on. She actually thought the foster carers were her family and had no idea that she would be leaving them and coming to live with us. Although the social workers and the foster carers had been helping to prepare her for the move and thought that she was engaging with the discussions and understood what was going on, this clearly was not the case.

---

As a parent your role is to empathise with your child's level of understanding and feelings, and to facilitate their emotional journey as they assimilate their experiences and memories and move forwards.

It is probably more helpful to assume that your child has less of an understanding than you anticipate and less of an understanding than they appear to have. This way you will not be working from an assumed base of knowledge and understanding that your child doesn't have. Listen for clues that indicate your child's level of understanding. No matter how confused or wrong their understanding of the situation appears to be, this is their perception, so start from that place and gently bring them forwards to a new and more accurate understanding.

## Put yourself in your child's shoes

As an adult, spending the night in someone else's house can feel awkward. If you didn't know the person it would feel even worse. It is hard to imagine how you might feel if you have lost everything that is familiar to you, you have had little say in where you are going, you are surrounded by different rules, different routines, different people, a different atmosphere, different smells, different noises...the list could go on!

The emotions of your child in response to this life change will differ depending on many factors, not least their age and emotional maturity. A slightly older child might be more aware and tuned in to the sensitivities of the situation, particularly if they have experienced similar moves before. They might project the context of previous moves onto this move. They may assume that what was expected of them in a previous move is what is expected of them here, and that what happened there will happen here. If young they will be less able to interpret their emotions, and these feelings may well manifest as behaviours, actions or outbursts that seem to indicate one thing but actually mean something very different!

If you think the first few days are going to be a challenge for you they will be nothing compared to how they are going to feel for your new child. Whether you are a single adopter or a couple, you were largely driving the decisions that led to the situation you are in. Also, if you have prepared well, you will have a support network of people to consult with, speak to and draw strength from: people to support and bolster you.

For your child, it couldn't be more different. They have probably had little or no say in their current situation. They will just move in and will need to cope with the new environment in which they find themselves. They have no immediate means to access a support network. They may feel alone and isolated.

Putting yourself in their shoes, with their background and experiences you may get an insight into how they might be feeling: Lonely? Confused? Frustrated? Scared? Numb? Depressed? Hopeless? Worried? Abandoned? Empty? Anxious? Cheated? Blamed? Uncomfortable? Lost? Rejected? Embarrassed? Powerless? Angry? Ashamed? Sad? Take even a few of these, mix them up and add in some sensory overload from the new environment and you could well have a complex mixture with unpredictable outcomes.

Empathise with your child's situation and understand their behaviour in context. Don't just react to the behaviours that may result from their powerful mixture of emotions, instead try to engage with the emotions that are causing the behaviours. You may then be able to identify ways to help soothe some of the emotions. If they are confused, you can help them understand. If they are grieving the loss of foster carers, have more photos around, and arrange Skype or telephone calls. If you can find different ways to reduce the intensity of some of their emotions, it may help smooth their experience of settling into their new home.

If your child is older when they join your family, they may well try to act how they think you want them to act, and be the child you want them to be. So although they may not have any challenging behaviour you might have a child who is hiding their true emotions and trying to comply, to ensure that they don't get moved on again.

## Reinforce the permanence of their new situation

If your child has experienced a number of moves, they may not understand the concept of permanence. Deep down, therefore, although they hear you saying that you will be their 'forever' family, and you will look after them and love them forever, they won't be able to understand what that means, as their life to date has only been in temporary chunks. Their life might only make sense to them if it is in a permanent state of transition.

---

### Reinforce your child's sense of permanence

Lucy, even after two years as part of our family, would get frustrated when she didn't get her own way over something, and would state, 'I'm going to get a new family now,' or 'I'm going to get another new mummy'. I remember it used to really hurt us to hear this, but it did give us the opportunity to reinforce the permanence of her situation.

We'd respond with phrases like:

'I can see that you're frustrated that you can't have what you want. If you did go and get a new family we'd all be very sad as we love you very much.'

'Do you remember the nice judge that we went to see on your special Adoption Day? He told us that we would be your family forever and that you'd never have to move again.'

> 'Sometimes when you're frustrated I can understand you might like to try another family, but that isn't possible. We are your family forever. You are our daughter forever. No matter what happens we will always love you and we will always be a family.'

Normally once we had reinforced the permanence of the situation, Lucy's feeling of transience would pass and she would move on to something else.

---

---

### How not to do it!

I remember one day after Lucy had been with us for a significant length of time, I received a relentless barrage of 'I go get another family now, another mummy would let me…' She was constantly saying that she wanted to leave and find a new family and a new mummy who would let her do all the things that she wanted that I wouldn't allow.

All day, I had been constant in my responses, acknowledging her frustrations and reinforcing the fact that we all loved her and would be a family forever. It was exhausting but I was consistent. But then after about the 30th time that day that she had told me she wanted to find a new family with a new mummy, my frustration bubbled up and instead of my usual reinforcing response I flippantly responded: 'Well, good luck finding a new family.' To which Lucy immediately broke down into inconsolable sobs, crying, 'You don't want me, you want me to leave and find a new family!'

It was awful. I felt terrible and so disappointed with myself. All of the positive messages I had been giving her, and I blew it in one throwaway sentence. I know, of course I should have continued with the approach that I believed to be right. On that day, clearly Lucy needed a lot more reassurance than normal. She was obviously feeling really insecure, she was testing me and the security of our family, and she had pushed me to my limit.

Later, when all was calm, I tried to repair the damage I had done with my flippant comment by discussing the situation with Lucy and explaining how my frustration had bubbled up. I then explained again and again how much we loved her and that, even if she got frustrated and wanted to move, it wasn't possible, as we were a family forever. Thankfully my flippant comment didn't seem to have done any lasting damage, but it certainly couldn't have helped her sense of permanence.

I later mentioned the episode to our social worker, who explained that research was starting to suggest that a seemingly settled child may experience feelings of insecurity after they have been in a placement for the same length of time as the age they were when first removed from their birth family. Although the children may not consciously remember how old they were when they were removed, their subconscious remembers.

At the time of the insecure day described here, Lucy would have been with us, almost to the week, for the same length of time she was with her birth family before being removed. It just goes to show what the subconscious part of the mind can remember.

Lucy still occasionally states categorically that she wants a new family, but I will strive never to let my frustration influence my response again.

---

## Narrative and metaphor will help your child process their life story

Your child will probably feel a little bewildered when they arrive and quite jumbled with their memories as they try to figure out what has happened, where the significant people in their lives have gone, why certain events have occurred and much more. Narrative and metaphor can help them make sense of their life so that they can better understand the key threads and develop a framework onto which they can pin their emerging understandings. A better understanding of their life story will give them a sense of grounding and stability to support their future development.

Repetition is very important and comforting to children. If you already have experience of children you will know that they rarely tire of hearing the same story again and again, its predictability offers comfort to their sense of understanding. A running narrative and repetition of what is happening currently for your child will help them understand the 'here and now' part of their life story.

---

### Repeating the day!

Lucy had been with us for about a week when she started to realise that she might not be returning to her foster carers. This emerging realisation was very unsettling for her as she firmly believed that they were her family and that their home was therefore her home.

From the point of this realisation Lucy continually asked us to describe every little detail of what we had done together so far that day. Every 15 minutes or so, she'd say 'Tell me the story about...' and she'd want us to tell her, in detail, about what had just happened in the previous 15 minutes. She wouldn't be happy if we didn't tell it in detail, and she would often want it repeated many times. Then she would choose certain parts as the day progressed and want us to describe that sequence of events over and over again.

Lucy would want the story of how I got her up, washed and dressed, then the story of how I made breakfast and how we sat together and ate, or how we got in the car and went food shopping and what we bought. All aspects of the day she would want to be told about repeatedly. This need for repetition of her reality was relentless and persisted every day for at least the first six months and then gradually reduced over the following six months, and now, three years on, only happens occasionally.

I have to confess that this constant need to have us replay the day back to her again and again did start to drive us all a little crazy. But every time she asked, we complied. It was clearly important to Lucy and we could tell she derived comfort from it.

Finally, we consulted our social worker, who explained the many benefits to Lucy of this repetitive practice. It was helping her to feel grounded, helping her make sense of her new situation, helping her brain to make new connections, and was helping her speech and language skills to develop through hearing the sequencing of words and sentences. And so we continued.

Knowing the extent to which it was benefitting Lucy helped us manage the frustration involved with spending huge chunks of our day verbally repeating huge chunks of our day!

---

Metaphors and stories are other powerful tools that can help your child make sense of their experience. Common wisdom advises that it is rarely too soon to start introducing your child to the fact that they were adopted. Indeed, if you are adopting a child over a certain age, they will be fully aware that you are not their birth parents as they will have memories of birth relatives and other significant carers. Metaphorical stories are a perfect way to gently start to communicate key aspects of your child's life story in an easily understandable and engaging way.

Adoption-related stories help your child consider other family models and the experiences of other children with whom they may feel a connection. Metaphorical stories allow you to relate aspects of your child's life experience in a story format using other characters, often animals, in place of the actual people. Using metaphorical stories can help your child remain open to learning about their history in situations where the hard facts presented in their raw form might cause them to resist listening. Stories and metaphors keep the communication channels open and thereby create the pathways for the messages to be heard. In turn this paves the way for your child hearing and becoming familiar with the narrative of their life story and coming to their own conclusions when they are ready.

---

### A story about rabbits

When Lucy arrived at age four, we had expected her to at least understand the basic steps in her life story, which were, simply, that her birth parents weren't able to look after her. At the age of two she moved in with her foster carers until a 'forever' family could be found. We were found as her forever family and then she moved in with us.

In reality Lucy had no understanding of this simple sequence of events at all. She was clearly remembering aspects of her past and had put her own inaccurate interpretation on them to make a different version of her life story. Over time Lucy's version of her life story had become very real to her and she was adamant that her 'truth' was correct.

We recognised that Lucy's truth *was* correct from her perspective. Directly trying to correct her understanding would have been confusing for her and would not have helped our aims of encouraging her to develop trust in us and to attach to us. Instead of correcting her, we acknowledged and accepted her truth from her perspective and simply started telling her a story about a family of rabbits.

The rabbit family had names similar to the main characters in her life. I told her the story of her life through the family of rabbits. Soon this story became a firm favourite and she requested it again and again, and soon corrected the names until they were exactly the same as the people in her life.

Slowly Lucy absorbed the stories and was able to understand the key steps. Lucy then started telling us the true story of her life and the previously fabricated story was never mentioned again. It was almost as if the rabbit story opened her mind and memory to make other versions of her life story possible, which allowed her to make more sense of the actual events in her life. Lucy soon started talking about different aspects of her life that she clearly remembered.

---

There are lots of adoption books written for children. These were great in helping Lucy understand the concept of adoption, but didn't help her understand her own journey through life. Every child's life story is different. It was the power of metaphor that paved the way for Lucy making sense of her memories and claiming her rightful life story. I know it will be different for all children, but consider exploring and using the power of stories and metaphor. It is an approach that may help your child make sense of their own life story.

## Your child's memory may be clear and confused

Your child has experienced their life through their five senses: sight, hearing, physical sensation, smell and taste. This is the only way any of us can experience what is going on around us. Our senses are also significant in how we make memories.

First we encode information received through our senses, then we store the information in our brains and finally we retrieve it as a memory.

Your child will be able to access those memories of experiences that their brains coded and stored in their conscious memory. They may have witnessed events of which they had no concept or understanding and so, depending on their age when they made their memories, it may be a challenge for them to make much sense of what they remember.

In talking with child psychologists I learnt that it is not only possible but is actually quite common for pre-verbal children to have memories imprinted so strongly that they later recall them when they have the language skills to talk about them. They may remember certain aspects of the events but might not have the capacity to understand the context of the whole event or the level of understanding to accurately interpret their experiences. As they grow up and time passes they will process their memories differently as they appreciate different contexts and have more experiences through which to process their memories. At any point in time they may interpret their memories correctly or incorrectly, but to them their memory and their interpretation of it will be clear and correct.

When your child recalls memories, therefore, they may try to attribute some explanation to help their memory of the experience make sense. As they grow up, gain experience and their knowledge of the world around them grows, they may try to interpret an old memory through a new awareness and attribute new meaning to it. This meaning may be accurate, but it may be completely false. Either way your child may well cling to their interpretation of a memory as, to them, their interpretation will seem accurate, valid and correct.

You may not know how much your child remembers unless they talk about it. They may not be aware of how much they remember until a memory is triggered by a familiar sight, sound, smell, taste or physical sensation.

Your child will probably be at least one year older when they move in with you than they were when they experienced many of their early life experiences. Therefore, they may be trying to process a younger child's memory through an older child's awareness and cognitive processing ability. This may cause them confusion.

If unsure how best to help your child process a particular memory, ask yourself:

'What can I say and do in this situation that will help my child know and feel that I empathise, that I believe them and their memories and that they can trust me?'

If your chosen response to a situation is guided by the answer to this question, then you will not have any regrets about how you have parented, as you will have done the best that you can in each situation given your current understanding of the situation, your child, your capabilities and the options open to you at that time.

## Validate and acknowledge your child's memories

Your child may try to tell you of an experience that seems highly unlikely, fanciful, or just not possible from your grown up understanding of the world, but from the perspective of their memory they may feel adamant that events unfolded as they remember them.

This is where your empathic approach will help again. Whatever memory your child chooses to share with you about their life before, make sure to let them know that you believe what they are telling you, because for them their memory is true.

Listen to your child and acknowledge their perspective and their memories. Give names to some of the emotions that they might have been feeling, and ask questions that enable them to expand and share their experience and memories to the extent that they would like. What your child needs from you is to hear that you believe their memory and their experience. Don't try to tell them that their memory is wrong – you weren't there – how can you be so sure?

You don't need to probe deeply or ask detailed questions. Just take what they offer and allow them the opportunity to share what they feel comfortable sharing. They will learn to trust you as someone they can share their thoughts with, someone who is non-judgemental and safe. The intent is to help them feel better about having shared their memories, not worse.

Think of some phrases to say to your child. These suggestions may help. But I am sure you will come up with your own too.

**Acknowledge your child's memories and feelings**

- 'You are working really hard to understand all of these memories you have.'
- 'You were very little when all this happened, and now you are older you are thinking back and doing a great job of trying to remember and figure out what it all means.'
- 'I can tell that was a very scary memory for you and you are being very brave thinking about all of this.'
- 'I can tell that this is confusing for you, but I believe what you are telling me and as you get older and keep talking to me about it I know that between us we will figure it all out.'
- 'You have remembered that really well from when you were little. To have that happen must have been very confusing and scary for you when you were so little.'
- 'I am sorry that you had to see/feel/hear that. I can imagine that that would have been very confusing and scary for you back then.'
- 'I wish I could have been there to protect you and stop any of that happening to you.'

## The bucket

One memory Ben would tell his adoptive mum was of his birth mum 'weeing and pooing' in a bucket and tipping it over his dad's car! Ben was almost two years old when he went into care and had just turned four when he first shared this story. It did seem a strange memory to have, and his adoptive mum struggled to believe it as, to the best of her knowledge, neither of Ben's parents owned a car.

Ben's adoptive mum did try to tell him that he'd probably made a mistake and that although lots of other things did happen, this memory probably didn't. After all, his start in life was bad enough without him adding false memories!

Ben got quite upset that his adoptive mum didn't believe him and kept repeating the story again and again, getting more and more insistent. Eventually he just stopped mentioning it. It wasn't until the adoptive mum had cause to contact the social workers regarding an issue with Ben's older brother that she realised Ben's memory might have actually happened. She found out that at the time the boys were removed from home, the birth parents were using a bucket for a toilet as their proper toilet was blocked, and so it was quite likely that such an unsavoury bucket did in fact exist! Also the fact that the birth dad had left the birth mum and used to be driven round by his new girlfriend to visit Ben added further credence to his story. Ben's birth parents were known to have a volatile relationship with physical arguments, so actually Ben's memory was entirely plausible!

When Ben's adoptive mum realised that Ben's memory was indeed possible, she apologised for not believing him and asked him to tell her what he remembered again. Ben was very relieved to finally have his new mum listen and believe him. Even if Ben's memory wasn't quite accurate, the relief that was evident to the adoptive mum when he finally felt believed made her wish that she had communicated 'belief' rather than 'doubt' at the outset.

It just goes to show, no matter how unlikely the memory that your child is trying to share, a version of their story may well be true. You will build more bridges and trust with your adopted child if you accept what they are telling you rather than refuting it. Their memories may be a little muddled, but it doesn't mean that they are wrong.

What we have come to realise through our experience with Lucy is that a child may well learn to live with their past, they will integrate it into their lives and move on. But as they grow up, develop, make different connections and mature in themselves, they will review and interact with their past from different perspectives and those past events may well have the power to hurt them at different levels and in different ways throughout their life. So as your child grows up you will always need to be there helping and supporting them emotionally as they remember and view the events through the eyes of developing child, adolescent and adult. They will make sense of it in their own way. Just be there for them and let them know that you empathise with whatever it is that they are feeling.

In all that I have read and been told, I firmly believe that the more you can acknowledge the validity of your child's memories and associated emotions, the more they are able to unstick and move forwards emotionally. Be patient, listen, empathise and make it safe for them to reflect on and feel their emotions in order to process them.

## Summary

★ You won't have an accurate idea of your child's emotional state when they move in to your home. Interact with them as they appear to be, not how you hope or think they should be. Assume they will have less understanding than you think they will have. Interact with them at their level of understanding and then gently bring them forwards.

- ★ Imagine how hard the transition must feel for your child. You are a grown up, emotionally mature, have been instrumental in this life change and have support to turn to. Your child is emotionally immature, has little or no control over current events and no immediate support network. Strive to understand their emotions and support them at that level rather than reacting to the behaviours they display as a result of these life changes being forced upon them.
- ★ Your child may not understand the concept of 'permanence' and may be expecting to move on at any point. Do all that you can to reassure them that you are their parents forever.
- ★ Narrative, repetition, stories and metaphors will all help your child make sense of their current reality and understand key steps in their life journey so far. Metaphorical stories may help them to be open to messages and truths to which they might otherwise be closed.
- ★ Much of your child's life experience will be stored as memories in their conscious brain. They may have memories that they don't fully understand and will interpret them through their current frame of reference. Depending on their age, it is likely that their interpretation may be factually incorrect but to them it will be valid and right. Don't refute your child's memory or interpretation. Let your child feel that you believe them and their memory. It is important for your child to learn to trust you and to be believed. As your child develops, their interpretation of their memories will evolve. Early on in your relationship listen, empathise and help your child open up and share.
- ★ Help your child feel secure in your reassurances. Let them learn to trust you by understanding them. Use stories and metaphors to help build their self-esteem.

CHAPTER 5

# Support Your Child Through Their Grieving Process

From the moment your child moves in they will be on an emotional journey at least equivalent to, if not greater than, yours.

Although much of the process of adoption is unpredictable, the one thing that you can count on is that your child will be very likely to experience some kind of grieving process. They may grieve for their birth family, their foster carers, the start in life they didn't have, the childhood that they wish they'd had but didn't, anything else or all of the above. The length and depth of the grieving process is influenced by many factors and it is unpredictable. It is difficult to know at what stage your child will be with regards to their grieving when they come to you.

The purpose of this chapter is to help you anticipate the grief process your child may experience and to help you think of ways to help them progress through rather than get stuck in their grief.

Often the child will be too young to understand what is going on, will be confused and have a mixture of unpleasant feelings. Some will be so confused and overwhelmed with different emotions associated with loss, that in order to make some sense of what is going on for them they will attribute the feelings of loss to an absent possession for which they will then grieve.

As a parent, adoptive or otherwise, watching your child hurt and grieve is an uncomfortable and unpleasant process. It can also be confusing as an adoptive parent, when you are aware of your child's life story and have an idea for what you think they should be grieving, yet you see them grieving openly for the absence of people, animals or inanimate objects that you hadn't realised were significant! You may also observe them grieving for family members whom you know caused them harm, and this can be confusing and hurtful for you. You may be tempted to voice your thoughts, but it would be better if your child didn't hear you judging their loved ones, as it is unlikely that this will encourage them to open up to you.

As uncomfortable as it may be for you, strive not to stem the flow of your child's grief or inadvertently make them feel guilty or uncomfortable for grieving. If they sense your disapproval, they may start to hide or stifle their emotions, which is not healthy for them or for you. An emotion buried is not an emotion resolved and will come back in some guise later in life. The more your child can grieve for the losses in their life, the more they will be able to settle and move on with their new life with you.

In the case of some children, the grieving may seem non-existent and in others it may be very pronounced. If your child's grieving is pronounced, be prepared for the extra emotional drain you may feel as a result. Be patient and kind to yourself. It can be extremely hard to support someone who is so patently hurting and grieving for an extended period of time.

## The five stages of grief

Elisabeth Kubler-Ross (1969) presented her concept of the five stages of grief. These five stages have been referenced internationally thousands of times over the past 40 years as an explanation of how people cope with different types of major change, ranging from the loss or death of a loved one to an organisational change that may impact them at work.

The five stages of grief have been validated time and time again. It is highly likely that you will notice your adopted child progress through some or all of these stages, though the sequence, intensity and duration of each stage will vary. As your child gets older and develops, it is possible for them to revisit stages of grief with new realisations and perspectives. The five stages therefore can be viewed as a guide and as a reassurance that what your child is experiencing is healthy, to be expected and is progressive. If your child becomes stuck for a long period of time in one stage, to the extent that it is causing you concern, then that would be the time to seek additional support from a professional.

These five stages of grief gave us a lens through which to interpret Lucy's emotions. We were able to recognise that, although she seemed swamped in sadness, her emotions and how she was interacting with them did change over time, and she was moving forwards and making progress.

## 'Denial' is the first stage of grief

It is easy to understand why a child might deny the reality of what is happening to them. If acknowledgement of their current situation brings the pain associated with losing everything and everyone familiar, along with uncertainty of the future, denial is certainly the easier option.

## Reaffirming the situation

In the early days Lucy clearly experienced some big emotions that were hard for her to process. With the few words she had, she would remind us every morning that her foster carers were coming to collect her that day.

> 'I go home. You not my home.'
>
> 'I no stay, I go home yesterday.'

It was hard for us to see her so confused, but we felt our role at this point was to help her move into her grief of which denial was the first stage. We gently acknowledged her confusion and how hard she was trying to figure stuff out, and gently explained the reality of her situation.

> 'I can tell you have some big feelings inside and you're trying to understand what has happened.'
>
> 'Mummy-Beth was your foster carer, who looked after you while a new family that would love you and look after you forever was being found for you.'

We would look at pictures with her of her foster family and explain:

> 'You did live there and now you live here. That was your bedroom and this is your new bedroom. Mummy-Beth was your foster carer and so was your mummy for a little while, and I will be your mummy from now on, forever. That was your foster family and we are your "forever" family. We will look after you and will love you forever.'
>
> 'This must all seem very confusing to you, you are doing some really good thinking about all of this, and I can see you feel very sad right now.'
>
> 'It's okay to feel sad, you miss Mummy-Beth and the rest of the family. I know they miss you too.'

We didn't feel it would benefit Lucy in the long run, to facilitate a short-term respite from her big emotions through letting her believe this situation was only temporary. We decided from the outset that we wanted our daughter to be able to trust us and believe what we said, so we didn't want to start out in our relationship by misleading her in any way.

---

After a few weeks Lucy moved from 'denial' squarely into 'anger'.

## 'Anger' is the second stage of grief

Once your child has been with you for a while and it isn't possible to keep denying the reality of their situation, your child may well start to have outbursts of anger caused by a combination of the emotional pain they are feeling, the situation they are in and the lack of control they have over their lives.

---

### Placating angry outbursts

Lucy's anger and lack of control over her current situation would result in some sizeable tantrums. However, we knew she was just an innocent four-year-old girl who didn't understand what was happening to her. She didn't understand why these new grown ups, who she met eight days before she moved into their home, would not let her go home to her own family! She truly believed that she belonged to her foster family. She had been there for a long time and she was attached to them.

When her outbursts gave way to sobbing she would repeat:

> 'I not need new family, I got family, I not need new family, I got family.'

It was heart-breaking for us to listen to her in pain. We couldn't take her pain away; all we could do was empathise with phrases like:

> 'I can see you're angry and upset, you don't want to be here with this family, and you want to be there with your foster family. If I were you I'd be angry too.'
>
> 'It doesn't seem fair that you can't go back there. You want to go back and no one will let you. That must be very frustrating for you.'
>
> 'You've got some big feelings inside and you don't know what to do with them. Sometimes shouting and stomping helps doesn't it!'
>
> 'I know you loved your foster family very much and they loved you too. They were looking after you until a "forever" family was found who would love you and look after you forever. We're really happy to be your "forever" family – we'll love you and we'll always look after you and keep you safe.'
>
> 'This is your new home now and it's completely okay that you love your other family and miss them. It's okay that you are angry, this must be very confusing for you.'

Finally, Lucy's anger stage subsided, which paved the way for the next stage.

---

Don't underestimate the emotional toll supporting your child through their grief will take on you. You, the adoptive family, will be going through your own emotions as a result of this change to your family, and you will have to find the reserves to help your adopted child progress through their stages of grief.

If your child's most painful emotions manifest at a time that coincides with your lowest energy and emotional reserves, this is when I fear that the adoptive placement could be at its most vulnerable. There were days when I hurt so much for the pain Lucy was going through that I almost started to feel that we were in the wrong for having her placed with us for adoption and that her rightful place was back with the foster carers. It is important if you hit this low place emotionally to get some perspective and appreciate the complexity of the situation and the causes of the heightened emotions. Call on your support network; take a break even for a couple of hours and physically get some distance between you and your home situation. Get some exercise, go see a film, catch up with some friends or just get some much-needed sleep. This low state is only temporary. Your reserves will refill, and your child will progress to the next stage, and so the vulnerability of the placement will pass.

Lucy didn't stay in the 'anger phase' for long and soon started mixing in some 'bargaining', which is the next phase of the grief process.

## 'Bargaining' is the third stage of grief

A normal reaction when feeling out of control is to try to regain some control of a situation. This is as true for a young child as it is for an adult – they will just bargain in different ways. Even if their former life with birth parents or foster carers was less than ideal, they may have found a way to cope with it. It was familiar and its predictability offered a semblance of comfort. 'Better the devil you know than the devil you don't' as the idiom goes.

It may be that your child will start to look for reasons to explain the changes. They may start to blame themselves, thinking that if they had behaved differently they could have stayed where they were. They may also start trying to think of what they can do to influence you to put things right, back to how they used to be.

## Empathising and explaining feelings

After several weeks with us, Lucy started saying:

'I not stay here lots, I stay here one lots then I go home.'

'I be good, then I go home.'

'You tell Mummy-Beth I good, Mummy-Beth come get me now.'

'I eat my peas. Now I go home.'

'I stay one night, then go home after.'

It was very frustrating for her, with her limited language skills to try to bargain her way 'home'. This in turn gave way to her experiencing more feelings of frustration and anger. All we could do was empathise with our daughter and help her make sense of her feelings by giving them names and explanations that she didn't have.

'I can tell that you really want to go back to where you used to live with Mummy-Beth and her family. You are thinking really hard about what you can do so that you can go back there.'

'You were at Mummy-Beth's for a long time and you felt happy there. You miss your bedroom. You don't understand why you can't go back there and that makes you feel sad and cross.'

'Mummy-Beth misses you too. But her role as a foster carer is to look after children while a new family is found that will look after them forever. Mummy-Beth has another little boy that she is looking after now, who couldn't stay with his first family. She is looking after him until another family can be found for him.'

'I wish that I could help you feel a little happier. Would you like me to read you a story or shall we do some colouring?'

At some point in the discussions, maybe when she felt understood, Lucy would allow us to help her change her focus onto something that would give her happier feelings.

We were careful not to deny her feelings of grief, but neither did we want her to be engulfed by them all the time and not feel anything positive. We were aware that there are stages of grief, and although we couldn't help her rush through them, we could help her experience some happier feelings along the way. The feelings of grief didn't go away, but they were quite exhausting for her, so to offer her periods of emotional respite from her mourning seemed appropriate.

---

Every child will be different. You will need to be guided by your child. Observe the clues and follow the cues as to what your child needs. Our daughter did a lot of hurting and from her perspective she clearly felt the world was very unjust. She wanted us to know that she was hurting and to feel that we empathised and could explain her feelings to her in a way that she could understand. The grieving was always there bubbling away under the surface, but over the first few months the periods of emotional respite for her got longer and the time spent hurting got shorter.

## 'Depression' is the fourth stage of grief

The feelings of denial, anger and bargaining will eventually pass and your child may be left with feelings of depression combining sadness for their loss and despair for what they now understand they cannot have.

As painful as it is for you to see your child so sad, don't be tempted to make false promises to cheer them up. Recognise that this is one of the grieving stages, which in itself is a process associated with healing that will allow your child to move on to happier times.

Find ways to help your child to express their sadness in ways that will help them engage with it and move through it.

---

### Giving feelings a voice

At times I could tell Lucy seemed resigned to a feeling of sadness, but she didn't have the words to express how she was feeling. I believed it would help if she could share how she was feeling, so there were a number of ways I enabled her feelings to have a voice. I am sure there are many more ways to do this, and that you would come up with what is right for you and your child. Here are some of the things that worked for us.

#### Happy and sad faces

I would sit down with Lucy with pencils and blank paper and I would draw simple circles or stick figures. I would put two eyes and a nose on the circle and ask Lucy whether the face was happy or sad. Usually a conversation would flow that represented her emotions.

This is how the first conversation of this type went:

Me: 'Shall we give this circle a happy face or a sad face?'

Lucy: 'A sad face.'

Me: *(while drawing on a sad face)* 'What makes this face sad?'

Lucy: 'It misses Mummy-Beth.'

Me: 'I can imagine if it misses Mummy-Beth it must feel very sad. What shall we put on that other circle?'

Lucy: 'A sad face.'

Me: 'Why is that face sad?'

Lucy: 'Mummy-Beth misses her Lucy.'

Oh how my heart went out to Lucy. Not only was she deeply missing her foster carer, she was also feeling sad that her foster carer was missing her. At four years old, Lucy was adding to her own despair by assuming the sadness that she anticipated her foster carer was feeling as a result of the separation as well.

Following this simple interaction I was able to talk with Lucy about how happy the foster carer was to know that she was settled, and to let her know that I was talking to the foster carer about how well she was doing, and that although the foster carer was thinking about Lucy, she wasn't sad, she was happy for her.

This seemed to give Lucy the permission to be a bit happier herself. When we repeated the exercise a few times in different ways with stick figures or dogs or rabbits and other characters she was always able to share a little of what she was feeling, and I was able to communicate some important messages that she clearly needed and wanted to hear.

### Painting

I also used huge pieces of paper and paints. After letting Lucy play with the paints for a while, I'd give her a fresh sheet and a simple instruction:

'Let's paint about Lucy!'

'Paint a picture of those feelings you have inside.'

'How do you feel today? Paint it in a picture.'

Lucy would respond differently to those instructions on different days. But usually they would result in something colourful on the paper that was significant for her and around which I could facilitate a discussion that reinforced what she needed to hear at that stage.

One day Lucy made a right mess of the paints as she dipped the brush in every colour and made a big splodge in the middle of the paper. Another day we got pink dots! It really didn't matter what Lucy painted, it was the activity that gave her the chance to express what she was feeling.

Another time Lucy ignored my question and started painting and talking about the variety of significant people in her life, past and present. She put various babies in various tummies and different boxes around different people to indicate who lived with whom. She was clearly trying to figure out her life story. It was immediately evident to me that she had a completely scrambled understanding of who came from whom and who lived with whom, and so we were able to gently address this understanding through metaphorical stories as mentioned in Chapter 4.

**Stories**

Sometimes I would make up a story which clearly mapped onto Lucy's current situation in a way that she knew which character she was in the story; for example, it may be obvious that she is the Bunny. At some point I would ask, 'How is the Bunny feeling?' At this point Lucy would project her current emotions right into the story and explain why the Bunny was feeling that way. If sad, I could even ask what would make the Bunny feel happier. Sometimes she didn't know, and we'd agree that a hug and a cuddle might do the trick, at which point she would snuggle up for a hug. At another time, she might say that the Bunny needed to see a photo of her foster family, or she needed to hear a particular story, in which case we would do whatever we could to make the Bunny in the story feel better.

---

Using a variety of interactions can help your child share how they are feeling and give you more of an idea of what would help them progress. Drawing, painting and stories are very simple to do. You could also use toys and finger puppets or anything that enables your child to view their confusing emotions from another perspective or project them onto something else so that they can share them. I really believe this type of interaction helped Lucy process her grief.

## 'Acceptance' is the fifth stage of grief

Acceptance is not about your child getting over their loss and becoming okay with what has happened. It is more about them assimilating what has happened into the fabric of their lives moving forwards. Learning to live with the loss of their loved ones doesn't mean that they don't miss them anymore, it simply means that they have found a way to live with the reality and move forwards.

---

### Accepting and moving on

Lucy first started showing signs of acceptance after about eight months with us. We noticed that she spoke about people from her past without getting sad anymore. She'd mention people quite a lot and simply make comparisons between then and now and about how her life was different, mostly better. The sadness had gone and her predominant state was happy all of the time, even when she spoke about people she used to miss greatly.

---

## Grief is not sequential

How your child will process their grief cannot be predicted. It is likely that they will move through each of the five stages mentioned, but the stages may not appear in that order and they may present with differing intensity and periods of time. Your child may move through the stages in relation to their parents, they could repeat the process differently with regard to their foster carers and about anyone or anything real or fictional that they are missing from their lives. They may complete the five stages of grief, and then revisit different aspects as memories are triggered.

As an adoptive parent, your role is to support your child through their grief, however it presents. Trust that as they work through their confusion of emotions, with the right encouragement and support, they will move through the stages at a pace that is right for them and will emerge on the other side having assimilated their feelings and their journey into their sense of self.

## First foster carer visit

To support the grieving process, you will probably be encouraged by your social workers to arrange a visit from the foster carers sometime after your child has moved in. We were encouraged to arrange this visit six weeks after Lucy moved in. This visit may bring up all sorts of emotions for your child depending on where they are in their grieving process, but generally it is believed that it will help them move on with their grief.

After a few weeks of living with your child, you will know them much better than the social workers do. You will know when (and if!) such a visit from their foster carers would be beneficial for your child. I would encourage you to schedule the first visit with care and with respect to your child's emotional needs. Be proactive in taking control of the scheduling of this date and don't just take the first recommended date from your social worker. Some children may benefit greatly from a foster carer visit after only a few weeks; for others it may be a few months.

## Arranging the foster carers' first visit

Although we were encouraged to have the foster carer visit after six weeks, we knew Lucy was not ready for such a visit. Lucy was progressing through the stages of grief at her own pace and we knew as the sixth week approached that a visit from the foster carer would be wrong for Lucy and so we pushed back strongly, postponing the visit. At six weeks Lucy was still cycling through denial, anger and bargaining, and was still talking about the foster mother coming to collect her. We believed a visit from them at this stage would do more harm than good, as Lucy may think that leaving us to go home with them was an option.

We knew the time was right about eight months after Lucy had moved in, when, at bedtime one night she was inconsolable, saying that she wanted to say 'goodbye' to her foster carers. We reminded her of the day we collected her and of how they had said goodbye to her and she to them. Of course at the time we collected her she had no idea what was happening, or of the finality that the word 'goodbye' would have, she probably thought it was a temporary 'goodbye', as they would be coming to collect her the following morning.

The next day in the car she said to my husband that she wanted to go and live with the foster carers. Not wanting to deny her feelings, as hurtful as it was for him to hear after eight months he simply said:

'We'd be very sad if you went back to live there, we'd miss you very much.'

To which she replied that she didn't want to stay there, she just wanted to go and say 'goodbye' and then come straight back!

Later that week while with my mum, Lucy brought it up again, taking pains to explain to my mum that when she had said 'goodbye' to the foster carers on the day we collected her, it wasn't a real '*goodbye*, goodbye'. My mum described that Lucy said it with so much emphasis, trying to explain that she hadn't emotionally said goodbye to them, and that at the time she hadn't realised that it was a *permanent* 'goodbye'. She thought it was more of a 'goodbye, see you later' type of goodbye.

Lucy was giving us lots of cues as to what she needed. We knew without a shadow of a doubt that this was the time for us to arrange the visit from the foster carers. We took a lot of trouble to arrange it carefully, and took advice from our social worker as to how the meeting should be arranged to have maximum benefit for Lucy. Although the foster carers were keen to meet up, this visit wasn't for their benefit; it had to be carefully orchestrated to support Lucy as she progressed through the grieving process and not knock her backwards.

The foster carers were lovely but had unwittingly sent Lucy gifts in the eight months that she had been with us, which, had we passed them on to her, would have anchored her straight back into emotional stages we had managed to move her out of and on from. The foster carers had the kindest of intentions but not much understanding of the negative impact their gifts could have on Lucy's progress. We were a little nervous therefore, but following guidance from our social worker were very prescriptive about the visit. The guidance that we shared with the foster carers from our social worker was that the focus of the visit should be on:

- them wanting to come and see Lucy with her new family and to see how well she has settled
- them reassuring Lucy that they are pleased she is settled, and that she has a lovely home, bedroom, garden, etc.
- them being interested in how things are going now for Lucy, about her clubs, her new school, her friends, her family
- for Lucy to have the chance to say a proper 'goodbye' to them.

During the visit they should:

- not bring any gifts
- not bring messages from other people (other than their children)
- not share news with Lucy about any of her old life, her old friends, or of her extended foster family *unless* she asks specifically about people, events, etc.

The meeting was scheduled to last a maximum of one hour but if Lucy started getting too dysregulated, I warned them that the social worker advised we bring the meeting to an end.

The visit from the foster carers was perfect; they followed the guidelines that I sent them, perfectly. They were fantastic, and did their utmost to only bring positivity to the visit for Lucy. Lucy did regress during their visit and afterwards but this was short lived, and the benefits of the visit far outweighed any regression we experienced. We encouraged Lucy to give a really big 'goodbye' at the end of the visit. We all walked to the door as a family and waved the foster carers goodbye. Lucy occasionally mentions the foster carers to this day, but has certainly assimilated us, her new family and home, into her life and the role that the foster carers played in helping her get here.

After the foster carers' visit, Lucy seemed to settle even more. It certainly helped her progress through her grieving process and move on to acceptance.

---

## Summary

★ The grieving process is somewhat predictable in that there are the five stages, but how those stages will manifest, how intense they will each be and how long they will each last is completely unpredictable. Once your child had gone through it once, then they may well go through it again!

★ Your role as a parent is to facilitate the process, to help them try to make sense of the parts they don't understand, give names to the feelings they may be expressing but not able to talk about and to find ways for them to share what they want to share so that they can feel listened to and acknowledged by you, their new family.

★ Although what they are feeling and expressing may hurt you, strive to protect them from your hurt. They have too much emotion to handle as it is and they will progress through the stages of grief far more quickly if they can be open and honest and feel validated by you rather than having to worry about protecting your feelings and possibly being judged by you.

★ Also remember that no matter how much harm was done to them by their birth family or other people in their lives, your child may still feel love for them. So if and when they talk about them, show compassion for their loved ones.

★ Facilitating a visit from the foster carers can really help with your child's grief process. Be guided by your social workers, but most of all be guided by your child and by your feeling of what your child needs.

## References

Kubler-Ross, E. (2009) *On Death and Dying – 40th Anniversary Edition.* London: Routledge (original work published in 1969).

PART THREE

# Nurture with Compassion

*To nurture a child means to care for and protect them, keeping their best interests at heart at all times as they grow up. To nurture with compassion is also to be mindful of the gaps in nurturing that they may have experienced in their lives to date, and to nurture with a view to filling those gaps with complete understanding and lack of blame or judgement. To nurture your child will help them feel safe and develop trust, build self-esteem and a feeling of self-worth, and will ultimately help in their path towards attachment.*

CHAPTER 6

# Pay Back the Nurture Debt

It is fair to assume that the vast majority of children in the care system have not received appropriate levels of nurture and as an adoptive parent you may never know the complete truth about your child's background. So, if in any doubt, assume your child has a nurture debt and start paying that debt back straight away. Nurturing a traumatised child can take time and patience and, I believe, can help heal a child from the inside out.

The intent of this chapter is to share thoughts on how to pay back the nurture debt that may have accumulated as a result of your child's early life experiences.

## Ensure the basic building blocks of nurture are in place

There are certain very basic, yet essential ways of nurturing an infant and young child that come instinctively to most adults and help babies to feel safe, secure, comfortable and loved. Whatever the age of your child, if they have missed out on any of these essential elements of nurture, it will impact them as they continue to develop. The gaps in your child's development as a result of insufficient nurture could be anywhere and everywhere. Any gap will have an impact;

many gaps will have more of an impact on their development and their potential.

Infants need high levels of nurture to ensure strong foundations from which they can continue their journey of development from infancy, through childhood, adolescence and into adulthood. With solid foundations of nurture as your child grows up, their brain will develop to the best of its ability. Your child will then have the best chance to grow up to be a well-developed, balanced adult, confident in themselves and able to live life to the full, able to enjoy their achievements and handle life's disappointments.

No matter the age of your child, if they have experienced lack of nurture during their early years, look for ways to nurture them to help minimise the impact of any gaps that may appear. You might even find that an older child demands to be nurtured in some of the ways more akin to caring for an infant.

*Meet your child's physical needs* to help them realise the difference between comfort and discomfort. Some children may not have been fed when they were hungry, they may not have been kept at a comfortable temperature, some may have been left in soiled nappies, or had ill-fitting clothes or shoes. When babies are uncomfortable, they normally cry and their mother or father or other significant carer will figure out what is wrong and then take away the discomfort, for example, by changing their nappy or feeding them to make them feel comfy again. Unfortunately, this consistent and responsive care is not part of the early experience of all babies.

If your child hasn't had their physical needs consistently met in their early years they may not have the ability to correctly identify the cause of any discomfort they experience. Your child may appear dysregulated when all is not well physically, but they may not be aware of what is causing their discomfort.

---

**Understanding the causes of discomfort**

Donna had been severely neglected by her birth family and, although she had been removed from that environment when she was two and a half, the impact of her experiences showed frequently in many different ways when she first moved in with her adoptive family and persisted for over two years. Most of the time Donna didn't know what was wrong with her or why she wasn't feeling right, as it appears she'd never learnt to fully understand the causes of her discomfort.

Donna interpreted most physical discomforts as hunger, which would have been an overwhelming feeling for her when she was very little. Donna was also oversensitive to clothes touching her genital areas, which could be due to being left in dirty nappies for extended periods. In the early months with her adoptive family, she would react to the prospect of getting dressed with sobbing tantrums, refusing to wear clothes that even barely touched her. Everything would have to be loose and hanging, with underwear several sizes too big.

For over a year the adoptive parents consciously named what they thought Donna's discomforts were, and then removed the discomfort and helped her consciously make the connection between what they had done and the absence of the discomfort.

Eventually, Donna started to make connections for herself. After about two years she started to know the difference between when she was hungry and full, didn't interpret every discomfort as hunger, and she could also wear clothes normally.

---

*Engage in non-verbal and physical interaction* to help your child feel close, loved and wanted. Some children haven't basked under the loving gaze of a parent or other significant adult in their early years; they haven't held eye contact with those that love them; they haven't experienced the closeness and comfort offered by cuddles and hugs or the pleasurable sensation of having their body gently stroked or massaged; they haven't heard the soothing cooing noises or enjoyed having songs sung to them by their birth parents. Some children have not felt that they were loved and wanted, and they haven't enjoyed the all-important nurturing sensation of closeness.

Some children who have not experienced this form of closeness and non-verbal communication regularly from an early age may feel very uncomfortable with other people being close, looking at them, hugging them, and may do anything to avoid eye contact or physical interaction. Although this form of nurture is what you would expect to do with a baby rather than a child, if your adopted child has never experienced this kind of nurture, it is vital that you help them experience it in some way. Experiencing physical closeness may well be much too much for your child in the short term, so be led by them. Allowing you to sit on the same sofa as them may be just about as much as they can cope with. Find out what your child can tolerate and then slowly encourage a little bit more by being creative in your approach.

Although we didn't have this challenge with Lucy, if we did I would have shifted Lucy's focus away from us sitting close and I would have played a game with toys. I might have pretended that I had a favourite cuddly toy, and encouraged Lucy to play with hers. I might have staged a tea party near the sofa and got the toys to make friends and sit on the sofa next to each other, then transitioned to us sitting next to our toys, then the toys playing and us playing, maybe then swapping toys, and gradually as we played I would have shifted until we were closer together, being mindful all the time of Lucy's comfort levels. I would have stayed within her comfort levels, but each time playing a different game or initiating a different activity that resulted in us getting physically closer.

Also, engaging with your child and showing your emotions and responses to them through facial expressions, eye contact, body and hand gestures will help your child learn to understand you, connect with you and feel nurtured by you.

---

### Encouraging eye contact

Lucy would not or could not look any of us in the eyes in the early weeks and would do all that she could to avoid looking at us directly. It was strange but we felt like we weren't really able to get to know the real Lucy until we were able to look into her eyes and have her look into ours.

Getting eye contact with Lucy was very challenging in the initial months. We could tell this was a challenge for her so we played lots of games involving mirrors, cameras, mirroring each other and any game or means we could think of to encourage Lucy to look at our faces and into our eyes and to allow us to look into her eyes. To start with it was easier for Lucy to make this visual contact indirectly through mirrors than it was directly, but eventually she got carried away in the games and making eye contact became easier for her.

We wanted Lucy to look at us to see us smiling at her, and for her to know that we were pleased with her and happy in her presence. It was a challenge, but slowly she became more able to look at us and into our eyes. The feeling we sensed from her when she saw us smiling at her and knowing that she had caused the smile was heart-warming and filled us with absolute joy. Lucy now bathes in our smiles and positively delights in receiving them.

Eye contact now is not a problem for Lucy, and only presents itself again when she is feeling out of sorts.

---

As well-balanced adults, we are programmed to emotionally and physically care for the young, and it can be hugely frustrating when we are not able to provide the basic nurturing through the physical interaction that we instinctively know is so desperately needed and that we long to provide. Do not underestimate the feelings of rejection that can build up if you are continually pushed away and avoided by the child you are trying so desperately hard to love.

Get creative. It may take you many steps and days or weeks to help your child move from what they can tolerate in terms of physical closeness, to sitting next to you or on your knee enjoying a cuddle, meeting your gaze with theirs. However, little by little, one step at a time you can find ways to help them accept nurture in this non-verbal, physical form.

*Stay physically close to your child* to let them know they are safe and that you are there to look after them. Some children will have spent much of their early life feeling scared and vulnerable and may even have been left alone to fend for themselves. Some may have been regularly left with random people with no consistent carer; some of these people may have been kind and caring, others less so. Your child may have grown accustomed to being physically distant and feel more comfortable this way.

Making sure to stay close to your child while still giving them the level of independence and space that you sense they need will give them a sense of consistency with you and safety in your presence. At times your child may feel vulnerable, and your close proximity, company and reassurance will help in those times when they might otherwise feel scared and alone.

Help your child to develop awareness that they are safe and to experience the positive feelings associated with that realisation. This will help them become aware of their safe environment and they will begin to place trust in the people who are creating that safe environment and enabling their feelings of safety. This emerging awareness of feeling safe and protected will help in the transition of their feelings of attachment away from previous carers and towards you and your family.

It may be that your child needs to feel close at certain times of the day or night. Helping them know you are close, reliable, consistent and dependable will help them relax and feel safe.

---

### Transitioning from awake to asleep

For the first few weeks in her new home, the only way Grace's adoptive parents could get her calm enough to sleep was to stroke her back until she fell asleep; she needed the physical touch as reassurance that they were there and would protect her and not leave her on her own. Over a period of weeks, the parents managed to transition the connection through 'touch' to a connection through 'voice' as they took turns to sit by the side of her bed.

After a couple of weeks, they were able to move gradually from her bedside to outside her bedroom door. Still though, they'd be talking gently to her so that she knew they were there. Eventually they sat silently outside her bedroom door, but answered immediately every time she called out to them, so that she knew they were still 'close'.

After a few more weeks they managed to progress downstairs with a two-way monitor so that Grace could speak to them and they would answer whenever she wanted. After a few weeks of quite active chatting back and forth on the monitor, Grace didn't need that constant level of interaction anymore and just called out if she needed something. However, when she did call out, she would get anxious and distressed if one of the parents did not respond promptly.

Now, a few years on, the adoptive parents still have the monitor for Grace and on the rare occasion she calls out now, she is more relaxed if they take longer to respond, but is still very comforted by their response. She occasionally likes to test that they are still there. Having invested so many months in building up her trust in them, their proximity and their protection of her at her most vulnerable time, they are still working hard to maintain that trust, and anticipate that they will only remove the monitor when she asks them to.

---

Each of the nurturing building blocks described above are vital for the development of a baby, through toddlerhood into childhood and beyond. They are also vital for an older child who has missed these essential nurturing elements in their infancy. It is very common for an adopted child to regress slightly when they move into an adoptive placement, so be prepared and take any opportunity that presents to nurture your child. I assume that it is better to overnurture than to miss the opportunity of meeting unmet needs in one of the essential areas.

Look for the clues and follow the cues: your child may actively guide you and pull some of the nurturing that they need directly from you. You may be surprised at some of the inventive games your child will come up with, the sole purpose of which will be to allow them to receive some nurturing in the guise of role play.

---

### Child-led nurture

From the instant Jayden moved in with his adoptive family, he gave them lots of clues about the gaps in his nurture. They could tell by the way that he interacted with his toys, other children and grown ups, how he managed himself, how he spoke and how he ate that he had not received the levels of care and nurture that he deserved.

Jayden's adoptive parents were well prepared and consciously looked for ways to repay the nurture debt, but what they hadn't anticipated was the nurturing that Jayden instinctively knew that he needed and regularly pulled from them.

Jayden was emotionally very immature when he joined his adoptive family and liked playing with baby dolls. Jayden's play clearly showed that he didn't know what babies needed in the way of nurturing. Comments like 'you stay in dirty nappy naughty baby' and 'all you need is dummies lots and lots of dummies' gave clues to some of his past experiences. Using the baby dolls, the adoptive mum helped Jayden learn what babies need from their mummies and daddies.

As Jayden started to understand how to properly care for a baby he found any opportunity to incorporate the role of a baby into the games he was playing and would always want to play the part of the baby. He would pretend to be a baby with a wet or dirty nappy and would pretend to cry as he was uncomfortable. He would keep crying until the adoptive mum pretended to change his nappy to make him clean and comfortable. He'd pretend to be a hungry baby crying for food, and the adoptive mum would pretend to feed him milk or baby food. He'd pretend to cry as he was too cold, and the mum would pretend to make him warm. And so the games would continue, again and again. At one point apparently, it seemed to be all Jayden wanted to play for weeks.

As the adoptive mum was role playing tending to Jayden's needs, he would also want her to explain what she was doing as she role played the actions. It wasn't good enough for her just to do it, Jayden wanted to hear her telling him every step of what she was doing, why she was doing it, how she was feeling and how he, baby Jayden, was feeling at each step of the process.

Jayden was very insistent. Sometimes he also wanted to be rocked and stroked as he drank out of a baby bottle while his mum gazed at him and interacted with him as though he were a baby.

One day his mum was wearing a baggy jumper and, while she was sitting on Jayden's bed reading him a book, he crawled up under her jumper, curled into a ball and to her surprise stayed there for about 15 minutes pretending he was in his adoptive mum's tummy. He then repeated this for about 10 minutes a time, sometimes several times a day. Jayden knew that he hadn't grown in his adoptive mum's tummy, but she sensed that he wanted to have the feeling of safety and of being wanted, as though he had grown there.

The adoptive mum always stressed that Jayden hadn't grown in her tummy, but had grown in his birth mum's tummy, but he insisted that although he knew that, he just wanted to know how his new mummy would have looked after him if he had grown in her tummy.

The adoptive mum showed Jayden how she would have talked to him and how she would have stroked her tummy if he had been in her tummy, and how she would have gently looked after him as a tiny baby even before he was born. Time and time again he went under his mum's jumper and wanted her to talk gently to him. When he was ready he would emerge from the jumper as though being born and would bask in the love showered on him as though he were a newborn baby.

Jayden gave his adoptive parents clue after clue of the areas missing from his nurturing and he provided lots of ways for them to help him receive the nurturing he so desperately needed.

Apparently one day after about 10 months, Jayden had clearly derived what he needed from the baby play and just stopped doing it. It seems his debt in that area was repaid.

---

*Build your child's sense of belonging* to support their emerging sense of permanence. Some children will feel very confused about where they fit in and where they belong. It is human nature to want to feel 'wanted' and to feel like we belong. It is possible that your child, now separated from their kin, will feel alone and bereft. When you sense the time is right, start pointing out similarities between your child and members of your family to help them feel that they are 'like' you. The more your child feels like they have similarities with you and their new kin, the easier it will be for them to start feeling like they belong. You can point out similarities in food preference, colour preference, skills, likes and dislikes, habits, and other personal and family traits as well as physical appearance like eye colour, hair colour, shape of hands and feet, to name but a few.

While raising their awareness of similarities with your family, it is important to honour the similarities they have with their birth family, or other people to whom they feel some loyalty and love. Point out the similarities as an 'as well as' rather than an 'instead of'. It is perfectly natural for them to embrace your family and their new home while still remembering their previous family and previous homes. Be led by them – if they want to talk about similarities they had with members of their birth family or friends, be interested in this as they share their thoughts and memories with you.

---

**Point out similarities**

Lucy likes it when we point out similarities, and she points them out again and again asking, 'What else? What else is the same?' Lucy has the same eye colour as my husband, the same hair colour as our son, the same skin tone as my father, she loves beetroot like me and has the same interest in fairies as my mum. She actively looks for similarities, in looks, likes and dislikes. It comforts her and definitely helps her sense of belonging.

---

*Vary your style of interaction* to enable your child's developing sense of self. Many children will not actually have been interacted with on a regular basis and may have spent a lot of their time feeling like they were a nuisance, in the way and in the wrong. I spoke to one lady who told me of a three-year-old child, who, as a result of having so many siblings, had been deprived of interaction to the extent that she didn't appear to know her own name!

Strive to use structured and unstructured interactions with your child for care giving and play. This will enable two-way communication and self-expression, and will facilitate your child's growing confidence. One-on-one time with your child, patiently taking turns at games, doing household chores or having simple conversations will help your child become familiar with the rhythm of interaction, and develop an emerging sense of self and self-importance.

Interact with your child through formal board games (taking turns, following rules) and less formal games, like Play Doh, Lego, painting and drawing, as well as made up 'role play' games. Let them lead the play while you follow and encourage them to follow when you lead.

Sometimes you can just be with them as they play, and give a running commentary of what you see them doing.

---

### Connecting though verbal commentary

My capacity for playing games is nowhere near that of Lucy and so sometimes when I have exceeded my limit I just sit with her as she plays and engage with the play by commenting on what she is doing. I will simply give a verbal running commentary:

> 'Oh I see you are putting the dolly in the cot, and covering her up nicely with the blanket to keep her warm.'
>
> 'I like the Lego house you are making; you put the green one on top of the blue one. I can see you are looking for a

particular block. Which colour are you looking for? Oh, I see you found a red one, and are putting that one on top now. I can see you are taking great care to build a strong wall. I see you smiling; I can tell you are feeling happy right now.'

This works really well for Lucy, who will join in the chatter about what she is doing as well. This form of interaction, as well as helping Lucy feel connected, I feel sure has also helped her speech develop.

For Lucy it seems to validate the choices she is making in her games, helps her feel that I am interested and observing what she is doing, and by commenting on how I think she is feeling, I can also help her learn about some of her emotions.

---

## Don't underestimate the importance of paying back the nurture debt

Psychologically, a nurtured child will learn to know themselves, to trust their intuition, trust their sense of what is right and wrong and to understand the complexities of the world around them. Emotionally, a nurtured child will develop more of an ability to experience the full range of emotions and will develop the ability to feel appropriate emotional responses in different situations. Physically, a nurtured child will be able to distinguish emotional from physical pain, and to detect and interpret the appropriate level of sensation from physical touch as well as interpret internal physical sensations. Socially, a nurtured child will be able to interact with others in a way that is appropriate for the culture in which they live.

As your child gets older and continues to develop, giving them appropriate opportunities to make decisions and learn from their mistakes will help their growing sense of self-worth and emerging confidence. As they become more able to look after themselves, choose their own friends and meet their own needs they will be better prepared for life as an adolescent and eventually an independent adult. It is never too soon to think about the future development and nurturing needs of your child, but it is essential to get the fundamental building blocks in place as a stable base from which your child can start to thrive.

## Summary

- ★ To grow up and thrive as an adult, a child must be nurtured from infancy, through childhood, into adolescence and beyond. The most fundamental of nurturing activities are those that should be borne out of a natural instinct to love, protect and care for the young. Unfortunately, many children have been denied the most basic forms of nurture, which may result in gaps in their development.
- ★ If you are adopting a child from the care system, assume that there will be a nurture debt and actively look for ways to nurture your child. Be open to your child pulling nurturing activities from you that they missed out on as an infant. Look for the clues and follow the cues and strive to fill the nurture gaps to help your child progress and develop to the best of their potential.
- ★ Make sure to meet their physical needs so that they can discern physical sensations in their body that indicate the difference between discomfort and comfort. Interact with your child in a physical way and communicate with them through non-verbal means, including facial expressions, eye contact and gestures. Help your child feel safe through your close physical proximity. Help them realise when they feel secure and that you are the cause of that positive feeling. Help your child feel that they can belong to your family and help reinforce their sense of permanence.

★ Nurturing your child will help them to feel safe and develop trust, build self-esteem and a feeling of self-worth, and will ultimately help in their path towards attachment.

CHAPTER 7

# Nurture Through the Senses for Brain Development

While it is probable that your child has not been fully nurtured, it is also probable that they have suffered from a lack of appropriate opportunities to fully develop in other ways as well.

The intent of this chapter is to help you understand how a child's brain develops from infancy, and to make you aware of the very positive impact you can have by consciously helping their brain develop as soon as you are able to have influence. The brain is a wonderful organ and research suggests that it has a huge capacity to develop, even after years of neglect.

As mentioned previously, we have five primary senses through which we interpret the world around us: sight, hearing, touch, taste and smell. Your child will process their life experiences through their senses, and to date, at least some of what they have processed will not have been beneficial to their well-being and development, which is why they are in need of a new family.

Some of your child's senses may have been overwhelmed by overstimulation, completely understimulated or fed with inappropriate input. You can use your child's senses to enrich their everyday experience and their sense of well-being, heal some of the hurt that they may have experienced, as well as to proactively stimulate their brain in this vital childhood stage of their development.

## Brain development is influenced by early experiences

Your child's five senses report information to their brain about the environment immediately around them; this input stimulates signals to be passed around their brain; this is called neural activity. Neurons are the nerve cells that support neural activity by carrying electrical signals across the brain. When two neurons meet, there is a tiny gap called a synapse. Very basically, the effectiveness of a brain depends on the extent to which it has developed a dense and effective network of neurons and synapses (see Figure 7.1).

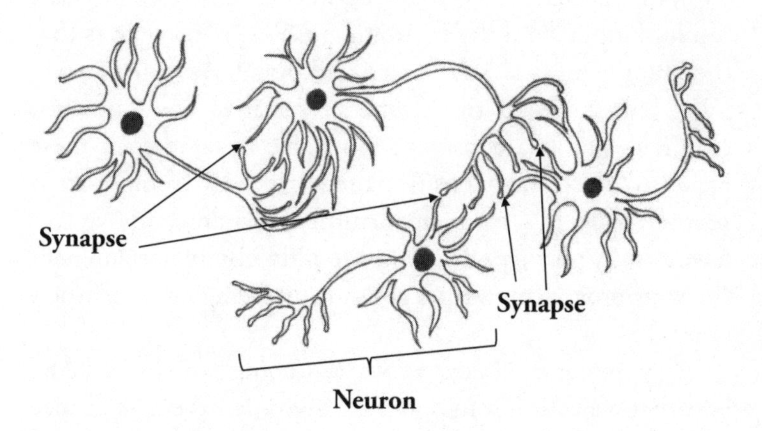


**Figure 7.1** Basic brain cell structure

Apparently, synapses that are repeatedly stimulated get stronger, and synapses that are rarely used will remain weak and are more likely to die throughout childhood and into adolescence. For example, speech sounds sensed by the ears will stimulate activity in the language-related regions of the brain. If more speech is heard, then the synapses between neurons in that part of the brain will be activated more often. If, on the other hand, as a consequence of neglect a child has not heard much speech, the language-related regions of the brain will be understimulated and your child will have delayed speech.

Nowakowski (2006) suggests that more than 99 per cent of all neurons present in the brain of an adult were already present before birth. It is the extent to which we build synapses and connect these neurons that enables efficient brain networks, which in turn support ongoing learning and other cognitive abilities. Your child's experiences not only determine what information enters their brain, but also how the brain processes information and how efficient their brain becomes as a result of the number and effectiveness of their synapses.

Brain plasticity refers to the brain's capacity to change as a result of input from the environment. Research suggests that the brain is most plastic during childhood. As well as being most vulnerable to the effects of negative environments, children's brains are also the most able to counteract these negative effects with positive input received through their senses. There is a great opportunity, therefore, for you to have a really positive effect on your child's brain development through proactive and purposeful nurturing through their senses.

We decided with Lucy that we were going to do the absolute best that we could from day one, to give her the best chance at being all she could be. Therefore, we paid great attention to everything in her environment that would be 'processed' through her senses. We wanted to make sure that as far as possible, anything that was going 'in' to Lucy through any of her senses was beneficial and varied.

We found that there are many ways to work with the senses to stimulate brain development and help close the developmental gap that may have resulted from a lack of appropriate stimulation early on.

## Develop your child through their sense of sight

There are many ways to ensure that lots of good visual input is received by your child to give them fresh visual images and visual memories on which to reflect. Good visual input can also affect their emotional state and stimulate the visual areas of their brain.

You could consider the following to help positively impact your child's visual experience and develop the visual parts of their brain:

- Arrange their living environment to be in calming colours, uncluttered, tidy and clean.
- Ensure their bedroom is visually comforting with familiar items.
- Ensure any television programmes are age appropriate and feed happy thoughts.
- Read books together, looking at and describing pictures.
- Provide photos of significant people with whom they have positive associations (birth parents, other relatives or foster carers, etc.) as needed to help them feel connected and calm.
- Let them see you smile in response to them, be pleased and excited to see them, this will positively impact their self-esteem.

- Help close the development gap with visual play, recognising shapes, numbers, colours, drawing and colouring, mixing paint, playing with torches, shadows, hand–eye coordination and any other age appropriate game that stimulates their eyes and thinking.
- Encourage them to sleep in a darkened room to promote healthy, deep sleep.

---

### More appropriate visual stimulation

Grace had been completely overstimulated by television from dawn until dusk in her life before her arrival with her adoptive family. In a busy foster family where she was the youngest foster child, it seemed she had mostly watched programmes that were appropriate for much older children and it was thought with her birth family she may have been exposed to programmes that were only suitable for adults. Much of what she had watched she appeared to remember and much of it came back to haunt her at night, giving her bad dreams, fears of ghouls and bad people.

As she was used to many hours of television every day in her previous life she initially demanded to watch it all day in her adoptive home – she wanted to do little else.

Over the period of a few weeks, the adoptive parents weaned Grace off television as they helped her learn to fill her time with other visually stimulating activities. While weaning, they made sure to choose programmes that they were happy for Grace to watch that were nurturing and/or educational and, they hoped, would only ever lead to pleasant dreams. They would record the programmes they favoured and would let Grace watch those in moderation.

Instead of television filling her visual field for all of her waking hours, they played lots of visually stimulating games, read lots of books and got mucky playing with paint, all of which Grace thoroughly enjoyed. Grace quickly lost her all-consuming need for television in preference for other activities and at the same time significantly closed her development gap in terms of recognising colours, shapes, number and letters. She soon wanted more and more of the nurturing, stimulating developmental type of interaction and was not so interested in the television.

---

## Develop your child through their sense of hearing

There are many ways to ensure that auditory input can help stimulate your child appropriately. Sound can help your child feel safe, and stimulate their curiosity, language skills and other sound sensitive areas of their brain.

You could consider the following to help positively impact your child's auditory experience and develop the auditory parts of their brain:

- Talk to your child a lot. Repeat phrases, explanations and stories. Pose questions. Give your child the chance to talk to you. Listen to them, give them time to answer and encourage them to express themselves. Frequently read them stories.
- Be consistent in your use of voice when interacting with your child so that they can learn to take cues from the tone of your voice as they interpret your message. Differentiate the voice you use when you are praising from the voice you use when you are chastising.
- Be mindful of the impact different music may have on your child; music can help stimulate or soothe. If you

are used to playing lots of music in your house or have older children who may be playing lots of loud music, anticipate how this may impact the internal state of your adopted child and consequently how they may react in situations.

- Encourage your child to listen to music and the sounds of different instruments. Help them think how the music makes them feel.
- Some children react badly to loud or sudden noises, or noises that they don't understand, so play games to help your child identify unfamiliar noises that may frighten them.
- Be careful of noises that might float into your child's bedrooms after 'lights out' and cause them concern. Raised voices and 'grown up' television may sound scarier for your child if hearing them from within their darkened room when they are feeling alone.
- Use a variety of ways to verbally reinforce messages that you want your child to understand, either speaking with them directly or indirectly by speaking to someone else while your child is within earshot. If it is difficult for your child to have you tell them directly that you are proud of them, for example, make sure they are close by when you are telling someone else how proud you are of something your child has done. It is surprising what children pick up on.
- Make sure not to have sensitive conversations about your child that you don't want them to overhear when there is any chance that they are within earshot. Again it is surprising what children will pick up on, even if they look like they are engrossed in another activity.

### Recalibration of the auditory sense

It was evident to both the foster carers and the adoptive parents that Donna was particularly sensitive to all background noises and became upset by unexpected loud noises or unfamiliar sounds. She seemed continually distracted by normal auditory stimulus and would react disproportionately to loud noises, either becoming very agitated and holding her hands over her ears, or becoming hyperactive.

Although the adoptive parents did all they could to provide a calming auditory environment for Donna at home, they couldn't control the environment when Donna was out of the home.

It became evident to Donna's school teachers that compared with other children, Donna was frequently disturbed by normal classroom noises and she could become quite disruptive in response to unanticipated noises.

Following a medical sensory assessment, Donna was diagnosed with a form of sensory processing disorder and was prescribed a 'Therapeutic Listening Programme', the aim of which was to help regulate the auditory part of her brain that appeared to be overstimulated by regular auditory stimuli.

Halfway through the 12-week programme both the school and Donna's parents started to notice some significant changes, which continued to the end of the programme and beyond.

As a result of the programme, Donna's auditory sensitivity had reduced and she was much more able to screen out the unimportant, focus at school and she was not so distracted or dysregulated by normal or unexpected noises.

## Develop your child through their sense of touch

Early nurturing 'touch' is beneficial for babies and children as it is essential to physical growth and development, emotional well-being, cognitive potential and overall health. It is well known that massage therapy benefits premature babies, and nurturing touch is one of the easiest ways of helping to develop emotional and mental well-being in children.

Most children will welcome the regular physical interaction involved with being parented, will interpret the bodily sensations correctly and will seek appropriate physical forms of interaction and comfort from you, their parents. Some children, however, will not, and it is important to understand these children and to help them develop and be nurtured through the sense of touch.

Some children will have experienced pain and/or inappropriate sexual touch from adults who should have been keeping them safe and therefore may shy away from your physical touch. Conversely, if your child seeks or initiates any form of 'touch' that makes you feel uncomfortable, then this is inappropriate touch. Simply explain to them that grown ups and children should not touch each other in that way, and show them some safe and appropriate ways of demonstrating parent and child love. If in any doubt, contact your social worker for more advice and support.

Consider the following when nurturing and developing your child through physical touch:

- Ensure your child's clothes fit well and are comfortable for them.
- Ensure they have soft and comforting toys to interact with.
- Be sensitive to the level of physical interaction that your child is comfortable with. Work towards helping your child to enjoy the calming 'touch' that is

naturally given from a parent to a child, in the form of arm and back stroking, hugs and being close. But be aware that this may take a while to achieve.

- Build your child's trust in your 'care giving' physical interactions. You may need to build their trust step by step before they will trust you to cut their nails, brush their hair, clean their teeth and bathe them.
- Help your child learn the boundaries for 'rough and tumble' physical interaction.
- Help them learn about their body and the parts of their body that are 'private' to them.
- If they are confused, help them learn appropriate 'touch' from a parent to a child and what is inappropriate.
- Encourage activities that require the use of big muscle groups: jumping, hopping on alternate legs, bunny hops, star jumps, crab walking, three-legged races, obstacle courses, leap frog, hopscotch, catching games, balancing, etc.
- Encourage activities to develop fine motor skills: picking up tiny objects, threading, playing with beads, etc.
- Make use of everyday stimulating textures and temperatures; for example, drawing in flour, moulding dough, playing with water and sand, stroking an animal, feeling ice cubes and warm water bottles.

---

### Feather stroking to build trust and attachment

Grace took longer to build a trusting relationship with her adoptive father than she did with her adoptive mother. As both parents shared all parenting duties it was important for the balance of their family unit that Grace was as comfortable being physically cared for by her father as she was her mother. After several months of very little progress, and active rejection from Grace towards her adoptive father, their social worker suggested initiating some 'feather stroking' for Grace.

To start with, Grace let her mum stroke her hand with the feather, and she seemed to enjoy the sensation very much. Then the mum stroked her cheek and neck, again she enjoyed this very much and wanted more. Grace's parents then explained that if she wanted more feather stroking it had to be her dad who did it now as her mum had to go and do some chores. Reluctantly at first, Grace let her dad stroke her hand, then arm, then neck and face. She then lay down very calmly with her eyes closed and asked him to do her arms, her face and neck, then her back and tummy.

This simple process allowed Grace to have some quiet relaxed time with her adoptive father, some special bonding time between them that allowed her to develop trust in him when she was feeling vulnerable. It was a simple process that they repeated many times over the coming weeks. It led to a significant step change in her being able to start to develop trust in and then attachment to her new father.

---

## Develop your child through their sense of smell

Nurturing and developing your child through their sense of smell may not appear to be as obvious as through some of the other senses, but for infants the sense of smell is their most significant sense as it is how they recognise their mother and their immediate environment.

- Make sure that you smell the same to your child throughout your introductions and in the first few weeks of your child moving in. Use the same deodorant, scent, shower gel and washing detergent.
- Ensure that your living environment doesn't smell strongly of bad odours.
- Be aware that your child may want their familiar smells around them in the first few weeks. So if possible use the same detergent as their foster carers, don't rush to wash all their toys and clothes to rid them of smells that are unfamiliar to you.
- Encourage your child to notice how things smell different, flowers, herbs, foods, soaps.
- Encourage exploration to find out how different scents make them feel.
- Be aware when a memory is triggered for them by a particular smell and either work to incorporate or avoid it in the future depending on the impact it has had.

---

### Being sensitive to smell

Both Connor and Ben seemed to be highly sensitised to bad smells, but especially Ben. Anything that was new to him in the early weeks was met with the comment 'it stinky, it scary'. The first time he went to the toilet at his adoptive home he was apprehensive before going in, and then quite relieved saying, 'it not stinky scary in here'.

Sometimes early on, Ben and Connor would both get quite distressed, smelling something that none of the adoptive family apart from them could smell. Once the family were out walking along a busy street going in between some shops, when both boys got quite distressed and upset saying it was 'stinky and scary'. The family never did identify the smell so don't know how to avoid it in the future, but it clearly triggered some memory for them that the adoptive parents didn't understand.

All of the toys and clothes the boys brought with them to their adoptive home apparently had a strong smell of their foster carers' home. The smell wasn't bad, it was just a different smell that seemed out of place to the adoptive parents, and didn't really fit in their home. Although they were tempted to wash everything, they resisted, feeling it was important that the boys were surrounded by smells that were familiar to them. A few weeks after moving in, however, Ben started pointing to his soft toys and saying they were stinky.

The adoptive parents didn't think they were actually 'stinky' but thought this was Ben's way of communicating that his toys smelt different and not like the rest of his new home. With Ben and Connor's permission the adoptive mum washed all the clothes and toys and very soon everything smelt like it belonged. When everything had been washed, the adoptive mum thinks that the boys seemed even happier with their toys and environment and seemed to settle even more.

As the boys seemed sensitive to 'stinky' the adoptive parents did pay particular attention to making sure that everything was clean and smelled nice and fresh.

---

## Develop your child through their sense of taste

Taste is important for children's emotional development. Familiar flavours may cause comfort or distress, certain tastes may calm or stimulate them, other tastes may trigger memories as well as additives triggering different reactions in their body.

Above all, a nutritious and balanced diet is essential for your child's physical development and mental well-being.

The extent to which your child will eat a varied diet will be largely down to the diet to which they have become accustomed, prior to moving in with you. Some foster carers are very aware of the importance of a healthy diet and have done wonders improving the eating habits and diets of the children in their care. Other foster carers don't seem so aware or conscientious, so you may have your work cut out for you in this respect. Changing your child's diet may be a challenge if they have lived on a diet of sweet sugary drinks and junk food, as these can be quite addictive.

In my view, it is never too soon to start improving your child's diet. Your child is going through great changes as they move in with you and, while everything is changing, I would encourage you to make any food changes you need to make straight away. There is never an easy time to encourage a change to their eating habits, but I don't believe it will be any easier for them or for you if you wait. If you start on the new eating regime from day one, it will certainly be hard for them initially, but at least they will be on the right track nutritionally from the beginning.

Here are some thoughts about how to encourage development through your child's sense of taste:

- Eliminate junk food from your child's diet.
- Be patient as you introduce as wide a diet as possible to your child.
- Encourage your child to appreciate the different textures and tastes of food.
- Try playing guessing games, using a blindfold and different foods.
- Remember that a varied and healthy diet will introduce them to a world of different tastes and textures and will ensure they get the essential

vitamins, minerals and nutrients that they need for body and brain development.

- Experiment with opposites: compare frozen foods with warm foods, salty with sweet, crunchy with soft, chewy with liquid.
- Experiment with making different smoothies, letting your child choose what combination of fruits and vegetables to use.
- Experiment with the impact certain foods have on your child. Do foods that require sipping or sucking calm your child? Do crunchy or chewy foods stimulate them and make them more alert?
- Always keep a supply of fresh fruits and vegetables and don't overload on biscuits and breads.
- Be aware of the potential impact of additives on your child's behaviour, and strive as much as possible for an additive-free diet.
- Cooking together is a great way to encourage children to stimulate many of the senses and to encourage your child to explore more tastes.

---

### Transition to a healthy diet

Bethany's adoptive parents were disappointed when they found the limited range of food that Bethany would eat and drink. Although able to eat a lot of food, Bethany's food of choice was limited and consisted mainly of junk food and sweets, and she point blank refused to drink water, demanding lemonade instead. She would have escalating tantrums if not given the food she would like, which seemed to have worked for her across her various foster families.

As a result, the early days were a real struggle for the adoptive parents as they decided to make all the changes to Bethany's diet effective from day one. Initially Bethany refused to eat the healthy food or to drink the water she was offered and they had their fair share of tantrums as a result.

They decided, however, to stick fast and with bags of patience, games and powers of persuasion they were able to encourage Bethany to try new foods and to drink water. It took a few weeks of patience and absolute consistency but finally Bethany started eating, and more importantly *enjoying* the food she was being given.

The adoptive mum loves cooking for Bethany now, and describes her as a pleasure to cook for, as she really enjoys her food and is much healthier as a result of her varied diet. The mum is relieved that they didn't cave in to Bethany's refusal to eat healthier options in the early days, although she was tempted to give in as the previous families had, she acknowledges that it certainly would have been easier in the short term, but knows it would have been much more difficult in the long term.

---

There are many different ways that we can nurture our children, and being more considerate regarding what is processed by them through their senses in their formative years is one way that we, as parents, can have a huge positive impact.

## Summary

★ Although your child may not have experienced the best conditions to develop in line with their potential they still have the opportunity to catch up.

★ Due to the plasticity of the brain you can still have a huge positive impact on helping your child's brain development.

★ Recent research shows that by focusing on appropriate stimulation of the brain through all five senses, the brain will continue to strengthen and develop.

★ Ensure positive and nurturing input is processed through all your child's senses, and that they experience varied sensory stimulation to help their brain develop a dense neurological network rich in effective synapses. This will help support your child's continued learning and cognitive development.

## References

Nowakowski, R.S. (2006) 'Stable neuron numbers from cradle to grave.' *Proceedings of the National Academy of Sciences of the United States of America 103*, 33, 12219–12220.

# CHAPTER 8

# Build Your Child's Self-esteem and Facilitate Their Attachment

There are many ways that we can interact with our children which can start to correct the impact of the wrongs that they have suffered in the early part of their lives. The positive impact of all of our efforts will be multiplied many-fold if our children have a positive sense of self-worth.

The intent of this chapter is to raise your awareness of the power of healthy self-esteem. I believe that if we can help our children feel worthy and take pride in themselves, all of the positive efforts we and they make towards overcoming any negative impact of their early life experiences will be multiplied.

Self-esteem is a term we use to describe our sense of self-worth, the extent to which we value ourselves as worthwhile human beings. Self-esteem involves feelings about ourselves that result from learning about ourselves in relation to our environment and those around us. It is widely acknowledged that self-esteem is an essential human trait that can pave the way for the normal and healthy development of a person.

Much has been written about the impact of neglect on a child's self-esteem and a lot of it is easily accessible through the internet. It seems that, due to the negative life experiences of children removed from their birth families, they are at a higher risk of experiencing low self-esteem than are those from a nurturing upbringing. Children with low self-esteem seem more anxious and frustrated when faced with challenges, have a harder time finding solutions to problems, can experience self-critical thoughts and have a tendency towards pessimism and depression.

By contrast, it has been noticed that children with healthy self-esteem seem more comfortable with their strengths and weaknesses, have an easier time handling conflicts, are better at resisting negative pressures, are generally more optimistic, smile more readily and seem to enjoy life.

You can positively impact your child's self-esteem in a number of ways including creating a safe and loving home environment, nurturing with compassion, listening attentively to what they have to say and communicating with a positive intent, to name but a few. However, I believe one of the most significant ways to encourage healthy levels of self-esteem in your child is simply for your child to know that you delight in them and that they make you happy!

## Delight in your child

One of the contributory factors I believe that can help build a child's self-esteem is when they feel that people are pleased just to have them around. Find ways to 'delight' in your child and let them know that you delight in them. Smile at them when they walk in the room, be obviously pleased to see them, laugh with them if they are doing something funny, find it amusing (yes, even for the hundredth time) if they hide behind the bathroom door to surprise you. If they've had a positive reaction from you once, they may well want to repeat it again and again to get the same response from you! As far as you can, let them repeat their new-found technique for delighting you and also make sure to show them other ways or other behaviours they can adopt to get their 'delighting need' met.

Praise all the little things your child does and acknowledge the effort they put into developing positive habits.

Most children thrive on praise, but you may find that your adopted child needs many more positive contributions towards building their self-esteem than a child who has been fully nurtured since birth. By delighting in your child you are really showing them that you enjoy them, and that you love them and I believe that this will help raise their self-esteem and will help them to love themselves.

## Help your children experience the feeling of pride

In order to help your child build their self-esteem and feeling of self-worth, it is important to help them recognise the sensation of pride. Pride is a feeling of pleasure and satisfaction derived from one's own achievements. It is important to help your child connect with the positive feelings that result when they do something well. Although it is nice to tell your child that you are proud of them, it should be about them and not you. If you always say how proud you are of them, indirectly you are making it about you and your achievement instead of them and theirs. Don't always say 'You did really well I'm so proud of you'. Though don't forget to say this sometimes as well! Instead encourage them to feel proud of themselves as this will keep the focus on them. You can feel happy and proud as well, but the primary focus should be on your child feeling proud of themselves. Try saying to them:

- 'You must feel so proud of yourself right now – I can only imagine!'
- 'Wow – you did so well, how does that feel inside?'
- 'I bet that makes you feel happy inside, I bet you are feeling proud of yourself right now, and so you should!'

If feeling pride is a new sensation for your child, experiencing it may feel uncomfortable for them at first and they may try to get comfortable again by doing something that they know you will disapprove of. Many people I have spoken to can identify with this situation, where their child was doing something well, they praised them and suddenly for no apparent reason their child then did something on purpose to get themselves into trouble. Sadly some children seem more comfortable handling feelings of shame than feelings of pride. I believe this can be changed. Certainly with Lucy we had to be sensitive not to overpraise her or she would react negatively. Small amounts of recognition that built up over time seemed to be manageable for her. Now, after a few years with us, she positively glows with pride as a result of her achievements and enjoys the associated feelings.

## Create the virtuous circle of delight

Positive feelings feed positive behaviours, which in turn feed positive feelings and positive reactions. The more your child feels good about themselves, the more they will be in a positive frame of mind. When they are in a positive frame of mind it is likely that their behaviours will be more positive, they will appear more lovable and in this state will trigger positive feelings in you. This in turn will keep you in a more positive frame of mind towards them, and you can truly enjoy each other's company.

As this virtuous circle escalates, you will develop feelings of bonding towards your child and they will start to develop feelings of attachment towards you. When your child feels that you delight in them, they will feel more likeable and lovable and this will feed their self-esteem (see Figure 8.1).

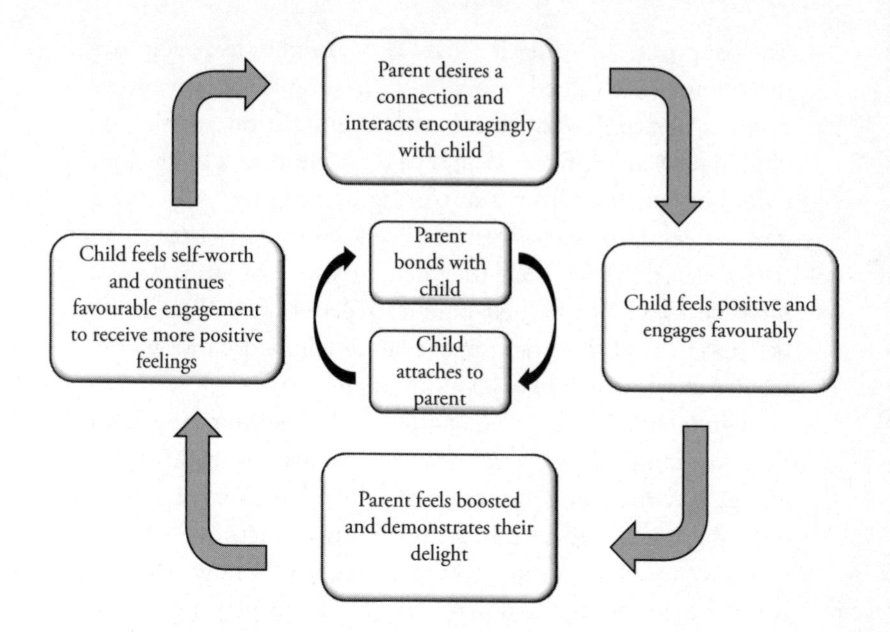


**Figure 8.1** The virtuous circle of delight

Everyone in your immediate family or permanently living in your household whose sense of well-being is directly impacted by your adopted child needs to experience positive feelings in relation to your adopted child. All members of an immediate family need to develop a sense of bonding, fondness and protection for your adopted child, and your adopted child needs to experience some sense of belonging with or attachment to all members of your immediate family in return. All members of your immediate family should strive to get on board the virtuous circle of delight as this paves the way for a successful adoption placement.

There will be days when nothing seems to go right, when you are a little more stressed than usual due to typical life and work balance issues. If those days coincide with your child demonstrating some challenging behaviours, it may be really difficult to communicate to them that you delight in them.

The opposite of this is that they might feel you are disappointed, irritated, impatient, frustrated or any other number of deprecating emotions. The impact on an adopted child may well be greater than on a birth child, as a birth child (who has benefited from a nurturing upbringing) will have a greater feeling of self-esteem and self-worth to bolster them when they don't feel that they delight you. The impact on a birth child who feels their parent's frustration will probably be shorter lived than the impact on an adopted child, whose feeling of self-worth may be more fragile.

If your child is being challenging, find something, anything that you can positively comment on and delight in them. Or just give them a hug anyway and admit 'Gosh we are both feeling grouchy today! But do you know something – I still love you no matter what. Come on let's have a hug.' Or stop what you are doing, sit down with them and play a game or read a book for a few minutes. Do what you can to change the mood, stop the downward spiral and create a virtuous circle of delight.

## Emotionally connect with your child

Children need emotional connection to thrive. In every interaction with your child, show your willingness to connect emotionally. If you are feeling emotionally overwhelmed and stressed following the placement of your child, it is a natural reaction to wonder if you made the right decision in entering the adoption process. You might start to question yourself and your capabilities and you may feel emotionally wrung out. You will still be able to give your child the routine care that they need, but it will be more challenging to do it in an affectionate way that communicates that you care for them and that you are growing to love them. You may find yourself giving routine care to your child without showing them any affection: you may feed them, clothe them, help them when they are hurt and go through the 'motions' without actually going through any '*e*motions'. This will not help your child build their sense of self-esteem or ultimately their feelings of attachment.

This is when the old adage 'fake it 'til you make it' comes into play. No matter what you are feeling, you have to communicate to this vulnerable child that you care for them, feel affection for them and are growing to love them. You need to get on board the virtuous circle of delight. The more they sense that you care for them and feel affection for them, the more they will show themselves to be lovable and the more you will want to love and care for them, and so it goes on.

You are the adult in this relationship, the one with the mature emotions. You have to be the one to create the virtuous circle, it is not your child's responsibility. You have to let your child feel that you enjoy caring for them, and even if you don't at first for whatever reason, once the power of the virtuous circle kicks in, you will eventually!

---

## A timely realisation

A few weeks after Lucy had moved in I was at my lowest point emotionally. My husband had returned to work, my son was at school and it seemed to me that Lucy was a challenge from the moment she woke up to the moment she went to sleep. I was feeling emotionally wrung out and exhausted.

Sometimes in the middle of the day I would put Lucy in front of the television and, once she was settled, I'd go into the other room and have a break, some Lucy-free time. In the early weeks, during these breaks I would frequently access the online Adoption UK discussion boards looking to see if anyone else was feeling what I was feeling and to receive words of wisdom and encouragement from other anonymous adopters.

These boards were a source of comfort to me and let me know I was not alone in what I was feeling.

I read one post from an adoptive mum seven years post-placement, who explained that she had never emotionally connected with her adopted daughter, her husband had emotionally connected but she never had. She remembered feeling really overwhelmed in the early weeks and, although she thinks her daughter was looking to connect, she (the mother) wasn't emotionally in the right place, so just went through the motions of caring for her daughter without connecting emotionally.

Reading this post really scared me – I couldn't bear the thought of being seven years down the line and not loving or feeling emotionally connected with Lucy. I know I was emotionally low, but she and I deserved more than that. From that moment on, I committed to making a real effort and 'faking it until I felt it' so that Lucy just felt 'love' coming from me in waves towards her.

I started by sitting next to her while she watched television and laughing with her (rather than taking a break in the other room), I'd get a bit closer and put my arm around her, I'd sit her on my knee, I'd laugh when she laughed at a character on the television. I made more effort every day to be close and to communicate to her that I was emotionally there for her rather than just there to provide for her.

It really didn't take long at all. Soon the little buds of love started to emerge and as I encouraged them more, they blossomed and I emotionally connected to Lucy and she to me.

I'll never know who put the post on the discussion board, but I thank them, as it jolted me out of a deep funk, reminded me that I was the adult, I was in charge and it helped me proactively connect emotionally with Lucy.

---

## Facilitate your child's attachment

According to much literature, children who grow up with a feeling of secure attachment to their carers are more likely to grow up able to trust people, develop self-reliance, attain their intellectual potential, cope with challenging situations, have greater self-esteem and mature emotionally. It is important, therefore, that you consciously strive to facilitate your child's feelings of attachment to you. Every interaction you have with your child is an opportunity for you to do this. If your child doesn't have a disorder that prevents attachment, theoretically they will be able to attach to you over time.

When you feel your child attaching to you it is the most wonderful feeling and creates a virtuous circle of positively reciprocated feelings. Your fondness towards your child increases, they feel it and become more open and warm towards you, and you in turn feel their warmth and become fonder and bond to them, and so on. What comes first? Who knows? It doesn't matter as long as you get on that virtuous circle.

---

### Delighting in Bethany

Bethany's parents really struggled in the early months to find any affection for Bethany as she had a number of undesirable behaviours that went against their values. Being on the receiving end of Bethany's spitting, swearing and general tantrums did get in the way of feelings of bonding from them to her.

However, they recognised the value of the virtuous circle of delight and realised that they needed to be the ones to get the circle spinning positively. They started to consciously put on a smiley face and communicate happiness each time they saw her. Although it seemed easier just to accept that she wasn't comfortable with physical interaction, they reignited their efforts to play games and gave Bethany attention in ways with which she was comfortable. They started to share more time with Bethany, often playing make-believe games that were led by Bethany.

Slowly but surely the virtuous circle of delight started turning, and both parents and Bethany were on board. After only a few days of conscious effort, the feelings of fondness and bonding started to stir, and soon after that they began to sense the beginnings of a feeling of attachment from Bethany towards them in return.

The parents noticed that when they really invested time interacting with Bethany, playing, reading and generally 'delighting' in her presence, this really seemed to boost her attachment to them, much more than anything else they did in terms of providing excellent care and nurturing.

---

## Anticipate an uneven attachment

It is quite common for a child placed for adoption to attach to one parent or family member more quickly than the other. This can result in a feeling of imbalance within the family unit. A few causes of this uneven attachment might be:

- The child may develop feelings of attachment first to whichever parent is providing more nurture, is meeting more of their needs or is spending time playing with them and delighting in them.
- The child may have had an abusive birth parent and therefore have a harder time opening up to, interacting with or trusting the parent of the same gender.
- It may be that the child was particularly close to their birth mum or birth dad and, therefore, for whatever reason, is not emotionally available to bond with the adoptive parent of the same gender as their favourite birth parent. They may, however, bond with the

adoptive parent who is the same gender as the birth parent with whom they didn't bond.

- It may also simply be that they prefer one parent or sibling to another for no apparent reason!

It is impossible to predict how your child might attach to you and members of your immediate family and in what order. It is prudent, however, to anticipate scenarios in which your child may attach to different family members at different rates. Anticipate how this may make you feel, and how you can manage those feelings to continue to try to board the virtuous circle of delight.

---

### The destructive power of an uneven attachment

Lucy attached to me more quickly than she did to my husband. It could be because I was doing most of the parenting in the early weeks after my husband returned to work, but there was no obvious reason for the uneven attachment.

It was very difficult for my husband when Lucy so obviously preferred me to him: she would actively push him away, verbally and physically rejecting him. As part of our adoption preparation we had theorised about uneven attachment, but we hadn't anticipated the strength of her rejection and the emotional and practical care giving consequences that we would experience in response.

With Lucy rejecting my husband so consistently and over many months, it was difficult for him to maintain a really affectionate disposition towards her. His natural defence against being hurt was not to seek active engagement with her as much in case she rejected him.

The consequence of this was that I had to do more of the parenting of Lucy, which left me less time for our son. This was a situation I began to resent, as I missed quality time with my son. I then became frustrated with my husband for not pulling his weight with Lucy. I also didn't want Lucy's attachment to me to get too far ahead of her attachment to my husband as this would upset the balance of the family even more. I found myself pulling slightly away from Lucy to slow down the emerging imbalance in attachment. This, in turn, slowed Lucy's attachment to me and caused noticeable regression in her behaviour, which fed my feelings of frustration towards my husband.

I was acutely aware of the knock-on effects of me pulling away from Lucy at this critical stage in her attachment, and I started resenting my husband for not trying hard enough with Lucy and for negatively impacting her progress and her attachment! My husband then started resenting Lucy as, from his perspective, she was the underlying cause of my resentment towards him.

It was a mess. We were in an emotional tangle that could have headed towards more stress or even disruption of the placement if not addressed.

We recognised the situation was serious and pushed for some external support in the form of a social worker who worked with us as a whole family unit, and focused on Lucy's attachment with my husband. The changes were very slow at first, but once the tide had turned and my husband was able to find ways to interact positively with Lucy, she responded positively back, and finally their relationship was mutually reinforcing and they were on the virtuous circle of delight. Lucy began to attach to my husband as well.

My husband stayed quite bruised emotionally for many months following the whole uneven attachment experience. But he hid his emotional bruises from Lucy while they were healing and today our attachment as a family is balanced and good. My husband and Lucy have a wonderful and close relationship, as do Lucy and I, and our family unit is completely balanced.

---

## Beware the vicious circle of rejection

The opposite of a virtuous circle of delight is a vicious circle of rejection. Negative feelings feed negative behaviours, which in turn feed negative feelings and negative reactions. As this vicious circle descends, you may develop feelings of ambivalence towards your child, who may pick up on those feelings and start to avoid you or reject your advances. When your child feels that you resent them, they will feel less likeable and less lovable and this will decrease their feeling of self-worth (see Figure 8.2).

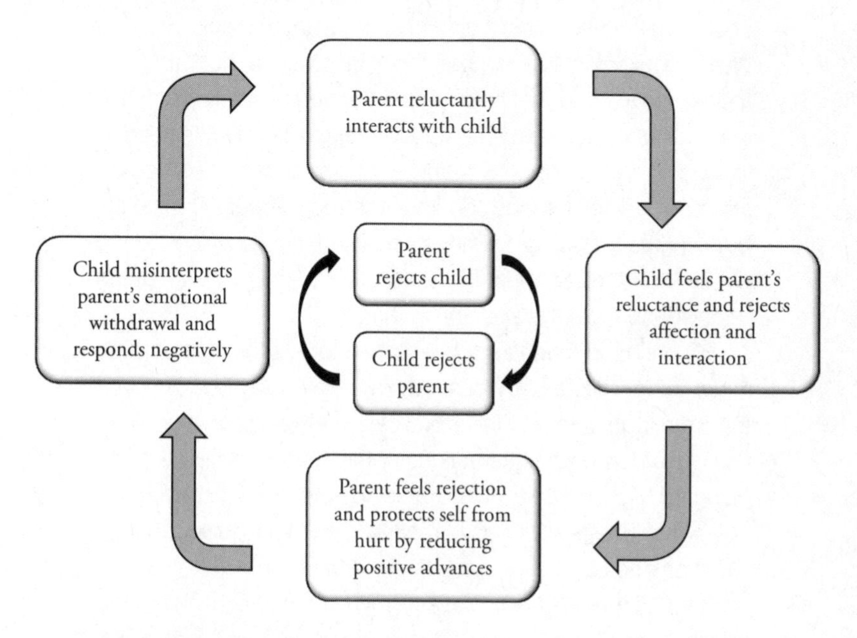


**Figure 8.2** Vicious circle of rejection

Sometimes when your child pushes you away, it could be that they are really testing you to see if you will stay no matter what.

---

## Refusing to board the vicious circle of rejection

Once my husband realised he and Lucy were on the vicious circle of rejection, he became resolute that he would not be pulled down by that vortex and looked for different ways to slow the circle down and to transition onto the virtuous circle of delight.

I remember one Saturday morning he went into Lucy's bedroom and asked her if he could read her a story, and she shouted at him to get out as she didn't want him near her. The easier choice would have been for him to leave, but he chose to stay. He told her that he cared for her and he really wanted to read her a story. Again she tried to make him leave. Instead of leaving he took a book from the shelf, sat next to the bed and started reading out loud to himself. It took about 10 minutes, but eventually Lucy got curious and came closer to look at the pictures and, after a few more minutes, transitioned to sitting on my husband's knee, enjoying the story.

My husband made sure to end the story reading session on a high note, before Lucy pushed him away. They both enjoyed that time together and the vicious circle started to slow down. A few more purposeful interactions of this type with my husband being gently stubborn, while voicing and demonstrating his positive intent, saw the vicious circle slow right down, change direction and become a virtuous circle of delight.

After 18 months Lucy was as firmly attached to my husband as she was to me. It may sound a long time, but it is a tiny fraction of the rest of their lives together.

---

The impact of your child developing uneven attachment within a newly forming family unit must not be underestimated. The tensions and stressors that uneven attachment can cause between different members of the family are difficult to fully appreciate and can be quite destructive. If the tensions and stressors within the family unit increase disproportionately and key family values are not being honoured, extreme feelings of frustration can result. Once the vicious circle of rejection intensifies, this can put the success of the adoption placement at risk. Therefore, as soon as you sense this may be happening for you or your partner, talk about it and strive to right the balance.

It is hugely important to get external professional support if you are not able to right the balance yourself. Contact the team within your adoption agency that is responsible for supporting adoptive parents post placement, and ask for their support and advice on how to address any emerging attachment issues.

When your child moves in with you, they will be emotionally vulnerable, immature and confused. Recognise this and do all in your power to delight in them, raise their self-esteem and encourage the virtuous circle of delight. It will facilitate trust, security and feelings of bonding and attachment, which are the most rewarding feelings to experience.

## Summary

- ★ Children who have suffered abuse, neglect or other similarly negative experiences necessitating their removal from home are at a higher risk of suffering from low self-esteem. A child with low self-esteem is far less likely to achieve their potential and lead a fulfilling and rewarding life.
- ★ There are many ways for you as a parent to positively impact your child's self-esteem but one of the key ways is simply for them to know and experience you 'delighting' in them, being happy to see them, smiling in response

to them and enjoying spending time with them. Help your child learn to identify the feeling of pride they may experience when they have done something they feel pleased with.

★ Strive to board the virtuous circle of delight: positive feelings feed positive reactions, which feed positive feelings, and so on. The more you feel your child attaching to you, the more you will naturally bond with them. A child who grows up with a secure attachment to their carers is also more likely to go on to lead a fulfilling life.

★ Either you or your child has to kickstart the virtuous circle of delight, so for whatever reason, even if you are not feeling positive towards your child, fake it 'til you make it! Once you interact positively with your child, slowly but surely the circle of delight will start turning and eventually will gain momentum.

★ It is not uncommon for a child to bond with one parent more than the other, at least initially. Do not underestimate how this can introduce unanticipated tension into family relationships and upset the dynamic of a family unit. Uneven attachment can lead to the vicious circle of rejection, which, if not reversed, can lead to a disrupted adoption placement. Once you feel yourself being pulled into this destructive, descending circle, focus on reversing the flow and if this is not possible, get some professional support for you and your family.

★ Recognise that your child is emotionally vulnerable and immature and do all that you can to help them raise their feeling of self-worth and trust in you as this will pave the way for bonding and attachment.

## PART FOUR

# Communicate Thoughtfully

*The quality of the relationship you are building with your child will be shaped significantly by the quality of your communications. The extent to which your child feels listened to and understood by you, as well as the extent to which they feel comfortable being guided by you will impact them as they develop. This section will share some thoughts on how to listen and communicate effectively, in the hope that when you are about to communicate ineffectively you may stop, pause, plan a different approach and communicate in a way that will help you achieve your intent while still building trust with your child.*

CHAPTER 9

# Help Your Child Feel Listened To

Listening is such a vital part of communication, but its importance is much overlooked. Many children, especially those from the care system, have been moved around from pillar to post, and it is probable that they have not felt really 'listened to'. One of the greatest gifts we can give to our children is to help them experience the feeling of really being listened to.

When a child feels listened to, they will feel more confident, comfortable and better able to 'open up' to reveal their emotions. They will feel understood and not judged, which will help release tensions, build trust and respect and have a positive impact on bonding and attachment. Improving your listening skills will greatly enhance the quality of the interactions you are able to have with your children, adopted or otherwise. Everyone likes to feel listened to and to feel that what they have to say is of interest. It is especially important for a child to feel listened to by their parents.

The purpose of this chapter is to highlight the importance of listening as a fundamental skill and to give hints about how to do it more effectively. I believe we all have room for improvement and can become better listeners, especially to our children. There are many books written on the topic of effective communication that include the all-important listening skills. I would recommend you browse the book shelves and read as many books as you can on the topic. We can all learn more, and the sooner you practise your new-found listening skills, the better.

## Practise empathic listening

Empathic listening is an 'active' skill that consciously engages our attention in the pursuit of really understanding another person's perspective and what they are thinking and feeling. It is different to 'passive' listening, where you simply rely on a person's words to tell the whole story. By listening actively to your child you are communicating 'I am interested to hear what you have to tell me. I want to understand what you are saying and how you feel about the situation. I am not judging or blaming you.'

By listening empathically to your child, you will use your voice, body language and eye contact to encourage your child to fully express themselves without being interrupted, criticised or judged. You don't need to agree with what your child is saying, as long as you can empathise, acknowledge and allow your child to believe that if you were their age, in their situation, with their life experiences you might well feel the same way as they are feeling now and act in the same way that they are acting now.

Empathic listening takes practice. Very few of us have ever been taught how to actually listen properly and most people are not naturally skilled at it. Many of us think we are good at listening, few of us actually are. We hear of people who are 'hard of hearing' because their ears don't work properly. Well, many of us are 'hard of listening': our ears work perfectly well but we don't actively engage with the person to whom we are supposed to be listening in a way that results in them feeling listened to. You are a good listener when the person to whom you are listening 'feels' listened to.

I have read widely on the topic of effective communication both for adults and for children and I firmly believe that empathic listening is the foundation upon which effective two-way communication between you and your child must build. One of the best books I have read specifically on communicating with children is *How to Talk So Kids Will Listen and Listen So Kids Will Talk* by Faber and Mazlish (2013 [1982]).

## Improve your empathic listening skills

Empathic listening will help your child feel listened to. It will help them feel understood more quickly and can help reduce any frustrations they are feeling. It can help your child contain an escalating tantrum, share experiences, reflect on feelings, seek guidance and much more besides. It is a technique that needs to be practised, but once mastered is useful for a wide application across life, not just with adopted children.

*Make time and look attentive*: If your child has not experienced 'being listened to' they may not be accustomed to talking much at all. When your child does want to share something with you, make time for them and give them your full attention so that you can really hear what your child is saying. Don't pretend to listen while trying to do something else. If at all possible pause what you are doing. Your time and your attention will encourage your child to share. There may be certain times of the day or certain activities during which your child feels more like talking. Lucy likes to open up and share her thoughts at bedtime, our son likes to share his thoughts and concerns over breakfast; each child will be different. Also, we should remember that there will be times when we are in the mood for listening and our children aren't in the mood for talking! As parents we need to be ready to listen when our children are ready to talk and can't expect them to talk just because we have time and are ready to listen.

*Listen with your ears*: Listen to 'what' your child is saying and 'how' they are saying it. 'What' your child says in terms of their choice of words, turns of phrase and the emphasis they put on different parts of what they are sharing, will give you most of the informational context of what they are telling you. It will also give you some key words to use when sharing your thoughts with them. Using some of the same words and turns of phrase will help your child feel more comfortable. Your child's non-verbal communication, or 'how' they are saying it, will give you the clues to their emotions as they are communicating. Non-verbals can be detected in their tone of voice, energy and enthusiasm conveyed, hesitancy, pauses and the levels of confidence with which your child is speaking. This will give you an idea of their priorities, the most important messages they have to share, whether they are sharing willingly or reluctantly, with excitement or trepidation.

*Listen with your eyes*: You will understand so much more about your child and what they are trying to tell you if you are able to observe them as they talk. Additional non-verbal clues can be observed through their body language, gestures and posture. What are their non-verbals telling you? Are they fidgety? Do they look nervous? Are they looking at you or avoiding eye contact? Do they look relaxed? Tense? Do they appear to be open and trusting or shrinking and cautious? If you observe them as they talk, you will get additional information to guide you in your responses to help them continue to open up and develop trust.

*Encourage your child to share more*: When listening to your child, encourage them to share and resist the urge to jump in with your thoughts. Instead, demonstrate that you really are interested in hearing all that they have to tell you. Simple encouragement like 'aah, I see, tell me more', 'uh-huh', 'what else?' or other such non-invasive encouragements may help your child continue talking and sharing. Nodding, shaking your head, smiling or frowning when appropriate to show that you are engaged with what they are saying and the emotion that they are communicating will also signal that you are interested and are empathising; this may encourage them to keep sharing. Giving your child time to fully express themselves communicates 'You are important. I have time for you. I am interested in what you have to say.' You can encourage your child to reflect and share their thoughts using pictures, paints, dolls and other props. Previously uncommunicative children may start to share their thoughts and experiences using props.

*Listen with your brain to assimilate what you are hearing*: Be mindful of what you are hearing your child say and the way they are saying it. Put yourself in your child's position to get a sense of any additional useful context. What might you be feeling if you were their age, with their insecurities, their challenges and their hopes in this instant? Listen to yourself and note any internal reactions to what you are 'hearing'. What feelings are coming up for you? Frustration? Compassion? Impatience? Which of these will be conducive to good listening in this instance and which do you need to keep in check as they may hinder your effectiveness?

*Summarise, reflect and clarify*: To demonstrate your attentive listening, engagement and understanding, summarise the key thoughts that your child has shared. Also reflect back to them what you sense they may be feeling. If you clearly sense an emotion from them: anger, frustration, disappointment, excitement, etc., acknowledge this as well. It will help your child feel listened to even more if you are able to help them verbalise what they are feeling. If there is something you don't understand, gently ask them to clarify. Ask them if you have understood them correctly and, if you haven't, seek to understand what they did mean. It may be that they are sharing something or are asking you for something that you don't agree with. By using empathic listening and good summarising skills to reflect back your child's thoughts, reasons and emotions, they can still feel listened to and acknowledged, even if they aren't going to get their way.

## Listen to your child before expecting them to listen to you

In my experience, people listen better when they feel listened to, and this also applies to children. Often it is practically impossible for a child to focus on what you have to say if they are bursting to tell you something else. If they are bursting with their own thoughts, concerns and ideas, there really is little point in forcing them to listen to you, as there is a high chance that what you have to say will not go in as they have their own ideas that are bursting to get out!

If you are trying to get your child to understand your perspective or learn a lesson, for example, in response to a situation, encouraging them to offload any thoughts that may be bubbling away for them will help them feel listened to, and will prime them to listen to you afterwards. At worst you will learn nothing new, but they are now ready to listen to you. At best, however, they will now feel listened to, you will learn something you weren't expecting – a different intent or reason for their action – which may actually change the approach you were about to take and the message you were about to deliver!

When your child feels fully listened to they will be more ready to hear your thoughts and accept your guidance. Depending on the context of the situation, it may be that they still can't have their way, but at least if they feel listened to, acknowledged and valued, it will be easier to influence them to accept whatever course of events, as their parent, you are proposing.

Using empathic listening to help you shape how you communicate with your child in any situation will help your child really feel listened to and can help them regulate their emotions quicker than if they don't feel listened to.

## Ground rules for helping your child feel 'listened to'

- *Do* make time for them to talk and help them sort through what they are feeling.
- *Do* encourage them to open up and think about their own experience or situation.
- *Do* help them feel acknowledged and valued.
- *Do* focus entirely on your child.
- *Do* use attentive body posture, comfortable eye contact, gestures and expressions that will make your child feel comfortable and will encourage them to open up.
- *Do* use your intuition to sense what their thoughts and feelings might be and interject occasionally with the essence of what you think they might be feeling.
- *Do* use non-committal words and a positive tone of voice: 'I see', 'uh-huh', 'that's interesting', 'tell me more', 'what else? 'then what?'.
- *Do* nod and smile, shake your head and frown in time with them when appropriate to show your understanding of what they are saying.
- *Do* restate the basics of what they are saying: 'What you're telling me is...'
- *Do* reflect back what you sense they may be feeling: 'You're feeling pretty disappointed...' 'I can hear in your voice that you are really cross about what has happened'.
- *Do* summarise their key points and feelings.

- *Do* clarify areas where you are not sure and check whether your child has anything to add.

• • • • • • •

- *Don't* get distracted by your own thoughts and reactions. Quickly acknowledge your reactions to yourself and then return to empathic listening mode.
- *Don't* interrupt with your own thoughts that may result in the conversation taking a different direction from the one your child had intended.
- *Don't* finish your child's sentences – no matter how long they take.
- *Don't* leap to conclusions and assume you know what they are talking about or how they feel. You may miss an opportunity to learn something new about them and/or for them to really feel listened to.
- *Don't* change the subject or move the conversation in a different direction. If the topic is making you feel uncomfortable, you may prevent them trusting you enough to open up again.
- *Don't* start planning your response while they are still talking. If you're rehearsing what to say next, you can't be listening.
- *Don't* give advice if all your child wants and needs is to feel listened to.
- *Don't* interrogate or judge.

## Summary

★ Listening with empathy will help your child feel that you are listening to them, that you are able to fully hear and understand them. This will help them build trust in you and will increase the chances that they will continue to open up to you. When you listen to your child, do so in a way that makes them actually feel 'listened to' and reassures them that what they said has actually been heard. Being a good listener isn't just about understanding what has been said to you, it is also about helping the other person feel listened to.

- ★ To listen with empathy: make time for your child, stop whatever else you are doing and look attentive; listen to the words being spoken to hear the information being shared; notice their non-verbal communication to better understand their underlying emotions; encourage your child to tell you more, give them space to continue with their thoughts; assimilate what you are hearing, think broadly and follow your sense as to how you should best respond to move them forwards while continuing to build trust; reflect back what you are hearing; clarify anything you are not sure about; and summarise back to them what you have heard.
- ★ Remember that children (and adults!) listen better when they feel listened to. Often it is difficult for children to listen to what others have to say, especially if they are bursting with something they want to share. Listening to your child in a way that helps them feel listened to will create space for them to take on new ideas from you.
- ★ Listening is a fundamental part of learning to communicate well, and is a skill that the vast majority of us could learn to do better.

## References

Faber, A. and Mazlish, E. (2013) *How to Talk So Kids Will Listen and Listen So Kids Will Talk*. New York: Avon Books Inc. (original work published in 1982).

CHAPTER 10

# Communicate with the Outcome in Mind

Absorbing your adopted child into the fabric of your family is a delicate process and one that is underpinned by a sense of growing trust, security and permanence. Developing effective two-way communications with your child is a fundamental skill that will help you achieve this. The ability to formulate your communications with the outcome you want to achieve in mind, to be understood, not to offend and to help your child feel good about themselves at all times, even when you are correcting their behaviour, is a skill to strive for. Most of us have room for improvement in our communication skills.

The purpose of this chapter is to help you become more aware of the subtleties of communicating and how the same message containing the same words can be interpreted in different ways depending on the emotions underpinning it as it is sent, and the emotions surrounding it as it is received. As a parent, you will help build trust with your child more quickly and achieve your desired outcome from your communication if you modify your communication approach with these emotional variables in mind.

When your child first meets you they have no idea of what type of person you are and whether or not they can trust you, let alone whether you will be a permanent person in their life. It is possible that everything and everyone in their life to date will have changed, so why should your child think you will be any more permanent?

Your child's expectations will have been shaped by their experiences of relationships with other adults in their lives. They will create an impression of you through the direct interactions they have with you as well as from what they hear about you from other significant people. Therefore, from your very first interaction, the way you are with your child and with those close to your child will help them form their opinion of you and their feelings towards you. Every interaction is an opportunity for you to help your child learn that you are someone who they can trust and with whom they can feel safe.

The early weeks following placement are crucial. This is when your child will feel at their most vulnerable and they will start to form an impression of you that will shape their interactions going forwards. They will be getting to know you as you are getting to know them. You can't be sure how they will respond in certain situations or what might trigger certain emotions, memories or behaviours, so you will need to think carefully about how you communicate with them.

To communicate thoughtfully, be fully aware of the outcome you want as a result of your communication, and then adapt your communication style to the specifics of the situation. This approach will increase the chances of you achieving your outcome and will encourage your child to move forwards in creating their emotional bonds with you. Even in situations where you are correcting your child's behaviour or reinforcing a boundary, this can be done in a way that they still move forwards emotionally in their connection with you.

## Learn from your child's response and level of understanding

In the early days you will be learning how to communicate with your child for best effect. You will be calibrating your communications depending on how your child processes what they hear. After you have shared some thoughts with your child, seek to understand the meaning your child has gleaned from your communication. Did they deduce the correct meaning from what you said? Did you inadvertently offend them? Did your communication impact their emotions in any way? Did you pitch the message correctly for the age at which they are presenting in the moment of the communication? Did you interact with them for who and how they are in the moment – not who and how you wish they would be? There is no time like the present to correct any misunderstandings that may have arisen from your child interpreting what you said in a way you hadn't anticipated.

If you feel at any time during an important discussion that your child has moved away from a resourceful and stable state, pause the conversation and ponder how to continue. If you continue beyond the point when you feel your child has become emotionally unstable or confused, you will not be having the conversation with them at their best and there would be little benefit in continuing your planned discussion. In the moment that you notice your child emotionally wobble, you are still at your most resourceful. If you continue and they become more emotionally confused and unstable, it is possible, and even likely, that their wobbling emotions will start to impact your emotions. Very soon the situation will start to destabilise and emotions may begin to escalate taking you both along for the ride.

## Manage your mood when communicating

One of the wonders of being a parent is the breadth of the range of emotions you will feel for your child. From rapture to despair, from pride to frustration – be aware that your child will help you experience all of them! It is vital when you are feeling more towards the negative end of the emotional spectrum that these feelings are controlled. Don't inadvertently let negative emotions taint your tone, behaviour and attitude towards your child while you are communicating with them, as this may feed the behaviour that you are resenting, which in turn may intensify your negative emotions.

Your emotional state when communicating will influence the words you choose and your style of communication. If you are angry, annoyed, frustrated and conveying high negative energy when you communicate a message to your child, you will naturally communicate in a different way than if you were calm, collected and considered in your message delivery. The quality of your mood when you deliver the message may impact the mood of your child and influence the outcome of the interaction.

Another variable to consider is the mood of your child when they receive your message. If you happen to choose a time when your child is in a highly charged or negative mood, they will receive and process your message differently compared with if they were feeling calm.

If your child is not in an appropriate mood to receive the message you intend, wait until a more appropriate time. If what you have to say is important and you really want your child to hear it and to understand things differently or to make changes as a consequence, it is in your interest to influence their mood until they are in an appropriate emotional state to receive the message.

Become more aware of your mood and how this impacts the mood of your child. You may be surprised to find that in order to create some positive changes in your child, one way is to get into a more positive mood yourself before interacting with them. Being aware of what influences your child's emotional state as well as what, when and how you choose to communicate will significantly increase your chances of an effective communication. At certain times of the day you will feel more patient, have more energy and will feel more able to handle sensitive conversations. Try not to initiate a sensitive conversation with your child when either you or they are feeling overly emotional.

Some communications need to happen right away, but if it is a conversation that can wait, look for a time that is convenient for you and your child. Many conversations fail because one person wants to have the conversation but the other person is actively engaged in another activity that is absorbing their focus or they're not emotionally ready for the conversation at hand. A convenient time for you may not be the most appropriate time to ensure the focus required from your child. Find a time that works for your child as well as you and plan enough time for the conversation. Don't squeeze an important conversation in between two other time-sensitive events or commitments.

---

### Conscious mood management

Lucy is now in school and at the end of every day, in Lucy's schoolbag, I receive a brief written report from her teacher telling me how Lucy has been that day. Most often she has a good day, concentrates well and is a pleasure to teach. On occasion, however, she will be more challenging, stubborn and difficult to manage. Many children may present similar challenges every day, but as Lucy is adopted and I am interested in how she has been at school, the teacher kindly makes the effort to tell me on a daily basis.

I quickly came to realise that what was written in Lucy's daily update drastically changed my mood towards her as I picked her up. If it was a good report, I would be bright and sunny towards her and we would go on to have a lovely evening at home. If I read a report indicating that Lucy had been challenging that day, I would feel frustrated with her. Inside I would be disappointed with Lucy's behaviour and unfortunately this did influence my interactions with her and often resulted in me grilling her as to what happened, why it happened and helping her learn how to make different choices next time. Given that the incident had already been dealt with at school, it wasn't much fun for Lucy or me to go over it all again while clearly showing my frustration.

Lucy's behaviour had been at school, not with me, yet there I was allowing the words that were written on the page about what had happened at school influence how I interacted with Lucy when she got home, which subsequently impacted Lucy's behaviour and the quality of the evening we had at home together. It didn't take me long to realise how my reaction to Lucy's daily report was adversely influencing Lucy's mood and behaviour for the rest of the evening when she got home.

It took much self-discipline, but I did manage to start reviewing Lucy's daily report from a detached perspective. I was able to maintain my sunny disposition and be pleased to see Lucy and interact with her as though she had had a positive day, regardless of the actual contents of the report. In turn, Lucy went on to have a good evening at home regardless of what had gone on during the day at school.

So, I am now much more mindful of how I interact with Lucy at the end of each day. We may discuss any incidents that have happened at school in a way that allows Lucy to reflect on what her options were at the time, but my mood is definitely happy and communicates that I love her and delight in her, regardless of what has gone on at school. It really has made a big difference to Lucy's behaviour in the evenings, but does take a conscious effort from me to actively manage my mood and my communications to achieve a more positive outcome.

---

## Actively manage escalating emotions

We all know that we are at our least resourceful when tempers are running high. What starts off being a simple misunderstanding about something relatively minor can quickly escalate to a highly charged situation resulting in reactions that are often out of proportion to the initial situation. Once a situation has become 'highly charged' it is inherently likely to cause unpredictable and disproportionate reactions on both sides.

A situation can escalate from normal to highly charged in a matter of seconds. As the parent, remember that the most important outcome when this happens is for your child to feel safe and secure and to trust that you can contain your emotions and handle the situation. Their trust in you will deepen when they understand that you don't escalate an already highly charged situation and that you can help them regulate their emotions.

As you get to know your child you will sense whether they are in an appropriate emotional state to handle the conversation you need to have with them. If they are not in the right state, don't try to have the conversation with them unless you are able to influence them to a state more conducive to engaging with, or listening to you. Meaningful conversations are more effective in calm situations where reactions are more predictable.

If a seemingly benign conversation suddenly becomes highly charged, focus on calming the situation and save the important dialogue for a time when you are both calmer. Empathic listening, as described in the previous chapter, can help calm a heated situation. Through use of the techniques described in previous chapters you will quickly sense what is going on for your child. Reflect back your child's emotions and let them feel you empathise with them by temporarily 'matching' them in their high energy state. 'Gosh I can hear that you are really angry!' said with a lot of energy, allows you to temporarily match them at their energy level and then, by gradually calming down the energy in your voice and gestures, you may be able to influence them to a calmer state.

All children have a stress threshold beyond which they aren't able to interact rationally. Typically, the younger the child, the lower the threshold, and if your child has experienced a lot of stressful situations in their earlier life, they too may have a lower threshold than usually expected for their age. All children, adopted or not, and many adults, will sometimes have seemingly irrational reactions to relatively ordinary situations or requests. The apparent cause of the situation may seem trivial to us as parents, but to our child, in that moment they feel entirely justified in their actions and reactions. In those instances it is futile to try to rationalise with your child, the only way to have a conversation with them is to empathise, and influence them to a calmer state, or to wait for them to calm down of their own accord.

---

### The wrong kind of paper

One day Jayden wanted some paper to draw on. His mum gave him some paper and his immediate response was a complete meltdown, sobbing, shouting and completely inconsolable as it was apparently the wrong kind of paper.

His mum didn't try to rationalise with him, as it was obvious to her that his response was nothing to do with the paper. She didn't think he was tired or hungry, so she assumed that for some reason Jayden was feeling a little emotional. Maybe something had happened to trigger some memories or some uncomfortable feelings for him that he didn't understand so he was looking for something to blame for how he felt. And so, it all became about the 'wrong paper'.

His mum believed that nothing she could have said or done about the paper in that situation would have been right.

When she realised what was going on, she picked Jayden up as though he were a toddler, straddled him across her hip and gave him a big hug. She took him to the sofa, sat him on her knee and gave him a big cuddle as she empathised with what he was feeling.

After a few minutes of cuddling Jayden calmed right down, got off his mum's knee and, without another comment about the paper, sat down and happily started drawing on it.

---

Sometimes the root cause of a tantrum or emotional situation is not what it seems to be. Don't always react to what is being presented. Pause, think about what might be going on for your child, empathise to contain the emotions and look to what else you can do that might help alleviate the situation from your child's perspective.

## Pause and ponder

To help manage your emotional state, a useful technique to perfect is simply...pausing. All too often we can experience a surge in frustration in response to a situation, which, if unchecked, may lead to us responding in a careless way that we may regret. Verbal 'knee-jerk' reactions do not allow time to get perspective on a situation and respond in the most appropriate way, they can damage trust and can unexpectedly change the course of an interaction for the worse.

Introducing a pause allows us to better appraise a situation, understand the underlying intent, appreciate differing perspectives, reflect back what we have perceived, seek clarity and ponder an appropriate response that furthers both the relationship and the situation at hand. Introducing a pause will greatly reduce the chance of you reacting to a situation in a way that you may later regret and increase the chance of you reacting in a way that, on reflection, you will be proud of.

Rather than just reacting to your child's undesirable behaviour, pause and ponder whether it was the 'consequence of' or the 'intent behind' their behaviour that is the issue from your perspective. At times a child will demonstrate an inappropriate behaviour or act thoughtlessly, as they just didn't know that what they were doing was wrong and they hadn't fully thought through the impact of their actions. In these instances, they didn't have a bad intent but the consequence of their behaviour has caused some concern. At other times a child may do something in full knowledge of the impact of their behaviour and that what they are doing is wrong. In these instances, it may be the wilful intent behind their behaviour that is more of the issue.

The way you handle the situation will depend on the intent of your child at the time of the incident. An innocent intent may necessitate re-education, while deliberate ill-intent may require further thought to gain insight into why your child is needing attention in this way. The way you communicate and interact with your child in these two instances will differ.

---

## Chair scribbling

Not long after she moved in, Lucy used a ballpoint pen to scribble on (I mean *really* scribble) and stab holes in a cream faux-leather chair. Inside, I was furious, frustrated and really cross with her! However, I knew that allowing my frustration to shape my communication would not help build Lucy's self-esteem, nor would it help build her trust in me. Despite my frustration, I was able to hold on to these overriding objectives and the outcome I wanted to achieve.

I managed to pause between discovering the incident and reacting, and in that pause was able to ask myself some questions to help me get clear on how I wanted to deal with the situation and shape my communication with Lucy. The discussion with myself went something like this...

*Question*: What do I think Lucy's intent was when she damaged the chair?

*Answer*: I honestly don't think she wilfully damaged it, I think she just found a pen and a blank canvas and set to work without thinking that it was wrong.

*Question*: What do I want to achieve with this conversation?

*Answer*: For Lucy to understand that drawing on any furniture or walls or indeed anything that is not paper designated for her drawings is not appropriate in our house or anywhere else. I want Lucy to learn that lesson while feeling good about herself, continuing to build her self-esteem and her trust in me.

*Question*: What 'emotional state' is Lucy in at the moment?

*Answer*: I can tell that she knows she's done something wrong and she is already showing the glimmerings of defiance, which means she is either going to have a full-blown tantrum or go silent and sulky, either of which means she won't be in an emotional state where she can listen to me.

*Question*: What can I do to get Lucy in an appropriate emotional state to listen and learn that it is never okay to draw on furniture or walls?

*Answer*: Empathise with her and acknowledge her.

*Question*: What emotional state am I in at the moment?

*Answer*: I am furious! How dare she scribble in ballpoint pen on the cream chair! It's ruined! I can feel that I have very little patience, and I want her to know that this is *not* okay and that I am cross!

*Question*: Am I in the right emotional state to achieve my outcome? And if not, what can I do to get into a more appropriate emotional state?

*Answer*: No I'm not. I need to pause, take a few breaths, look at the bigger picture, put this in perspective and focus on everything that I know about mindful communication, empathic parenting, implementing and reinforcing boundaries. Deep breath in – and out… I know that in Lucy's previous homes it didn't really matter what she did… I remember her foster carers joking and laughing about the fact that she used to draw on the walls…she's probably never been told that it was an undesirable behaviour…and in…and out… Okay – that feels a little better now.

*Question*: What does Lucy need from me during this conversation to continue to develop trust in me, to feel good about herself and to feel that we love her?

*Answer*: For me to be understanding, not cross, and to let her know that here is an opportunity for her to learn something different.

I allowed this conversation with myself to help me formulate my approach and the way I spoke with Lucy.

I explained to Lucy that drawing on furniture and walls wasn't acceptable behaviour, but that I understood she didn't know that as no one had helped her learn it yet. I explained that first we had to clean the chair, and then we would play a game that would help her learn where is was okay for her to draw and scribble.

I explained to Lucy that as she had scribbled all over the chair, she had to help clean it and try to remove the ink that she had put there. Lucy didn't like this one bit and made it quite clear that she'd rather do anything but clean the chair. However, with bags of empathy, patience and encouragement, Lucy did clean the chair and in the process realised that the fun she had experienced in the scribbling on the chair was far outweighed by the boredom of cleaning it; however, she did feel good about helping clean up the mess she had made.

After the chair was clean (or as clean as it was ever going to be) and the incident was considered 'over', we reminded Lucy that drawing on or wilfully damaging any walls or furniture was not acceptable behaviour wherever she was, and that if in doubt she could always ask us before she did it. We played a fun guessing game that helped reinforce the message of where and on what it was okay to scribble, paint, draw, stab holes and stick stickers. We made sure that when the episode was over, it was truly over. We didn't keep harping on about it, and made sure that Lucy's self-esteem was not harmed through the process.

We also took the opportunity when we saw her drawing and scribbling in appropriate places to congratulate her on her choice of where to draw. Needless to say the lesson was learnt and Lucy has never scribbled on (or stabbed holes in) anything inappropriate again, and her lesson was learnt without her being made to feel naughty.

---

With the chair scribbling incident shared above, after I had paused, I truly believed that Lucy did not have a malicious intent behind her actions, and so I crafted my response and actions accordingly. If, however, this behaviour had continued, I would have followed other avenues to better understand why Lucy was seeking a connection in this challenging way, and would have shaped my communications accordingly.

## Focus on the key words

It is possible that your adopted child will have some developmental delay and at times may be confused with mixed emotions. They may also be in a hypervigilant state and/or experiencing an overstimulation of their senses. It is difficult to know the internal world of your child at the time you are communicating with them. Therefore, until you really understand your child, assume you are communicating into a jumble of confusion and mixed emotion. This should naturally lead you to being more patient, clear and concise with your communications.

Many parents use too many words with their children, especially with younger children. When you have something you need them to understand, try to use only key words and don't confuse the essential message with superfluous words. The more words your child has to work out, the harder it will be for them to get the key message. Repeat the key message several times if necessary.

Here's a simple example. Your child wants to watch television, and they have lots of toys all over the floor that you would like them to put away. You don't need to say, 'Gosh look at all the mess. I don't know why you get so many toys out, if only you would get one out, play with that and then put it away before you got the next, out the floor wouldn't be so messy. If you tidy all the toys away quickly now, then we can put the television on but you must tidy everything away first. I can't be tidying up after you all of the time, I have enough tidying to do without all this mess.'

Instead simply say, 'Put the toys away now, then you can watch television', and repeat it a few times: 'Put the toys away now, then you can watch television'. This will be much easier for your child to pick out the essential words and understand what is expected of them.

## Focus on what you want, not what you don't want

Be very aware of what you would like to achieve with your communication and focus on moving towards that, rather than dwelling on the problem at hand. Remember that your emotions may impact those of your child. If you express anger and disappointment about their behaviour, for example, they may feel a dip in their self-esteem as a result. If you communicate concern and worry about their action, this may momentarily impact their self-confidence and therefore their performance.

Although your intention may be to create a positive outcome, it will be easier for your child to focus on what you want if you direct them there with your focus rather than expecting them to mentally leap there by implication. If you want your child to do something, focus on what you want them to do rather than on what you don't want them to do.

'Keep tidy' and 'Don't make a mess' both have the same intended outcome. With the first one, however, your child will hear the word 'tidy' and will focus on that, with the second one they will hear the word 'mess' and may inadvertently focus on that. You may find a child with the second instruction will make more mess than the first.

'Carry it carefully' and 'Don't spill it' both have the same intended outcome, but the first one focuses on 'careful' and the second one on 'spill'. You may get more of the negative result you are trying to avoid, if that is where you focus your child's attention!

---

### An unintended outcome

During some voluntary work I did with young offenders I came across a 12-year-old boy who was a repeat offender for theft and criminal damage. This boy was positively excited that the hard work he was putting into his misdemeanours with the law was finally getting noticed!

During our first meeting, he proudly explained to me that finally coming to the attention of the Youth Offending Team was an important step on his journey to the local Young Offender Institution and, ultimately, prison. His mother, who accompanied him to the meeting, was horrified and hadn't realised the significance to her son of him living in an environment where his two older brothers, his father and uncle were in and out of prison for repeat offences.

It came to light in the discussion that he didn't feel able to be considered 'grown up' until he had served a significant stint 'at her Majesty's pleasure'. His mother's comments like 'if you keep on like this, you'll end up like your brothers', and 'if you want to end up like all the rest of the men in this family you're on the right track', and 'oh, that's just what I need, another one of you in jail', were not being perceived by him as deterrents, but rather as encouragement and confirmation that he was on the right track!

This was one seriously confused boy and a great example of a parent naively focusing their child's attention on the wrong outcome.

---

Comments can also impact how your child feels; for example, if you want your child to get dressed more quickly, you will have a different result if you say 'Why are you always so slow to get dressed? Can't you speed up?' rather than 'I know you can get dressed quickly. I will have the biggest smile on my face when you have surprised me with your speed!' Both are said with the intention of getting your child to dress quickly and, depending on your child's expectations and their association with the comments, one or the other may work. However, it is more likely that the first one will reinforce any feelings of worthlessness for your child, compared with the second, which is giving the opportunity to bask in your delight!

Focus on the positive behaviour you want and not the negative behaviour you don't. If the purpose of your interaction with your child is to help them learn a new way of doing something, don't give way to your frustration and focus on the negative of what they have done wrong. Instead, help them focus on correcting the situation and moving forwards learning a new approach.

Strive to develop a positive communication style with your child that is mindful of how you want them to develop and doesn't constantly remind them of the difference between where they are now and where you want them to be.

## Forgive and move on

Start each communication 'afresh' and be careful not to allow previous frustrations to influence how you interact with your child.

Once an incident is over and you have had the discussion with your child, don't harbour frustration. Find a way to let it go. Otherwise it is possible that your pent up frustration could fuel future conversations, resulting in a reaction from you that is disproportionate to the situation at hand. Your mood of frustration and impatience may impact your child's emotional state and so impair their ability to deduce your intended meaning. It can be quite frustrating for a parent to have to communicate the same thing again and again. Just at the time when the message may finally be about to stick and their behaviour change, you could blow it by allowing previous unresolved frustrations to negatively influence your style of communication.

Managing your mood is so important for each and every communication. If you can adopt the most appropriate mood for the delivery of a particular message each time you deliver that message the chance of your child interpreting that message correctly increases. Consistency is key. The more you are able to do this, the quicker your messages will get through. Be prepared though, you may have to communicate the same message many times. Depending on your child and the extent to which their brain has developed normally, the message should eventually get through.

As well as not letting previous frustrations build up and impact your communication, it is equally important not to let assumptions about your child impact how you interact and communicate with them. Just because they have acted in a certain way before, doesn't mean they will do it again.

Imagine a teacher having a persistently challenging child in their class who always plays up during a certain activity. Each time the activity comes around, the teacher assumes they know how the child will behave and readies themselves for the challenging behaviour. As we communicate both verbally and non-verbally, it is entirely possible and even probable that the child will pick up on this teacher's anticipation of their challenging behaviour and that the negative energy perceived by the child as a result may actually play a part in encouraging them to be disruptive in that situation.

Likewise the child may realise that during that same activity the teacher always becomes stricter with them than during other activities, and so gets ready for the stern interactions by acting a little more boldly and defiantly than usual.

The teacher is negatively influencing the child's behaviour and the child is negatively influencing the teacher's behaviour. Both are basing their behaviour on previous experiences, and both are allowing those previous experiences to impact current assumptions, future expectations and behaviour. Teacher and child are each reacting to and having a part in causing the other's treatment towards themselves!

As a parent, beware of this vicious circle and don't get caught in it with your child. It will only ever prolong and escalate frustrations and negative behaviours. Far better to take control of your mood, consciously decide not to let previous interactions carry over to future interactions and to treat each interaction afresh with the expectation that this time it will be better. This will give you the best chance at truly effective communications and will help your child unlearn certain ways of being and learn new ones.

I've said this before and I will say it again. As parents we try so hard to do the best that we can, but we will not get it right all of the time. You won't get it right all of the time. I don't get it right all of the time. It is important to reflect on what happened, forgive yourself and move on with a little more wisdom than you had before.

## Reinforce your message with your style of delivery

Help your child understand what you are saying by using your tone of voice, facial expressions, body language and proximity as well as the actual words you use.

Communicate in a manner that distinguishes when you are reinforcing a boundary or correcting behaviour from having fun and messing about. Your style when you 'chat' will be different to when you are empathising and discussing a sensitive subject. Help your child distinguish between the different types of communication by varying *how* you communicate.

You will have your own styles of communication but it will be very confusing for your child if they are picking up the same emotional vibes from you when they have fun with you as when they are being corrected by you.

---

### Distinct communication styles

In the early days with Lucy I consciously made my styles of communication with Lucy very distinct to help her understand the intent of what I was communicating:

*Reinforcing a boundary*: I sit in close proximity to Lucy, either next to her or in front of her in a position where I can encourage good eye contact. If standing, I get down to Lucy's physical level so I am not towering over her. I use short matter-of-fact sentences with no superfluous words delivered with more of a 'flat' voice with a dip in tone at the end of the sentence. I use minimal head and facial movement and am a lot less smiley than usual, which gives the impression of a more serious face. I give regular summaries of what has been said with definite points being made along the way as I keep the direction of the conversation on track moving towards acknowledgement of the actions and agreement of consequences. I discourage Lucy from taking the conversation off track and am careful to bring her back to the point in hand. I don't intersperse this short conversation with hugs but do engage in big hugs at the end.

*Engaging in chatty dialogue*: Physical proximity isn't important, it's not important for me to be right next to Lucy. As long as we are in the same room we could be doing different activities in each other's presence; on the other hand she may be sitting on my knee! I use and encourage longer sentences with some superfluous words and a more interesting 'sing-song' undulating voice. I demonstrate more head movement and facial expressions and am much more smiley, giving a friendlier and appealing face. My language is less direct, chattier, without definite points being made. I ask lots of questions and encourage connections to be made, which may take the conversation in different directions. I express interest in whatever Lucy wants to talk about and am comfortable if there is no particular direction to the conversation. I freely give hugs at any point when Lucy indicates that she wants them, and at plenty of times when she doesn't ask!

*Empathising over a sensitive situation or disclosure*: Often I am sitting next to Lucy with my arm around her or she's sitting on my knee for a cuddle, or it is bedtime and Lucy is lying in bed with me sitting or lying on the bed next to her. Close physical proximity and physical touch is important as this is when Lucy seems to open up. Eye contact is not as important in these situations as physical proximity, and Lucy is able to open up more without direct eye contact. In these situations, I don't usually seek to engage visually with Lucy, it is more through a reassuring use of voice. I use a soft, quiet voice and give lots of non-verbal encouragement mixed with short gentle questions. Much of my talk is reflecting back what I have heard Lucy say and what I sense she felt or feels. The whole conversation often takes part in some form of a hug.

Cultivating different styles of communication has worked for Lucy, who found communication challenging in the early months.

---

## Choose the best vehicle for the communication

Depending on the purpose of your communication, there are many different ways that you can achieve your outcome. Talking with your child and helping them try to understand a concept or a lesson may work for some children all of the time, or for all children some of the time. Finding complementary ways to communicate the same message may help your child understand or learn the message more effectively.

Stories, use of metaphor and play are all excellent vehicles to reinforce your verbal messages and help deliver the message in an unthreatening and easy to process way. Purchasing specific books, making up your own stories, and using puppets and toys are all easy ways that engage children and help carry messages.

---

### Teaching lessons and reinforcing messages

We frequently engage in playful games using Lucy's dolls, cuddly toys, Lego and Playmobil characters to help her understand messages, learn lessons and anticipate situations. Here are some examples.

**Increasing awareness of stranger danger**

At five years old Lucy was still not securely attached to us, her new family, and would trust and walk away with anyone without a second thought. Normal explanations didn't register with her, and it began to present as a very real danger for us. As vigilant as we were, we couldn't watch Lucy every minute of every day, especially at times that we weren't with her, for example, school trips.

Using a combination of Lucy's dolls' house, Playmobil characters, a simulated park and a Lego car, we played a game of a little girl wandering off with a complete stranger and the little girl's parents frantically looking for her and getting worried as they couldn't find her. The little girl in the story was called Lucy. Lucy kept saying to the Playmobil parents, 'It's okay, I'm over here with this lady!' and pointing to where her character was in the simulation. We explained that the parents couldn't hear her or see her, as she had been driven off in a car and was now not within hearing distance. Lucy wanted to play that the little girl got to come home and we explained that the stranger wanted to keep the little girl and wouldn't let her go home. We asked Lucy how the little girl in the game might be feeling, and Lucy explained that she missed her new family and wanted to go home and that she was sad. Lucy did get a bit upset, but the game achieved its purpose, and Lucy became more aware of strangers and started to exhibit appropriate stranger awareness for her age. Lucy remembered the game, and we referred back to it several times to help her understand the message.

### Encouraging collaborative play

We have played similar games with her toys to explain how other children might feel in certain situations if she behaves in a certain way; for example, not sharing may result in children not wanting to play with her, and being very bossy may result in children not including her in their games. To play this with the Playmobil characters and to have them not want to play with the character that represents her does help get the message through and has helped with her mode of play.

**Learning different approaches**

We have also done role play with Lucy if she has communicated in ways that were not polite at home. We discuss more acceptable ways of her getting what she wanted that didn't upset other people. We would then role play them a few times, with Lucy playing the part of herself and us all going through the paces acting out the scenario a few times as she approaches it in different ways, to support her in her learning. These lessons through role play really work for Lucy and she is better able to remember different ways of 'being' in different situations compared with if we just repeatedly 'tell' her.

---

I believe that when you tell a child something they can try to understand it, but unless they can really comprehend the significance of what you are talking about, it will be difficult for them to remember the lesson for long. If you can help them connect emotionally and feel the potential consequences of the lesson that you are helping them learn, in my experience the message or the lesson seems to sink in more effectively and starts to take root.

If you use an approach with your child similar to those just described, make sure to do this sensitively, gradually, with care, and with lots of love and support. The games and lessons need not be too harsh and realistic – remember it is a game. Be guided by your child and be sensitive to what is appropriate for them. This should be a game with a lesson or a moral to the story with which they can emotionally engage. Then you can support them as they explore the stories further, make the connections and learn the lessons. These should not be games that upset them and leave them in a bad place emotionally; rather, they should be games with happy endings, with your child feeling empowered that they now know the right decisions to make and how to act in certain situations.

## Anticipate and communicate

Anticipate upcoming situations or events that will be new for your child and as a result may take them out of their familiar routines. In these instances, invest time in communicating with your child ahead of time, help them think through the situation that is approaching and encourage them to anticipate what they might hear, see and feel in that situation. You can explain a sequence of events that is going to happen and help your child role play certain aspects that you anticipate may be problematic for them. You can then better understand what may be needed to help the actual scenario unfold more smoothly. You may find that having role played the situation, when the real scenario unfolds, your child is more prepared and feels more confident as it is less likely that there will be any unanticipated surprises.

We have successfully anticipated situations and role played with Lucy many times; for example, her first day at school, birthday parties, extended family gatherings, food shopping in supermarkets, a camping trip, sitting through a Christmas carol concert, sitting through a christening church service, travelling on planes, trains and tubes, and many changes to normal routine including sleeping over at friends' and families' houses, to name but a few!

In all cases, helping Lucy anticipate what she was going to experience and what might be expected of her helped her prepare and helped the events run smoothly. In the absence of previous experience, effective communication, scenario planning and role play can give your child the understanding they need to bolster them when they are feeling confused and vulnerable.

## When you say 'no' – mean it!

No chapter on communicating with children would be complete without a comment or two on the effective use of the word 'no'.

I read an online article, in which the researchers claimed toddlers can get told 'no' an average of 400 times a day! Exhausting for them and their parents. It must be demoralising for a child to be told 'no' so many times in a day, not to mention confusing as to when it is really meant and when it is not meant.

It is easy to understand how that little word 'no' can become overused, as there are so many scenarios when it is useful to employ!

- No you can't.
- No I can't.
- No you don't.
- No, not like that.
- No, not yet.
- No, because I said so.
- NO!!!

Anything that is overused can lose its potency and so it is with the word 'no'. Not to mention the fact that some people use the word 'no' when they actually mean 'maybe', or even worse, they mean, 'If you cry enough I'll eventually give in and say yes!' I've even heard some people say, 'No you can't, and I really mean it this time!' And even then giving in after the child had persisted long enough. Decide when it is appropriate for you to use the word 'no' and mean it when you say it each and every time, and think of some alternatives for the other situations.

As well as letting our children know that they can't have what they want, 'no' is also used frequently in situations when we are trying to encourage our children. With homework, for example, it is so easy to get in the habit of saying 'no' every time they read or spell a word incorrectly or get a word or a sum wrong. Alternative more supportive phrases might be:

- Not quite, try again.
- Nearly, the correct word sounds similar to that.
- Great try, have another guess.
- Almost, can you work it out again?
- You are trying really hard with that one. It is a bit tricky. Shall we work it out together?
- Good try, it's not quite right, can you see if you can fix it?

Be mindful of the amount of times you find yourself saying 'no' to your child. There are so many other ways to achieve the same outcome in a different and often more positive way that will come quite easily with practice. Using the word 'no' more sparingly means that it can retain more of its potency. If saved for the times you absolutely want your child to understand that the answer is 'NO!' or times of danger when they need to stop their current action immediately, it will have more impact.

## Summary

- ★ A thoughtful communication is a communication shaped with an outcome in mind and an awareness of all variables that may impact how a communication is delivered and how it may be received.
- ★ Early in your relationship with your child it is vital that your communications help your child feel that you are someone worthy of their trust, you help make them feel good about themselves and you are someone around whom they can feel safe and who helps them feel secure.

- ★ The mood you are in when you communicate and your child's mood as they listen to you will impact both how your message is delivered and received. Therefore, manage your emotions when communicating and encourage an appropriate mood in your child to increase the chance that they receive the message that you intend.
- ★ Avoid 'knee-jerk' communications by developing the habit of…pausing. Simply introduce a break: time to take a few deep breaths and to ponder the situation before reacting. This will give you the chance to make your response 'thoughtful'.
- ★ Help your child pick out the essence of your message by speaking clearly and precisely and stripping out the superfluous words that may cloud the message. The more important your communication, the fewer words the better.
- ★ Remember to focus on what you want and not what you don't want. Spending a lot of words talking about what you don't want to happen will take your child's focus to where you don't want it! Instead, plan your communication so that you are moving your child's focus onto what you do want.
- ★ Be forgiving. Don't let previous frustrations bubble up and influence your mood for subsequent communications. Remember that your expectations may alter how you interact with your child, which will impact how they interact with you, and so on. A cycle of negative reinforcement can make situations worse. By starting each interaction afresh, with positive expectations you can get on a positively reinforcing cycle, which can break bad habits and lead to positive interactions.
- ★ Reinforce your messages with your communication style. Your child will learn to understand your non-verbal

forms of communication and this will help them more accurately interpret the meaning of what you say.

- ★ There are many ways to communicate, including games, books, metaphors and stories, as well as speaking. Choose the best vehicle for your communication and reinforce important messages using a variety of means.
- ★ Anticipate and role play situations that you think may present challenges for your child. The more familiar they can become with a situation through role play, the more comfortable and at ease they may feel when the actual situation comes around.
- ★ Be careful not to overuse the word 'no', it can be very demotivating when used frequently and will lose its potency.

PART FIVE

# Enable Your Child's Development

*It is very common for a 'looked after child' to come on in leaps and bounds with their development once they feel settled and secure with their 'forever family'. Children respond well to structure, they feel secure within it and take comfort from knowing what is expected from them, and what is and is not allowed. Providing structure in terms of consistent boundaries and routines will provide the environment within which your child can develop and flourish.*

CHAPTER 11

# Provide Structure and Consistency

Unless your child was removed or relinquished at birth, it is highly likely that they will have experienced different living environments with different rules and expectations. It is highly probable that your child will arrive in your home not knowing exactly what is expected of them now.

It is well noted in most parenting books that children respond well to structure.

By consistently and consciously parenting with empathy and communicating effectively, you will be supporting your child in the best way possible and giving them a firm foundation from which to progress. Your primary focus will be to pay back the nurture debt and to support your child through their grieving process. At the same time, however, it is important to address any challenging behaviours that may cause tension and/or harm if not resolved. You can help your child learn new habits and ways of being through a framework of structure and consistency.

The purpose of this chapter is to talk about structure, and to help you think about how you might use it to help your child settle quickly and to stay settled.

Implementing structure and consistency for a child who has been used to living life with neither can be a challenge, but your child will settle more quickly if you help them understand their new environment in terms of what they can expect and what is expected from them. It may be tempting to introduce soft boundaries with a little more flexibility than you would like just to help get them settled. Flexible boundaries and arbitrary guidelines, however, will not lead to your child feeling safe and comfortable and will not facilitate their process of understanding their new environment.

From the first minute of the first day that your child moves into your home strive to be consistent in your expectations regarding behaviour. In my experience children feel safe and develop well when given structure. Don't wait until they are settled to introduce structure and consistency. Structure and consistency are the two things that will help them settle. By structure, I mean boundaries and routines that are well communicated, well explained and encouraged through patient reminders, incentives and consequences.

It is not an easy challenge to introduce consistent boundaries and routines. You may well falter in your endeavours many times. We did. But it can be done. We did it and you can too. Patiently explain any boundaries as they arise and work with your child to develop routines that work for you both. This approach will help to guide your child's behaviour and the choices they start to make for themselves.

## Introduce boundaries to guide behaviour

A boundary is a rule; it is the distinction of what is and what is not allowed. Boundaries are fixed and your child should learn that if they choose to cross a boundary, there will be a consequence, be it natural (they touch something very hot, they will get burnt) or applied (if they hit or bite then they have to 'sit out' of the game they are playing for a few minutes). With careful consideration and discussion, boundaries can be relaxed or removed as appropriate to support your child as they develop. Boundaries are there for a reason – your child may not agree with the boundary or the reason behind it, but they can learn to acknowledge that the boundary is there through the consequences they experience when honouring or breaking it.

Boundaries provide children with:

- simplicity in the form of unambiguous rules for what is and is not acceptable
- consistency, as they learn which behaviour elicits which response each and every time
- certainty, as they learn what is expected of them in different situations and the parameters within which they can make their choices.

## Sensible boundaries are made from a calm state

Sensible boundaries are easier to implement and enforce than those that are random and ill-considered. There is a higher likelihood of a boundary being sensible and well-considered if you are in a calm state when you make it.

As a parent you will frequently be challenged by your children to revisit boundaries, and all children are particularly gifted at badgering parents to give in and change their mind regarding boundaries or to reverse a decision they have made. I would encourage you to stand firm. Do not set a precedent for caving in, relaxing a boundary or reversing a decision in response to your child's persistent badgering or tantrums.

When feeling hassled and stressed, it is more difficult to apply the same decision-making rigour that you can apply when you are calm. Many ill-planned precedents have been set by people in a state of stress, only to regret their decisions when all is calm again.

So, strive to review boundaries when you are calm, and consider whether it is in fact appropriate to change a boundary that is causing an issue, or is it actually in the best interest of your child for the time being to remain firm? Be consistent, and when you are under duress or feeling stressed by your child, take this as a signal to reinforce your boundaries. If you give in when they have a tantrum, be aware that you are teaching them 'Hassle Mummy or Daddy when they are stressed and you can get what you want!' Once you give in, it will be far more effort to re-establish that boundary than would have been required to reinforce it in the first place.

Know that most children have excellent memories, they only need you to give in once for the precedent to be set, and you could find yourself on a downward spiral with them exerting more and more pressure each time until they get what they want.

Be supervigilant – if you want to minimise the build-up of stress and frustration and move to a state of settled families in the shortest possible time, set and adhere to well-considered boundaries. Appropriate boundaries will vary from household to household and child to child, but consistency within your home is key.

---

### Meal-time rules

It became quickly apparent to the adoptive parents that Donna had not experienced any boundaries around eating. She had clearly become accustomed to snacking throughout the day while playing, never sitting down to meals, refusing to eat what she was given and having a tantrum until she got what she wanted, and drinking lots of sugary drinks.

The adoptive parents introduced some boundaries around eating and meal times. Some of their rules were:

- No toys at the table.
- No random snacking during the day. There were three planned meals and three planned snacks: breakfast,

mid-morning snack, lunch, mid-afternoon snack, tea, evening snack, bed.

- There is no getting up and down from the table to play during meal times. Once at the table you stay at the table unless you have permission to get down, to go to the toilet, for example. If you get down from the table without permission, your food gets taken away and there is nothing else to eat until the next meal or snack.
- You eat what you are given, there are no choices.
- You don't have to eat everything on your plate, but if you don't eat all your vegetables you don't get dessert.
- There is only water to drink with meals.

These rules were really challenging for Donna in the early weeks; however, with patient explanation and reinforcement, it did not take long for Donna to realise that her parents meant what they said. Within a couple of months Donna adhered to each of the boundaries above and meal times became stress-free.

---

Boundaries are effective when:

- *Based on careful consideration and not impulse*: Put thought into which boundaries are important to you as a parent to safeguard your child. Focus on those that will help them learn to behave appropriately and fit in with the norms of your family, and will give them the opportunity to develop to meet their potential. Boundaries decided on impulse may not be 'fully agreed' among those expected to enforce them, they may not be well communicated and, if made in the heat of the moment, they may cause frustration and confusion.
- *Age appropriate and relevant*: Some boundaries will be absolute, for example, 'never play in the kitchen near

the stove', and others, like bedtimes, will change as your child grows up.

- *Applied fairly and consistently*: The enforcement of a boundary should not depend on variables such as who is in charge, who is visiting the house, your stress levels or how much your child has cried and pestered you to change your mind. If you have a boundary relating to eating, for example, 'You don't have to finish all of your tea but you can't have any pudding unless you finish your vegetables', this must be applied consistently regardless of who is visiting your home for tea. It is not important who is asking you to make an exception, whether it is your child, the visiting child or indeed the visiting child's parent. The boundary should stand firm. If this is the boundary, then it is vital that visiting children also adhere to it otherwise it can cause confusion and upset for your child. Once you calmly explain the reason for the boundary in your home, you will find most visiting parents will respect your wishes and support you in reinforcing the boundary. If they don't, then you can decide not to invite them back!
- *Easy to explain and easy to follow*: It is important that your child understands how they can comply with any boundaries, and what meets and does not meet expectations regarding the boundary. Boundaries should not be open to interpretation, that is, 'You must eat all of your vegetables' is better than 'You must eat some of your vegetables'.
- *Introduced when needed*: Communicate a boundary as and when you notice one is needed to give guidance regarding expected behaviours and to encourage healthy habits. Don't dump a large number of boundaries on your child as they move in, they have

enough to assimilate when transitioning to your home without feeling overwhelmed by boundaries that won't seem relevant to them at the time. Start as you mean to go on by introducing a boundary as soon as you perceive that it is needed.

- *Noticeable*: It should be obvious when your child respects a boundary so that you can acknowledge and praise them.
- *Definite*: Clear boundaries are easier for younger children to follow as they don't have the experience or critical thinking skills to work out ambiguities. For example 'no hitting' is quite definite. If you then allow gentle hits, or hits that don't result in another child crying, where is the boundary? A hit is a hit and all hitting should be treated in the same way. As your child gets older they will be able to interpret subtleties, but not when they are young.

---

### A much-needed boundary

Connor and Ben used to wake up very early in the morning, every morning and go through to their adoptive parents to wake them up. The parents knew that in the early months it was important for Connor and Ben to know that they were there for them, and so let this happen, building their relationship with the boys.

After the first six months had passed the boys were appearing more settled. At about this time the parents decided to introduce a boundary to discourage the boys from waking them up at 'silly o'clock' in the morning. After six months of feeling relatively sleep deprived, they were desperate to secure the amount of sleep they needed to continue effectively parenting these two lively boys.

In order for the parents to have the energy for the day, adequate sleep was vital for them. They explained to the boys that the change was going to happen and then together they went to buy a sleep-trainer alarm clock. The clock had a light that could be set to turn off at a particular time. As long as the light was on, the boys needed to stay in their room. When the light turned off the boys could wake up their parents.

The parents made sure that Connor and Ben understood they were always welcome to wake up their parents regardless of whether the light was on or off if they had a bad dream, felt insecure or poorly, or in the case of any other emergency.

While learning the boundary, each morning the parents would have to take one or both of the boys back to their room several times, encouraging them to play with their toys and look at their books quietly while waiting for the alarm clock light to turn off.

Rewards were introduced for when the boys were successful in staying in their room until the light went off. Little by little, Ben and Connor did learn and after about two months they got it completely. The boys now wake up and play happily in their room, and then go through to their parents when the light on the clock turns off.

At the weekend the parents set the clock so that the light would turn off a little later to allow themselves to sleep a little longer. The parents explained that sometimes at the weekend they would wake up before the boys' alarm light has turned off, and on a few occasions while Ben and Connor were learning the boundary, they still went through to their parents' room when the alarm light was on. Both parents were tempted to relax the boundary 'just that once' and let the boys stay. They realised, however, that this would introduce confusion for the boys, as they would have been allowed to go through to their parents' room and stay even though their alarm light hadn't turned off and there was no emergency. This would have introduced confusion and precedents, so although the parents felt a little strict, they always took the boys back to their room and made them stay there until the alarm light had turned off.

This boundary took a couple of months of persistent reinforcement until the boys would respect it. It took a lot of patience and consistency but the benefits were huge! The adoptive parents now get the appropriate amount of unbroken sleep and enjoy a lie-in at the weekend. Happy days!

---

## Develop routines to help your child feel secure

A routine is a sequence of events that can help complete an activity, or transition from one activity to another. Routines provide children with:

- a sense of safety and confidence that they can cope with what is expected of them and that there will be no unexpected surprises
- predictability, as they learn to understand a sequence of events and the sense of security that comes from knowing what will happen next
- smooth transitions between states and situations; for example, from home to school, from playtime to sleep.

Some routines may comprise smaller sub-routines; for example, a routine of events to calm your child down from a state of high energy at play, to a calm state in bed waiting for sleep, might involve a 'tidy away routine', a 'tea routine', a 'bath routine' and then a 'bedtime story and light out routine'.

---

### Routine success

Jayden's parents quickly realised that Jayden yearned for routines. Once they did something one way, he would want it repeated the same way, and the familiarity of steps seemed to give him comfort. Some routines were initiated by Jayden for his own familiarity and comfort, and others were put in place by his parents to help him transition more smoothly from one situation to another.

Soon after Jayden moved in with his adoptive family, he shaped his own bath and bedtime routine, which comprised many little steps that together took him from being fully clothed downstairs to bathed, relaxed and ready for sleep in his bedroom. Jayden's routine included specifics as to exactly what toys he would have in the bath, how the towel would be wrapped around him when he got out of the bath, which direction he would face while sitting on his mum's knee getting dry, to exactly how many kisses on each cheek and how many hugs he needed from each family member before he would settle ready for sleep.

Jayden wanted and created many familiar routines in his early months. As the months went by, some of the smaller steps in his self-imposed routines fell away, but this was led by Jayden, not by his parents.

Other routines that were put in place by Jayden's parents still persist today. These include the steps involved from rising in the morning to walking out of the front door to arrive at school on time and relaxed! This routine is now familiar, ingrained, prevents tension and arguments, and results in stress-free mornings as they all get ready to leave the house on time.

---

## Combine boundaries and routine to provide structure

Together, boundaries and routines provide structure, which leads to reliability, trust and ultimately a feeling of security. Your child will start to feel safe knowing what is expected of them and what they can expect from other significant people involved with their care giving and nurturing. They will learn that they can both rely on and trust you. Structure may also help them to manage themselves and their own internal emotional state. Over time your child will feel comfortable in a routine and will know what is expected of them, and you may notice your child appearing more regulated. It is when routines depart significantly from the norm or when unexpected events occur that your child may feel dysregulated and display some chaotic and challenging behaviour.

---

### Reinforcing structure

In the early days following Lucy's arrival she was hyperactive and demonstrated chaotic behaviour much of the time. We quickly introduced structure to her life in the form of boundaries and routines. Lucy took well to the routines, but initially rallied against many of the boundaries with crying and tantrums.

As a family we were very consistent in our application and reinforcement of boundaries, and were surprised by Lucy's will in continuing to resist. However, after resisting the boundaries for many weeks, Lucy finally realised that no matter how big her tantrums became, a boundary was a boundary, a decision was a decision, 'no' always meant 'no' and no amount of screaming was going to change it.

This was not easy for us as a family but we really believed that Lucy would thrive with structure in her life, and so we persisted. At times when we began to feel worn down by enforcing a boundary, we mentally took a step back, reminded ourselves why we were doing what we were doing, and carried on. We consciously prevented our frustration from building by focusing on the outcome we wanted to achieve with Lucy rather than on the challenge of getting there. The types of boundaries we were enforcing for Lucy were the normal ones introduced by most parents for their children and were around bedtimes, amount of television, meal times, food, sweets and general behaviour.

After only a few weeks, Lucy started to respond well to the combination of boundaries with routines and adapted to the structure we were putting in place. As a consequence, Lucy became regulated, happier and relaxed. She seemed more settled and actually started enjoying life like a four-year-old should. She began to thrive.

However, even once settled, when Lucy was in the throes of wanting something she wasn't allowed she could work herself into a tantrum. This, by the way, is not just a talent of children from the care system. Most children at some point will try to use tantrums as a means to get what they want. When in a tantrum, no amount of reasoning with Lucy would work. We would simply empathise with her, showing that we understood her frustrations, and repeat the course of action that was going to happen or the boundary that was being reinforced.

An example would be:

Lucy: 'I want telly.'

Me *(calm and matter of fact)*: 'You want to watch the telly, but the television doesn't go on until after tea, Lucy. Let's see what other game we can find to do together.'

Lucy *(shouting)*: 'NO! I WANT TELLY!'

Me *(a bit more high energy to match a little of Lucy's high energy)*: 'You like telly and you want to watch it. But we're not putting the television on now. The television doesn't go on before tea time and it isn't tea time yet. Let's play a game instead.'

Lucy *(yelling and crying)*: 'I WANT TELLY NOW – I HATE YOU!'

Me *(responding with a lot of energy to match her state)*: 'I can see that you're very frustrated that I won't put the television on because you want the telly on right now. I can see that you're angry with me.'

Lucy *(still yelling and crying)*: 'I WANT TELLY, I WANT TELLY, I WANT TELLY!'

Me *(still high energy, but starting to come down towards the end of my sentence)*: 'Gosh, I can tell you REALLY want to watch some television! But that isn't going to happen, as the television does not go on before tea. I will play a game with you though. What shall we play?'

Lucy *(already starting to calm down a little)*: 'I don't want to play game. I WANT TELLY!'

Me: 'I can hear you are upset. You don't want to play a game; the only thing you want is the telly.'

Lucy *(calmer)*: 'I want telly now.'

Me *(reaching to Lucy to sit her on my knee for a cuddle)*: 'The television doesn't go on before tea. We have time for one game now. Then tea. After tea you can watch the television.'

Lucy *(happy)*: 'I want to play Incey Wincey Spider game.'

Me *(happy)*: 'Great choice, you like Incey Wincey Spider game, that is a good game.'

Lucy: 'Yes, I good at that game, I like that game.'

Me: 'I can see you're happy about playing Incey Wincey Spider.'

Lucy: 'Yes, Mummy you get it now.'

In this interaction I was careful to let Lucy know that I knew she was feeling frustrated and angry, but that what she wanted wasn't possible.

Sometimes these types of interactions would last a lot longer, but over the months, they would escalate and then normalise in a quicker period of time as Lucy felt listened to and acknowledged and realised that a boundary would never be moved in response to a tantrum.

---

Be aware that when all becomes calm and you can't believe the positive changes in your child, it may be going so well largely as a result of the structure and the routine you have diligently put in place. Now is the time to maintain the structure, not relax it. The boundaries and routines are important ingredients to the positive changes you are experiencing. Structure is a long-term approach not a short-term fix.

---

### Some unanticipated results of relaxing the structure

Several months after Jayden had joined his adoptive family he seemed to be getting more settled and as a family they were getting on well. They decided one evening that they would let Jayden stay up later than usual so they could all watch a family film together. The film went on a little later than anticipated, so as it was then quite late for Jayden, the adoptive mum decided to put him to bed by shortening the usual bedtime routine. In a matter of minutes as a result of changing the bedtime routine the family had a full-blown episode on their hands with Jayden having a complete meltdown, and clearly not understanding why.

The adoptive parents could instantly see the problem. Jayden was a little more tired than normal and they had taken away the predictability and comfort of his bedtime routine that helped him transition from active and awake to restful and ready for sleep.

Jayden was a little emotionally delayed and did not have the maturity to accommodate the sudden, unplanned changes to his routine. The predictability of the familiar steps that would have offered him comfort in his tired state was removed as the adoptive mum hastily got him ready for bed. It was clear that Jayden no longer felt calm and secure inside.

Jayden's reaction was not a normal, tired four year old's reaction. It was way above and beyond any normal reaction you might get from a tired child and the impact lasted for a couple of weeks, during which he remained unsure and overly emotional around bedtime. Eventually, however, by sticking to Jayden's routine the adoptive family managed to get him back to the settled place he had been in before they let him stay up later.

---

### A nightmare holiday

Bethany had been with her adoptive family for six months when they went on their first family holiday. As advised, they took time to prepare Bethany for all aspects of the holiday. They role played packing their cases, played games about the airport check in process, and even found story books explaining in detail what happens when you get on a plane and fly to a holiday destination. They'd discussed the hotel room, looked at pictures on the internet from the hotel website, helped Bethany visualise where she would be sleeping, where they would be having their meals and what they would be doing on holiday. Bethany was very excited, the preparation paid off and the journey to their holiday destination went without a hitch.

What the parents hadn't anticipated, however, was that Bethany had no concept of a 'holiday'. Although they told her they'd all be away for 14 sleeps and then they'd be coming back home, Bethany had no experience of going away for a period of time and then returning to the same place. All her experience of sleeping in a different place meant *never* returning to the home she had just left. So, although she could repeat back to her parents what was happening, in her body she was preparing herself for something very different. After five days on holiday when it was clear that all of the routines had changed, and the boundaries were slightly different (later bedtimes and more ice cream), Bethany's behaviour spiralled downwards, with many of her old habits and behaviours that the family had worked so hard to change, coming back. When Bethany's behaviour regressed, her parents' frustrations rose and they found themselves in a vicious circle of negative emotions, which resulted in a stressful holiday that none of them really enjoyed.

When they finally returned home, Bethany was obviously surprised to be home, running from room to room clearly expressing surprise that she had returned home and that her bedroom with all her stuff was just as she had left it and was waiting for her. It became immediately obvious to her parents for the first time that Bethany truly thought that she wouldn't be coming back to their home again. This is something they hadn't anticipated, and they immediately understood the change in her behaviour while they had been away.

Bethany's behaviour didn't revert immediately to her pre-holiday calm and settled state. It took another month to help her settle again and get her back to the state she had been in before the family went away.

A year later when Bethany's adoptive family planned their next holiday, in full consideration of Bethany, they arranged to go back to the same holiday resort, in a room that appeared to be the same, and did lots of preparation with Bethany again, including reminding her that they would be returning home at the end of the holiday. This time, as Bethany already had the experience and memories of returning home from this location, and she was a year more settled, the holiday was a huge success and did not negatively impact Bethany at all.

---

I can only imagine how unsettling it must be for a child, just when they are starting to feel comfortable, familiar and secure with their routines to be thrown into the unknown again by an unexpected change and experience the turmoil of their resulting emotions; it's no wonder they exhibit dysregulated behaviour. The impact on an adopted child of changing a well-established routine may be far bigger than on most nurtured children from stable homes. Only change your child's important routines on purpose and after thorough consideration and preparation with your child. Eventually when your child feels fully settled and secure you may be able to adapt the routines at short notice. You will know when the time is right.

## Reinforce the boundaries

One of the responsibilities of being a parent is to help your child learn the boundaries for what is and is not acceptable behaviour. There will be some minor transgressions and there may well be some major ones. It might be that your child repeats a certain behaviour over and over again, and no matter how you try to help them learn a particular boundary they just continue breaking it. They may need many repetitions of the same lesson before they learn a particular boundary, in which case a consistent reaction from you, time and time again, over the long term is vital to helping them learn that boundary. Various factors will impact your child's ability to understand boundaries – their developmental age and their appreciation of action and consequence being just two factors. Patience is key.

---

### Reinforcing boundaries and facilitating behaviour change

When Lucy first moved in with us, she displayed behaviours that indicated that she wasn't used to behavioural boundaries. We developed a routine that we followed every time Lucy behaved in a way that was inappropriate for the norms of our family. We assumed that at her young age, and given her history, she hadn't been shown how to behave properly and therefore didn't know that what she was doing was wrong.

We simply tried to help her replace some behaviours that were undesirable from the perspective of our family, with new ones.

We followed a 'time out' type approach with Lucy each time she transgressed.

- At the time of any transgression, we removed Lucy from the situation or activity, listened to her if there was anything she wanted to share and explained why we had removed her from her activity.
- After a brief dialogue we sat Lucy on her bottom in an appropriate place, away from things she could fiddle with, but always in the same room as us. If we were in a supermarket or elsewhere, we would just find a suitable space out of the way of other people, for Lucy to sit down.
- As Lucy was four years old we would sit her down for four minutes (one minute for every year of her age). If we were at home, we would set the kitchen timer to measure the time and to 'ping' when the time was up. If we were out, we would just measure the time on our watch or set an alarm on our phone. We would not interact with Lucy for the duration of her 'thinking time', and would not start the timer until she was cooperating and calm.
- Immediately after the time was up, I would go over to Lucy and ask her to stand up. I'd crouch down to her level and explain again why I had sat her down to 'think', explaining what was inappropriate about the behaviour she had demonstrated, and how she could try something different next time. I would help her feel listened to if she had anything she wanted to share. Then I'd give her a big hug, and I'd reassure her that I loved her and I would always love her no matter how she behaved, and I would encourage her to give an apology.
- We would then consider the matter to be over.

The first few times I tried the time out process with Lucy, she completely resisted it, and would run off every time I tried to sit her down. However, my persistence was greater than hers, and I repeatedly explained the process as I retrieved her from wherever she had run, and placed her back on her bottom again. The first few times it must have taken me 20 or so attempts before she would sit still and we did the 'time out' for only two minutes. Once she got used to the process, and realised I wasn't going to change my mind or give in to her running off, we were quickly able to raise it to three and then four minutes. Whatever length of time you choose, it needs to be significant enough to your child, so that they realise they have been removed from their activity, and long enough for them and you to have some space to calm down and for you to consider your words and your next steps.

Those first few times were the hardest and, although I was calm on the outside, I was anything but calm on the inside! I felt exasperated and tired and began to question whether the process would work. But, as I was determined not to set a precedent of giving in if Lucy kept running off, I committed to continue no matter how long it took. I continued until Lucy sat in time out whenever she was put there. Outwardly I communicated quiet determination and ultimately I was just more persistent than Lucy, as I realised what was at stake if I gave in.

In the grand scale of things, it didn't take Lucy long to learn the time out routine and to follow it. After about two weeks of focused effort Lucy learned the significance of and the process involved with us 'putting her on her bottom' and would participate fully, if not happily. It was a hard couple of weeks, but it was worth persevering.

Initially, once Lucy learned the process, we were surprised that although we were following the process it took many, many iterations of the process to correct a behaviour that Lucy would simply keep repeating.

After Lucy had been placed on her bottom for a transgression, and the time out process was completed as described, Lucy would always say something like, 'I sorry, I never ever do it again', at which point she would run off and play, and within five minutes may well have repeated the very same behaviour or something similar. So the cycle would be repeated and she would sit on her bottom again. As she was starting to sit down she'd say something like, 'I said I sorry, I never ever do it again! I not sit here!' She would not want to sit, but she would sit down, we'd repeat the whole process, she'd say sorry, she'd get up and, even then, soon afterwards she might do the behaviour again.

In the early weeks, there seemed to be no connection in Lucy's mind between her actions and the consequences she was receiving. It was as if there was no 'action–consequence link', as though her brain were missing some connections. I have subsequently found out through reading and attending conferences that this is probably the case. Lack of nurture and structure had probably prevented Lucy's brain developing the neural pathways to process the connections between action and consequence that other children might make. She did not connect that her action was leading to the consequence that she was experiencing.

We were diligent in applying the time out routine for inappropriate behaviours and breaking boundaries. There were many times when we thought 'what's the point?' but we continued anyway in a belief that Lucy would eventually make the connections. Our repeated and consistent response to her behaviour did help Lucy make connections and form neural pathways. It was exhausting in the first few weeks, but the alternative of putting up with the behaviours or giving in to the boundaries being stretched would have demonstrated that we accepted the behaviours we were trying to change, and were willing, when really pushed, to stretch the boundaries.

Giving up would also have led to us feeling increasing levels of frustration, and this could have escalated into other less resourceful emotions, which would have negatively impacted all that we were trying to achieve with Lucy. So in order for us to feel in control and positive, our belief in the routine kept us strong and gave us a sequence of events into which we channelled our energies rather than allowing the energies to grow into frustration.

It was reassuring to us to follow the routine and made us feel as though we were doing something positive in helping Lucy learn new ways. So we stood firm with the boundaries, believing that eventually Lucy would learn different ways to behave, and eventually she did. It just took many, many more repetitions and weeks than we could possibly have anticipated.[1]

I am sure, as I think back now, if we had bowed to the pressure put on by Lucy and put up with some of the behaviours and slackened or eliminated the boundaries, or even had we given up on the time out routine and just repeatedly told her 'no', we would not be in nearly as good a place as we are in now, which is a *very* good place.

---

## Prepare for boundaries to be tested

Boundaries should only be introduced for good reasons: normally to protect your child from harm, help your child develop healthily and to observe your family and wider social values.

It is natural for children to explore the world around them, learning the many different ways, positive and negative, to interact with it and impact on it. In doing this they also learn about boundaries: what is and what is not acceptable to themselves and those around them. A boundary can be played with in many ways, while being explored and understood.

Once a boundary is understood, it is natural for children to want to push for it to be changed to fit in with what they

---

1 One interesting resource on the 'time out' approach is: '10 Time-Out for Children Techniques.' www.askdrsears.com/topics/parenting/discipline-behavior/10-time-out-techniques

want to do, or to test your reactions in certain situations to get to know you better!

There will be times when your child fully understands a boundary and is using it to test you and your reactions. Only by thoroughly testing certain boundaries can they come to rely on those boundaries and feel safe within them. Does 'no' always mean 'no'? Are you reliable? If you say you'll do something – will you? Can they count on you and trust your word? How bad do punishments get? Will you ever harm them?

---

### Testing me

When Lucy first moved in with us, she couldn't talk very well and would express her frustration and anger in many ways, one of which was spitting. She quickly learned that spitting was not an acceptable behaviour in our house and stopped. One day when she had been living with us for about six months, and knowing that spitting was not allowed, she deliberately spat on her brother during a game.

I made her stop her game and used the time out approach to help mark the fact that spitting is not acceptable. I sat her on her bottom for four minutes and set the kitchen timer to mark the time. It was time out of her game, rather than time out of the room. Lucy was still in the same room as me and could see me, she just had to sit for four minutes without playing to think about what she may have done that was not acceptable and what else she could have done instead.

As I approached Lucy at the end of the four minutes she deliberately spat on the floor, looked me in the eye and calmly said, 'What now Mummy? More four minutes?'

I have to confess to being a little stuck for words, and also frustrated, and started to feel myself getting cross inside, but I calmly (through a clenched jaw) replied, 'Yes Lucy, another four minutes', and I reset the timer for four minutes. Again, immediately as the timer pinged, signalling the end of the four minutes, Lucy looked at me and spat on the floor. I couldn't believe she had done it, twice on purpose while looking at me – it was so controlled and deliberate! This time she followed the spit with, 'Now what Mummy?' to which I explained she would have to sit there for another four minutes, and I set the timer yet again.

This time, however, after resetting the timer I turned her around so she was no longer facing me, but instead was looking out of the glass doors into the garden. She didn't like that, and protested loudly, but did stay facing in the direction in which she was put. Again the four minutes ticked away. This time, however, immediately after the timer pinged she swivelled on her bottom until she was facing me, looked me in the eyes and boldly and deliberately spat on the floor again. I was confused, shocked and starting to feel really frustrated. This was now uncharted territory for me and I could feel a swell of negative emotions rising. Worse still, I knew Lucy was doing her behaviour deliberately, and she knew that what she was doing was deeply offending me and making me angry.

It took a few mental deep breaths to clear my head and quell the rising frustration. I kept calm, and decided not to be drawn into her game any further. I managed to pause and think behind her behaviour to the potential root cause. I sensed beyond a shadow of a doubt that Lucy knew she had found a behaviour that was totally unacceptable to me and wanted to see how bad the punishment would get by repeatedly offending. I sensed that she was testing me to see if she was safe, or whether I would resort to physical punishment and hurt her.

This time instead of resetting the timer, and keeping her in 'time out' I went over to Lucy, sat next to her on the floor and gave her a *huge* hug, and simply said to her, 'Lucy, it doesn't matter what you do, or how bad your behaviour is, I will always love you, I will always be your mummy and I will never hurt you', at which point Lucy burst into tears, clung to me and through her sobs, apologised repeatedly, saying, 'I so sorry Mummy, I never, never do again, I sorry Mummy', in response to which I simply stroked her hair, soothed her and told her she was safe.

Lucy has never, to this day, spat inappropriately again.

---

When your child is pushing the boundaries, you may find yourself experiencing such frustration that you won't know what to do with yourself! In these instances, steel yourself, pause and ponder, take a few deep breaths and strive to remain calm, look to understand the intent behind your child's actions and try to respond in a way that will help them feel safe, secure and that you can be counted on to keep yourself in control and them safe.

If you find yourself struggling to control the feelings of frustration, or are unsure how to respond, please realise this is perfectly normal! In these instances, get some distance: make sure your child is safe where they are and then remove yourself from the situation. Sometimes just leaving the immediate situation and going into another room, or for a walk around the garden, can help you regain control of your emotions, get in a better frame of mind and return ready to deal with the situation at hand.

## Be consistent

Assuming you have introduced well-considered boundaries and routines, be consistent and diligent in their use and enforcement.

Children who suffer severe neglect and/or other forms of maltreatment do not develop in the same way as children who are nurtured in their early months or years. Their brains may fail to develop normally and may not make nearly as many connections as nurtured children, and as a result parts of their brain may be severely underdeveloped. The extent of the neglect is linked to the permanence of the damage to the brain. The brain is magnificent, and it is my understanding that in all but the most dreadful of cases a child's brain will develop in leaps and bounds as soon as they start to experience a truly nurturing environment.

As your child's brain develops, so will their ability to understand boundaries. To start with, as we did, you may experience extreme frustration over the number of times you have to explain a particular boundary. Each time it may seem as though your child is hearing you explain the boundary for the first time! Eventually, however, it is highly likely that your child will start to understand and honour the boundaries, though it may take many weeks or months to see the progress.

Develop a routine to handle the breaking of a boundary. Beware of the 'naughty chair', the 'naughty corner', the 'naughty step' or other such 'naughty' locations. Sitting your child in these locations and naming them as 'naughty' may reinforce their negative perception of themselves and be counterproductive to all the other positive esteem-building foundations you are laying through effective nurturing. If you do want to use a place for them to sit consider calling it the 'thinking chair', the 'pausing corner', the 'calm step' or something that will reinforce what you hope they will do while they are sitting there. Also be aware that if you choose to use a 'time out' approach, it means time out of the activity they were doing, not time out of the room separated from you and feeling isolated. Sitting out of a current activity to break a behaviour pattern is one thing, but banishing them to another room to be on their own may trigger other unwanted memories or behaviours. At no time should your child feel rejected by you.

Develop a routine that will work for you and can be applied equally and consistently by the primary care givers in your family. The routine should involve a marked pause in the current activity, an encouragement for them to share their thoughts and an opportunity for them to feel listened to, an explanation of the impact of their behaviour and why it was inappropriate, and a reminder of the boundary and why it is important.

## Explain don't blame

Don't blame and shame. Seek to understand and explain. It will be easier for your child to engage with you following a transgression if they are not feeling shameful and blamed for what they have done wrong. If you accuse and blame this may put them in an undesirable and unresourceful state where they just feel 'bad'. You may even trigger old memories, which will compound their feelings of low self-esteem. Instead talk to them about their behaviour, the choice they made, the impact of their choice and the options open to them for choosing differently next time.

Help your child understand the reasons behind the boundary, and why you are reacting the way you are in response to their behaviour. Consistently explaining and demonstrating the thinking behind your behaviours and decisions will eventually help your child to make associations between behaviours, beliefs and values, and will ultimately help them develop confidence in their decisions.

It isn't always obvious to children why we grown ups do what we do and why certain rules and boundaries are in place. Patient, consistent explanations will help your child learn why their action or behaviour was inappropriate and will empower them to do something differently next time. Just blaming them and telling them off may further lower their self-esteem and will not help them learn or progress.

Take every opportunity to reinforce to your child that you will love them no matter what, that you know they are a good and kind child and that you will always be there for them.

## Notice and encourage good behaviour

Noticing, praising and rewarding good behaviour is at least as important as correcting the unwanted behaviours. Make sure to help your child develop awareness of when they are behaving appropriately, making the right choices and demonstrating the behaviours you have been encouraging.

If you notice your child doing something well, or exhibiting a behaviour that you would like to encourage, acknowledge it out loud to them and name the behaviour. This will help them become familiar with what they are doing and the reason why it is desirable.

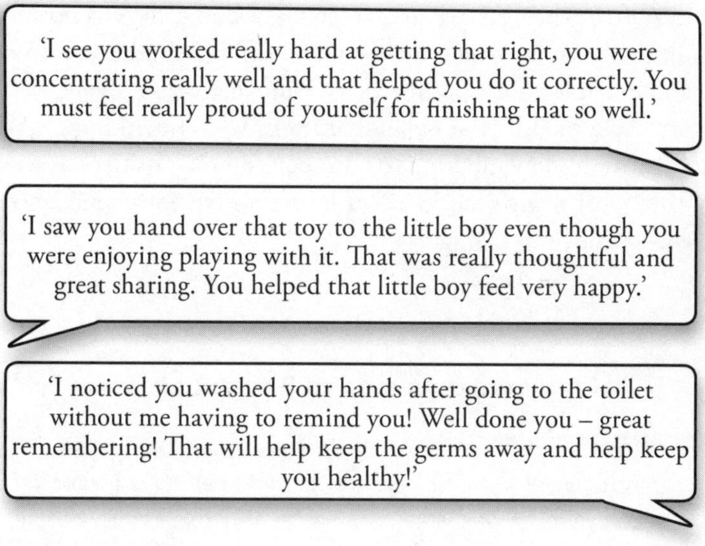

'I see you worked really hard at getting that right, you were concentrating really well and that helped you do it correctly. You must feel really proud of yourself for finishing that so well.'

'I saw you hand over that toy to the little boy even though you were enjoying playing with it. That was really thoughtful and great sharing. You helped that little boy feel very happy.'

'I noticed you washed your hands after going to the toilet without me having to remind you! Well done you – great remembering! That will help keep the germs away and help keep you healthy!'

**Figure 11.1** Acknowledge and name positive behaviours

You can consciously reinforce and name all of the key traits and behaviours that demonstrate your values and those of your family as and when you see them displayed; for example, thoughtfulness, helpfulness, patience, diligence, politeness, creativity, curiosity, open mindedness, etc. By noticing when your child is demonstrating those behaviours or attributes you can highlight them, and help your child link the positive emotions or outcomes they are causing or experiencing in that moment to what they are doing and how they are behaving.

Becoming more mindful of the way you communicate and on what you choose to focus will help you notice when situations are unfolding in line with your hopes and expectations. When your child is behaving well or demonstrating a new desired behaviour, remember to comment on this and acknowledge their actions and behaviours and the efforts that they are making.

It is easy to notice each instance where your child does something 'wrong' that is not in line with your expectations, but often when behaviours are going well and there is nothing untoward we fail to comment on how well our children are doing and to reinforce the positive behaviours that we are seeing.

Strive to shift the balance from only commenting on the negative to remembering to comment on the positives as well. The boost it gives children to hear positive comments about their behaviour is huge.

---

### Happy feelings lead to happy behaviour

When Lucy first joined our family, understandably it was quite a tricky time for our birth son, who had been an only child for seven years. It was vital for us, as an emerging family of four, that Lucy and our son started playing well together, sharing and enjoying each other's company. The more the children bickered, the more we felt frustrated, became short tempered and found ourselves in negative emotional states.

There were plenty of negative interactions on which we could have continued to focus, but we began to sound like a broken record. Our frustration fed their bickering, which fed our frustration, and so on. It didn't take long for us to realise the error of our ways and we consciously decided to focus on the positives.

When we saw the children interact well and share, or pass a toy, we commented on the positive behaviours we had observed and praised them. Occasionally after really good play we would reward them with treats. Soon they got used to the praise and the treats and what they needed to do to get them and consciously did these things more, and they genuinely started enjoying each other's company and seeking each other out as playmates.

I also drew their attention to how they felt when they were getting on well: how did they feel inside themselves? They spoke about the nice feelings that made them feel happy inside, not grumpy, bad tempered, mean feelings that made them cross with each other. They decided that they preferred the nice, happy feelings and that they responded to each other better when they were happy, and that made them happier!

> 'I can see that you are both really enjoying the way you are playing. I can see you smiling and hear you laughing, so I know you are feeling happy inside. When you are nice to each other it makes the other one of you be nice back! Isn't that great? Well done both of you for playing nicely. I think you both deserve a treat.'

We helped them make a connection between their kind and sharing behaviour and their happy feelings, and soon they transitioned to playing well because of the positive feelings they were giving and receiving. They also realised that when they were playing well and interacting kindly towards each other, this positively impacted me and my husband, and they were surrounded by positive feelings as well. At that point the treats weren't so important!

Conversely, if we noticed a silly, petty squabble that would eventually burn out on its own, we'd try our best to ignore it, so the interaction they were getting from us was when they were being good. This was very difficult and we didn't always manage it! However, when we did intervene, we made sure to give them both time individually to talk about what had happened, ask them how they would like to fix what is going on, and would help them come to some agreement. We'd also help them think about how the squabble had made them feel inside and to acknowledge that it wasn't really a nice feeling.

We still give treats occasionally when they have been playing really well for a long time and generally getting on well, but this isn't expected anymore and is now a nice bonus for them.

---

Our approach above worked really well, and continues to work today, but it takes consistent conscious effort to only focus on the positive behaviours that we see and to nurture those, while at the same time resisting the temptation to leap on each negative interaction that we observed. It has taken continuous effort and control of our reactions, but we did not give in and the results have paid off.

Lucy and her brother still squabble occasionally but they can also play well for hours at a time. I believe they have a regular brother–sister relationship, which doesn't seem to be any different because one of them is adopted and the other one isn't.

## Motivate your child with appropriate rewards

Different children will be motivated by different rewards. Find a reward routine that works for your child. For some children it will be stickers, for others it will be doing certain activities, and so on. Whatever you choose, make the rewards desirable, manageable and frequently attainable. A reward that builds into something big that can't be enjoyed for weeks or months is not motivating and may actually be demotivating. Rewards simply for 'good behaviour' can be too general and difficult to attain. Be specific about what your child can do to earn the rewards.

Once earned for good behaviour I don't believe a reward should be removed for poor behaviour. The impact of this may be hugely demotivating to your child. A reward earned is a reward to be enjoyed. We chose to develop one routine that rewards good behaviour and a separate routine that enforces boundaries and corrects poor behaviour. Once a behaviour is learned and continually demonstrated, we embed that new behaviour with lots of recognition and acknowledgement, and then encourage another new behaviour with the reward scheme. If the scheme that you choose is not motivational to your child, work with them to find one that is.

The following is an example of a reward scheme chosen by Grace's parents.

---

### Screen credits as a motivator

Grace is motivated by computer games and time on the Wii. Her parents choose not to allow her to spend a lot of time on computer screens, but do allow some time at weekends. Good behaviour is rewarded with 'screen credits'. Each credit is worth five minutes, and these credits can be cashed in at the weekend for time playing games on the computer or the Wii.

Grace took to this reward system very well when she moved in with her adoptive family at the age of five. She enjoyed counting her credits during the week and actively looked for ways that she could earn extra credits. Screen credits certainly helped Grace learn new behaviours and her parents made sure to recognise and acknowledge the positive behaviours she demonstrated as a way to further encourage the desired behaviours.

As Grace spent her screen credits at the weekend, her parents made sure to remind her of all the good behaviours she had demonstrated to earn her credits. This reminder helped her connect the fun she was having on the screen with the good behaviours she had demonstrated during the week.

Once Grace consistently demonstrated a new behaviour, her parents found that the incentive of the reward for that particular behaviour was no longer needed. At that point they transferred the opportunity to earn rewards to another behaviour they were trying to encourage.

---

Remember that boundaries and routines combine to form structure, the introduction of which will allow your child to feel secure and will support them as they develop. Please don't fall into the trap of relaxing the structure surrounding your child just at the point where all of your hard work in introducing and reinforcing structure is starting to pay off!

As second time parents we thought that introducing structure and boundaries to Lucy's life would be easy, but it wasn't. On reflection I realise we were supported by some principles that helped us. It may help you to come up with your own principles, but in case it helps, here are some principles that guided us.

---

**Principles that supported us as we introduced structure**

- *Start as you mean to go on*: A clear approach from day one helped Lucy understand the guidelines associated with her new home and family.
- *Don't get cross – get curious*: We found that getting curious and looking to understand the situation helped keep our focus away from getting cross! We were more resourceful and patient when we turned our attention to learning about the situation rather than reacting to it.

- *Proceed with confidence*: Although sometimes we didn't feel it, to Lucy we exuded confidence in our parenting approach. We reflected on and refined our approach as we progressed.
- *Reinforce positive behaviour*: We strived to reinforce the behaviours we wanted by focusing on those and linking Lucy's positive feelings to those also. We felt that the benefits of this approach far outweighed the impact of constantly criticising her negative behaviour.
- *Pause and ponder*: Frequently we became aware that our initial reaction to a situation was not the best way forward. So we learnt to pause, think more widely around the situation, the emotions and moods involved, and to think of what outcome we wanted and the most appropriate way to act to help us achieve that for us and for Lucy.
- *Be consistent in action and reaction*: Initially my husband and I, and after the first few months my mum as well, made sure we were absolutely aligned and consistent with our approach and the boundaries we upheld when parenting Lucy. Even our son patiently helped Lucy adhere to the boundaries. The fact that Lucy had consistent rules and reactions, no matter who was in charge, really helped her feel secure and adapt.
- *Implement firm boundaries with lashings of love*: Every boundary we introduced remained firm and we remained calm and compassionate even in the face of tantrums or major sulks.
- *Tune in and be guided*: Once tuned in to your child you will be able to anticipate their needs more accurately and build trust and attachment.
- *Be forgiving*: Both you and your child will make mistakes as you learn to live together. Don't harbour frustration for your child or yourself. Forgive and move on.

- *Shoot for the stars*: At all times, we assumed the best for Lucy was possible. We chose not to limit our expectations for Lucy, as we felt that would be denying her the opportunity of realising her true potential. So we maintained our high hopes, while at the same time being realistic in our observations and refining our approaches and expectations accordingly.

---

## Summary

- It is widely recognised that children respond well to a certain level of structure provided in terms of boundaries and routine. Structure enables them to feel safe to explore their world and their relationship with it. Structure can also help *you*, the parent, to feel secure in your parenting, so develop some principles that help guide *your* behaviour, and in times of doubt your principles will help guide you.
- Boundaries are the guides for what is and what is not acceptable in terms of behaviour. Boundaries should be set by the parents to keep the children safe, help them grow and help them understand how to behave. Boundaries should be simple to understand and follow, and should be applied consistently. Boundaries can be reviewed and either relaxed or removed as a child matures. However, boundaries should only be set and reviewed in a calm and relaxed state and never under pressure from a state of high tension or a situation being caused by your child getting upset or having a tantrum.
- Routines are sequences of steps or events that become familiar to a child and help them to feel secure as they transition between states, as well as helping them feel comfortable in the knowledge of what is happening and what is about to

happen. Long routines may comprise smaller sub-routines, each of which is familiar to your child.

- ★ Children are programmed to test their environment, which includes the structure within which they live. For the boundaries to work they need to be enforced. A child should experience natural or applied consequences to help them learn a boundary. It may take many iterations of the same consequences for a child to learn a boundary, but eventually if their brain is developing normally, they will learn it. Patience is key.
- ★ Sometimes you may be tempted to break a routine to which your child has become accustomed. A small change in routine may be easily tolerated by one child, yet might introduce untold levels of anxiety for another. If a change in routine, however well intentioned, ends with chaotic and emotional behaviour, be patient. Realise that the challenging behaviour may be a direct result of the insecure feelings caused by the change in routine rather than because your child is being wilfully naughty.
- ★ Helping your child to learn the routines and honour the boundaries may take some time, and will be related to the development of their brain and their capacity to learn, as well as your patient approach. Patient, consistent explanation and enforcement of boundaries should enable most children to learn, honour and feel relaxed within the structure provided.
- ★ Noticing, encouraging and rewarding good behaviour and the honouring of boundaries is as important as enforcing the boundaries following an attempted transgression. Most children have something that motivates and encourages their good behaviour. Find out what your child's motivator is and introduce a reward routine around it.

CHAPTER 12

# Close the Development Gap

It is highly likely that your child will be behind in some if not all areas of development when they come to you. Their personal medical history and life story to date will give you a level of understanding as to what their potential may be, and what may be realistic for you to hope for, regarding their future meeting of developmental milestones.

The purpose of this chapter is to encourage you. Small efforts by you will result in almost imperceptible changes in the first few weeks, but these changes will occur, and they will accumulate until you notice your child making progress in many different areas. Depending on your child's history, you may be cautioned by social workers not to have high expectations regarding their development and to temper your expectations regarding the speed with which they can develop. But this doesn't mean to say that you shouldn't try to give your child every opportunity to develop. Small and frequent stimulation and encouragement in many different areas will help them grow and develop, and enable them to be all that they can be – no matter what that level is for them.

As mentioned in Chapter 7, due to the power of brain plasticity your child's brain can make new connections and develop, but as they get older, the opportunity for influencing their development decreases. Therefore, the earlier the better. There is never a better time than 'as soon as you can' to start helping your child develop, using fun and engaging activities in small bite-sized periods of time, you may be astounded at the power of incremental change. We were.

---

### Helping to close the development gap

From the first time we met Lucy it was evident that she was a four-year-old child operating as a toddler in all areas. We assumed from the beginning that she had as much potential as any child from a stable background and we encouraged her accordingly.

We noticed instantly that Lucy responded really well to the framework of structure that we introduced to her life. She clearly started to feel secure and, over a number of weeks, we noticed her responding positively in many areas.

We wanted to give Lucy the chance to be all that she could be and to fulfil her potential. We knew that at four years old there was still time to help her brain develop, to stimulate her curiosity and her love of learning.

We hoped that Lucy would be able to catch up and start reaching the appropriate milestones for her age. If this wasn't possible for her, then at least we knew that she would be accomplishing everything possible for her. She would be fulfilling her potential, whatever that might be.

Within a couple of weeks of Lucy moving in, in addition to the usual time we spent playing with and caring for Lucy, I dedicated a period of slightly more structured time being with her at the kitchen table, playing games to support her learning and development.

We'd play games involving different colours and shapes, holding pencils, colouring and scribbling, using scissors, picking up small objects, following patterns with her finger, describing pictures, spotting the difference. Anything to help

Lucy develop her fine motor skills, or recognise, process and remember information.

Initially Lucy couldn't and wouldn't focus her attention on anything, but after only a few days, she started to engage more with the games. Only for a minute at first, but after a couple of weeks one minute had become 10 and then 15 minutes. After about a month, Lucy seemed thirsty for learning opportunities. It seemed that the more she could engage, the more she wanted to engage, and the more she found that she could actually do. Soon she wanted to learn more and more.

After a couple of months Lucy was recognising colours, then numbers and shapes. We built this learning time up to 30 minutes. Every week day after breakfast for half an hour, Lucy and I would play learning-related games. During the rest of the day we regularly played games to help Lucy develop her curiosity, thinking skills and resourcefulness. Lucy got used to our daily routines and would look forward to our half hour when we would play learning-related games. Often she would take out the games we played during those times, and would also want to play them at other times in the day too.

It is such a fixed part of our morning routine that we still do it today three years on. Every week day after breakfast we spend 30 minutes together playing games that support Lucy's learning.

---

## Help your child to develop through play

I got very interested in 'developing through play' and I learned that the brain is stimulated through many different forms of play. We made sure to incorporate all of these elements into Lucy's life to pique her interest, keep her attention and help her develop.

## Learning through creative play

You can encourage drawing, painting with brushes and fingers, Play Doh, finger drawing in flour, decorating with stickers and feathers and anything brightly coloured. Any game that encourages greater manual dexterity is wonderful for brain development and also makes learning to write letters easier for your child when they start school. Activities can include threading laces through holes, playing with and sorting beads, sewing and shape sorting.

## Learning through being active

You can encourage active play, toddler activity groups, gymnastics, body awareness, acting out games and role playing, jumping and/or rolling around on a trampoline, and coordination through pedalling and balance. Consider getting a 'balance bike' (toddler bikes without pedals or stabilisers that encourage early balance) or a two-wheeled scooter. These remove the reliance on stabilisers to start with and encourage better balance in your child at an earlier age. The initial frustration they will experience as they learn to balance is far outweighed by the fun they will have and the better sense of balance in the long term.

## Learning through music

You can encourage singing nursery rhymes and other songs, listening to music and lullabies, making and playing basic percussion instruments, banging drums, shaking bells and playing along to the rhythm of music.

## Learning through social interaction

You can encourage playing and sharing with other children at toddler groups, attend a nursery and spend lots of time encouraging your child to talk to you about anything.

Get or make toys that encourage role play and dressing up, this allows your child to try out different roles and different personas. It is surprising what they may share or ask when they are dressed up in a role, compared with being themselves.

## Learning through entertaining themselves

Create space every day that is not filled by some other activity – some time for your child just to bumble around entertaining themselves. This may be a challenge for them at first if they need to be stimulated all the time or aren't comfortable in their own company. Over time this may change and they may transition to being as happy playing on their own with their toys as they are interacting with others.

## Learning through word play

You can encourage your child to love books. Spend time with them touching and looking at books, pointing out letters and words, describing the pictures, playing with different words. Playing I-spy and other word games also helps. When your child is old enough they will probably love time playing computer games and using various applications on iPads and similar devices. There are many educational games for children. Of course there are guidelines that govern how much time is appropriate. When you know your child you will judge this for yourself.

## Learning through numbers and logic

You can encourage your child to recognise and play with all sorts of patterns, puzzles, counting, numbers, sizes, weights, comparisons, etc. Everything from sorting the laundry to unpacking the dishwasher can be turned into a matching or counting game.

## Develop your child through conversation

One piece of advice I was given very early on by a health care professional was simply to continually engage Lucy in conversation. Conversing with all children is important but arguably more so for those children who are developmentally delayed. Talk to your child, encourage them to talk, let them know that you are interested and listen patiently to what they have to say. This advice paid dividends for us and I know it has for many other adoptive parents as well.

---

### From speech impairment to speech success!

When Bethany moved into her adoptive home she was almost five years old, had the speaking age of a two-year-old, and the same desire to share her thoughts as a regular five-year-old; this understandably was very frustrating for her, and her adoptive parents. Taking time to really listen what she was trying to say, and summarising back to her what they thought she said, took much time and patience.

Bethany's frustration levels would rise quickly at not being understood, so her parents patiently tried many different versions of what she was saying until eventually they would get the meaning of the message that she was intending them to hear. Once Bethany felt understood her tension would usually evaporate.

Bethany's speaking ability was described as 'severely impaired and delayed' by specialists three months after she moved in with her adoptive parents, though by this time her parents had already noticed a significant improvement in her ability to communicate.

Bethany's parents believed that her speech would continue to improve through dedicated one-on-one attention. When speaking with Bethany they consciously used very simple sentences with one noun and one verb where possible, building in adverbs and adjectives, which then led onto more complex and compound sentences over time.

Bethany's parents patiently listened to her as she struggled to make herself understood. They recalled being tempted to answer for her when people asked her questions to which she didn't respond quickly enough. They were tempted to leap in and finish her sentences for her, or guess what she meant to say to get to the point of her communication more quickly. But they resisted these urges. No matter how long it took, they allowed her to struggle through her sentences, encouraging her and responding to her as they would in any other conversation.

Most importantly they made time to listen to Bethany to help her feel listened to. When she phrased sentences or questions incorrectly – which was much of the time – they would simply state the correct way of saying it and then they would respond to that. They never made her repeat the correct phrasing – they believed that through modelling correct sentence structure Bethany would learn. And she did.

Another speech assessment at six months' post-placement concluded that Bethany's speech had 'improved significantly', and within nine months she was exceeding speech milestones for her age. Soon there was no stopping Bethany, and now at age six she can talk for England!

---

Not all children will develop as well or as quickly as Bethany, but if you interact with your child in a patient way, letting them practise talking and experience feeling listened to, you will help them on their way to achieving their speaking potential.

## Enable a healthy body and a healthy mind

It makes sense that in order to give your child the best chance at realising their potential and catching up in their development it is essential that you help them to become as healthy as possible. Strive to give your child a healthy well-rounded diet and help them get appropriate exercise and sleep.

This may be a challenge to implement on day one, but if you hold it as your focus, you will find that within a few weeks your child will be eating and sleeping better than they were when they arrived and that will already be positively impacting their development.

Along with healthy eating, you may choose to supplement your child's diet with fish oils, vitamins and minerals if their early life of neglect and lack of food has left them nutritionally deficient. If in doubt, contact a nutritionist or consult with your child's doctor for the latest thinking and advice in this area. With a healthy body and an alert mind, your child will have a firm foundation from which they can develop.

The same principles apply to you too! In order that you can be the best that you can be for your child, be mindful of your own diet, rest and exercise. A healthy body and a healthy mind are equally important for the parents as for the children.

## Summary

- ★ It is likely that your child will exhibit some delays in their development. You may be surprised how quickly some or all of these delays can resolve themselves when your child experiences the nurturing and well-rounded parenting that you will provide.
- ★ Different forms of play are excellent ways to stimulate your child's brain and encourage learning and development. Play is fun and engaging for your child, and beneficial to them in closing the development gap.
- ★ It may be that you have to help your child learn *how* to play. If they have spent much of their time being entertained by the television, they may have to learn how to engage and interact with toys.

★ Fundamentally, if your child is well nourished and well rested they will have the basic building blocks to benefit from the other interventions you will be providing. If they are continually tired, or undernourished through a poor diet, progress may be hindered.

★ Make sure to look after yourself as well. A good diet, rest and exercise are just as important for you as for your child.

PART SIX

# Prepare Carefully for Your New Arrival

*Once you have been matched with your child and the placement is approved, time will seem to speed up. Before you know it you will be meeting your child – possibly for the first time – and soon after that, your child will be moving in. Once your child arrives you may feel you are in uncharted territory, managing situations and emotions that, at best, you had only imagined. The more you can anticipate and prepare both practically and emotionally, the better you will feel and the better equipped you will be to manage the situations and your emotions. This section highlights some areas of preparation that, given time constraints, you may overlook or leave to the last minute. In my experience, and the experience of others with whom I have spoken, the more effort you put into the preparation, the easier those first few weeks and months with your child will be.*

CHAPTER 13

# Involve Family and Friends

When you adopt a child into your immediate family, you are also adopting them into your extended family and into the community in which you live. You alone, or you and your partner or spouse will have done the preparation and thinking around assimilating this child into your life, yet other people close to you and affiliated with your lives to differing degrees also have to embrace, welcome and understand your child. They also need to know what role they play and how they should play it to contribute to your child's sense of attachment and feelings of security in their new life. You can't do this alone; you need to involve your family, friends and certain people within your community.

The purpose of this chapter is to help you think more widely about whom you might consider involving and how you might involve them in preparing both for the arrival of your child, and helping assimilate them into your life.

## Prepare other children for the new arrival

If there are children already in your family, preparing them is critical to the success of the placement process. Your patience as a parent is one factor, but any existing children in the family also need to be prepared for what to expect and to have practised some coping strategies for the situations they may experience and the emotions they may feel.

Ideally you will start preparing other siblings as part of the adoption approval process to help them understand why some children need new homes, and why these children may exhibit some challenging and/or unusual behaviour as a result of their life experiences.

There are many books available and different ways you can talk to existing children. As well as using those with our son (we particularly liked *Adopting a Brother or Sister* by Hedi Argent (2014)) we also chose to use a metaphor from our life.

---

### A cat called Jak

We were fortunate enough to have two cats living happily in our home when another cat came through the cat flap one day and decided to stay. This stray cat would come in, scruffy and hungry, eat the cat food, and curl up under a cupboard to sleep. As soon as he saw us, he would bolt out of the cat flap, only to come back the next day and repeat the process. He was unfriendly and would hiss and try to scratch us if we got too close. Our existing cats were territorial and made it quite clear that they did not want to share their space, beds or food with him; they were hostile towards him and did not want him around.

After a few weeks of this cat turning up every day, we managed to catch him and take him to the vet, who was able to put us in contact with his owners. The owners confessed to being 'dog people' more than 'cat people' and were unable to protect the cat from their large dog, who attacked it every time he saw it. They were glad their cat had left home as they were fearful for his safety if he remained with them.

We were asked if we would adopt the cat, called Jak. Well, we didn't have much choice as it had already decided to move in! So we said yes.

When Jak moved in he was dirty and unfriendly, scavenged for food, was hostile towards our two cats. If we tried to stroke him, he would bite and scratch. We and our cats were quite wary of Jak in the early weeks and he was obviously wary of us, though he had chosen to stay with us. We could only imagine what his former life had been like on the basis of what we had been told by his past owners, but we knew that he had not received much care or affection at his last home.

Over many months of being patiently looked after and cared for by us, Jak completely changed. Within a year during which Jak experienced compassion, patience and unconditional love from all of us, he became the friendliest, cuddliest, happiest, softest and purriest cat you would wish to meet and is adored by us and both of our other cats. All of the cats get along really well, playing, eating and sleeping together.

The story of Jak and his assimilation into our family provided many parallels that were easy for our son to grasp. We discussed how our existing cats might be feeling with this intrusion, and how the stray was feeling as he tried to fit in and settle down. We anticipated how we all might feel in certain situations with a new child in our family, as well as trying to understand how a new child might feel when they moved in with us. We discussed possible undesirable behaviours and situations that may occur with a new child moving in. We were amazed at the capacity for compassionate thinking that our son demonstrated, all born from a powerful metaphorical story about a cat called Jak.

Jak was a gift to our family and definitely helped pave the way for our son's understanding regarding the arrival of his sister Lucy.

---

You can start to prepare any existing children, and help them think through what life may be like for them post-placement, as well as what it may be like for your new child. However, it is difficult to prepare existing children for the actual child who may join your family until you have passed the matching panel and are certain that the child will definitely be joining your family.

I have met a few adoptive parents whose first match did not work out. Often they had fully prepared their new child's bedroom and had fully informed other children of the imminent arrival of their new sibling, only for the situation to change just before or during the matching panel, resulting in the prospective child never joining the family at all. As adults we are better equipped than our children to cope with the powerful emotions associated with a failed placement. It is not fair on our existing children to expose them to having to cope with these powerful and confusing emotions.

Second time round, none of these adoptive parents breathed a word about the imminent arrival of the new sibling until the matching panel had approved the match and the introductions were planned. Once you have passed the matching panel, then and only then can you really start preparing your other children in earnest for the specific child joining your family.

When we knew that Lucy was definitely joining our family we were able to tailor our discussions with our son and build upon the earlier, more general preparation, to help him anticipate, more specifically, what life might be like for him, for us and for Lucy after she joined our family.

## Involve existing children in the practical preparation

As well as the theoretical and emotional preparation for your other children, another way to help them prepare is to involve them in the practical preparations for the arrival of their adopted sibling. Enlisting their help when preparing the bedroom, soft furnishing, fixtures and fittings is a great way for them to feel valued, included and part of this new change.

Remember to include some treats for your other children too. A new bedroom 'makeover' or new items for their bedroom can help existing children feel special and excited about the changes taking place as well.

---

### A new bedroom for our son

While our son was helping us choose items for Lucy's room we managed to glean from him how he would like his bedroom changed to make it 'awesome'. Then, a few days before Lucy moved in, while he was out, we transformed his bedroom into the 'awesome' room he had described. He was thrilled beyond belief. He understood that Lucy was important so she was getting a new bedroom, but he also felt important as he was getting a new bedroom too. This certainly helped seed positive associations with Lucy's imminent arrival.

---

## Educate and involve significant people

Significant people are all people who will spend chunks of time with your child either with or without you. You will know far more about your child and about the potential challenges adopted children may have than any of your family, friends or other contacts who have not encountered the world of adoption. It is important to help these people anticipate and prepare for their part in positively influencing your child. It is easier to ask people in advance to interact in a particular way than it is to ask them to correct unhelpful interactions after they have happened.

Your friends and family will be excited for you. In many cases they will have lived through your adoption approval journey with you and will be wanting to support and help your new family unit succeed. The best way for these significant people to support you will depend on your child; specifically, their age (both chronological and emotional), their life experience to date and any physical, emotional or psychological challenges they may have. Without specific guidance from you on how to support you and your growing relationship with your child, your friends and family may not know how to interact with your child, and may inadvertently interact in a way that does not help.

There are books you can give friends and family to help them prepare generally for the arrival of your child. We found *Related by Adoption* by Hedi Argent (2010) to be an easy read and a good introduction for extended family members. It will be up to you, however, to decide what specific information on your child's background it would be pertinent to share and to explain why you need to make certain requests.

All children regardless of their background will need to learn that you are their close family, that you can be relied on to meet their needs and care for them, and that it is to you that they should be forming their primary attachment. It could be very confusing for your child, therefore, if all your friends and family, in a bid to be welcoming, are over-friendly and inadvertently act in a way that suggests they are there to care for your child as well.

---

**Preparing friends and family**

We knew that when Lucy moved in there was no way that she was going to feel attached to us straight away; we anticipated that she would probably feel confused and would be grieving.

We were overt in our preparation and communication with our friends and family. We explained that it was important for Lucy to learn that my husband and I were her new mummy and daddy and that she needed to become aware of the positive associations and the importance of those nurturing parental relationships. We wanted her to learn that we were the appropriate people from whom she should seek her care giving attention, hugs and cuddles, comfort and food.

We gave specific guidance to all our extended family, friends and acquaintances about how to interact with Lucy the first few times that they met with her. We explained that Lucy would be trying to learn to trust us as her new family, and it would really help her attach to us if they could support the forming of these new bonds. We asked people to:

- Just say hello or shake hands when they met her for the first few times and not hug and kiss her.
- Avoid reciprocating her affection if she offered it, but instead be a little more formal and redirect her back to us for affection.
- Avoid meeting any of her needs, but rather direct her towards us, her new parents, to get her needs met. This included not giving her food, drink or treats, as well as no cuddles or hugs or comfort if she hurt herself. In each case we asked them to redirect her back to us, we would only ever be a few feet away!
- At school pick up, don't lavish her with disproportionate amounts of attention because she is new to the circle and is 'different' as she is to be adopted, instead treat her like you would treat any other child.

When Lucy moved in, as we anticipated, she didn't attach to us immediately and actually sought attention and caring from all the people she met in this, her new life. We, her adoptive parents, were but two of many potential care providers as perceived by Lucy. As she had not experienced beneficial nurturing from a mother or father before, Lucy had no idea of the significance of these people in her life. She was not mature enough to understand the importance of certain relationships in relation to herself.

With the help of our friends and family, we were able to make the differences more obvious to Lucy, and she started to feel the benefits of the parental relationship compared with other acquaintances. In the early weeks we kept it simple: Lucy could seek comfort, nurture and physical affection from her immediate nuclear family (me, my husband and our son) only.

It took many months but we eventually managed to guide Lucy in creating relationships and appreciating the differences between the types of relationships she was forming. She understood how a close relationship was different to a vague acquaintance and, therefore, how her interactions with those people would differ.

All of our friends and family were gracious in accepting the guidance, grateful for the guidelines and honoured our wishes, even though it sometimes made them feel uncomfortable to gently push Lucy away from them and encourage her back to us. Some didn't really understand why we were being so strict, but did it anyway as we were very open about what we needed. On occasion we would need to remind friends and family as they would forget and pick Lucy up for a big cuddle. We were consistent, and we strongly feel that this expedited Lucy's attachment to us.

Lucy is now firmly attached to us, seeks affection only from close family and shows appropriate stranger awareness. The change in her is remarkable. It took two years of constant vigilance, and the changes were really slow, but we know that Lucy is securely attached to us now, which bodes so well for her future development.

---

Anticipate what type of interaction from others will best support your child's development and their growing attachment to you. Be explicit to your friends, family and contacts about how they can help your child's future development by interacting in specific ways. Even when you have explained it to people, you may need to remind them a few times, and gently step in to encourage the appropriate interaction from them if they forget. But your constant vigilance will be effort well spent.

If you notice a person interacting with your child in a way that you would prefer they didn't, intercept as soon as possible. Gently explain what you are trying to achieve for your child, how you are trying to help them, and how their behaviour and interaction with your child can help or hinder. Most people will also want the best for your child and when taken into your confidence will be happy and relieved to be guided by you. It is really important to educate those around you so that they don't unwittingly undermine your efforts and your child's progress.

You may feel awkward offering guidance or stepping in to guide an interaction, but better to suffer the temporary feeling of awkwardness in the short term, than the impaired attachment of your child in the long term.

---

### A well-intentioned friend

One adoptive mum I met explained that her close friend, another lady who had birth children, and whom she saw often, would frequently pick up and cuddle her newly placed little boy.

The adoptive mum was trying to bond with her little boy and encourage attachment, and he was clearly confused about whom he should be bonding with given the frequent cuddles he was receiving from this other lady. The close friend, an experienced mother, thought she was doing the right thing. As the little boy came from a neglectful home she assumed the more hugs and cuddles he had from anyone the better!

This was hugely frustrating for the new adoptive mum, who felt awkward correcting the practice of her friend who had so much more parenting experience than she did! Consequently, the adoptive mum did not offer any guidance to her friend about how to interact with her new son. As the adoptive mum didn't mention it at the beginning, by the time it had been going on for a few weeks she then felt too uncomfortable mentioning it!

The situation went from bad to worse and at the time of the discussion the adoptive mum seemed convinced it was impacting the progress of the little boy's attachment. This adoptive mum could have averted this situation by educating and involving her friend, and asking for her support *before* her little boy arrived, explaining that she could best help the little boy and support her, the adoptive mum, by *not* offering physical contact and comfort to him.

---

## Influence your friends and family just in case!

The vast majority of the people you know will have heard of adoption but will have no idea of the challenges some of today's adoptive children will have faced in their past or will continue to face as they develop. Some people assume babies are still given up at birth by perfectly well functioning parents who simply want a better life for their child. Naively, many people have no idea that almost all children are taken away due to various forms of neglect and/or abuse.

It is important that those people closest to you in your support network, be they friends or family, are aware of the types of challenges that may be common for adopted children. You may well forget how much you have learned as you have gone through the approval and matching process. By comparison, your friends and family will be quite innocent of the facts.

Some people believe that children who have come from the care system are all troublesome and will exert a bad influence on those around them. They might even believe these children are less worthy and deserve fewer rewards and less recognition than children from stable homes. You may be astounded by some of the heartless and ill-founded beliefs held by some people.

I heard an experience from one couple with two adopted children, who told me some of their friends wouldn't let their own children come and play with their adopted children as they didn't want the 'bad influence'. A friend of mine described the deep hurt he felt (and still feels) when as a teenager he found out from his cousins that they received better Christmas and birthday presents from their mutual grandparents than he did, as they were biological relations and he wasn't. Yet another family had to move their daughter from her school after another school mum corralled a group of mums and their children into alienating the little girl and her family as apparently 'all adopted children are good-for-nothing trouble makers'.

I was horrified by these stories and, in shock, I shared them with my friends and family; thankfully they were as shocked as I had been that such discrimination existed. The chances of you coming across such narrow mindedness are very slim, but it does exist. So be aware and proactively educate and inform those around you.

## Summary

★ Before your child moves in there are many aspects and situations that you can anticipate and prepare for. The more anticipation and preparation, the better. One of the most important aspects is ensuring that other children in your immediate family are prepared for some of the potential behaviours your child may demonstrate, and to help them be patient while your new child learns not to demonstrate some undesirable behaviours and learns new ones instead.

★ Although you can prepare your other children generally about adoption, the specific preparation regarding the child you plan to adopt should only start in earnest following confirmation at the matching panel.

★ As well as theoretical preparation you can involve your other children in the practical preparation of changes around your home in anticipation of the new arrival.

★ Be bold, and help prepare any other significant people in your support network who will be interacting with your child. Help your friends and family understand how they can best interact with your child to support their behavioural changes and the process of attachment to you, their new family.

## References

Argent, H. (2010) *Adopting a Brother or Sister – A Guide for Young Children.* London: British Association for Adoption and Fostering (BAAF).

Argent, H. (2014) *Related by Adoption – A Handbook for Grandparents and Other Relatives.* London: British Association for Adoption and Fostering (BAAF).

CHAPTER 14

# Plan for the Introductions and the Transition

Everything may seem to have been in a state of limbo as you wait for your adoption matching panel, but once you have officially been matched with your child it is all systems go! It is time to prepare your child's bedroom, and talk things through with other children in the family, your friends and extended family members, not to mention making plans for the introductions, the long-anticipated time when you actually get to meet your child and spend time getting to know them.

You will be so busy from the point of being matched with your child, to meeting them, that you may not have time to fully anticipate the emotional demands of the 'introduction period'. The introduction period is that time when you visit your child daily, allowing you to get to know them, them to get to know you and for their care to be gradually transitioned from their current carers to you. The end of the introduction period culminates in you collecting your child and bringing them home to live with you. The introduction period can be emotionally intense and energy-draining, which can mean that your child moves into your home when you are feeling emotionally and energetically exhausted.

The purpose of this chapter is to help you think through the different elements of preparation that will reduce the pressure and tension for those first precious few days and weeks after you meet your child for the first time and they move in.

## The introductions can be emotionally challenging

Depending on the location of your child, you may need to travel to a different part of the country for the duration of the introduction period.

As Lucy lived within a two-hour drive from our home, we decided to do the drive each way every day. We opted for the inconvenience of the long drive but with the benefit of being able to return to the comfort of our home each day and demonstrate some normality for our son throughout the process. It did mean a few very early starts and late finishes, but for us it was worth it not having the added stress of having to stay in a hotel along with the added disruption for our son.

I know that for many it is not possible to do the introductions daily from home. For some, staying away from home for the introduction period causes additional stress as they have to make arrangements for other children. For others, however, staying away from home for the introductions can mean a more relaxed approach that allows them time away from daily responsibilities of children and home. Staying away can offer the emotional space to focus on your new child and to rest and reflect in between meetings. Whether you drive back and forth every day or choose to stay close to your adoptive child, do not underestimate the emotions involved with the introduction period.

You will probably have been very busy from the day of the matching panel to the day the introductions start. Not much time to stop, take stock and reflect on your emotions. Then suddenly there you are at the front door of the foster carers, about to meet your child possibly for the very first time. This is a huge moment and the start of an intense week!

The introduction period will follow hot on the heels of the matching panel. Do make time to think through what arrangements would work best for you, and what would minimise your stress and anxiety during this crucial time, allowing you to be emotionally free to focus on your new child.

Years of waiting, assessment and planning have all been working towards this point in the process. These emotions are added to the emotions of how you will feel about your child when you first meet them, what you sense they feel about you, any uncomfortable feelings about spending time in the foster carers' home and trying to bond with your child in front of strangers. All the emotions add up and can be quite overwhelming.

## Be prepared for any greeting

Meeting your child for the first time will involve a mixture of emotions and expectations for you and for your child. How your child will react to you and interact with you during that first meeting will depend on so many factors, not least of which is how they are feeling on that particular day. If your meeting goes well and meets or even exceeds your expectations, then treasure the memories. If, however, your meeting does not go well and does not meet your expectations, then try to forget it and move on, looking forward to the next meeting. The success of the first meeting is not a predictor of the success of the relationship that is to follow.

Your child may fling themselves at you, wanting to sit on your knee and play with you, or they may cling to their foster carers, not wanting to interact with you at all. If your child flings themselves at you this will give you a wonderful feeling that you will enjoy and reciprocate, yet this behaviour from your child may or may not be indicative of an underlying attachment issue that could cause challenges later. If your child wants nothing to do with you and clings to their foster carers, this may make you feel unwanted, especially as you have been looking forward to this moment, yet this behaviour may or may not be indicative of a strong attachment to the foster carers that, if present, could bode well for your child being able to develop feelings of attachment to you.

You really can read nothing into the greeting your child gives you in those early days, so be prepared for anything and everything and just take it in your stride.

---

### Meeting Lucy for the first time

We had been texting the foster carers updating them with our expected time of arrival. As they lived in the middle of a dense complex of flats, one of them was going to come out to the road to show us the way to their flat. We saw the foster mum approach and in her arms was this little girl. Was that really her? Lucy? Our daughter? We couldn't believe it – here she was after all the years in preparation and months of waiting to be matched, the moment we were going to meet our daughter had arrived!

As the foster mum put her down, Lucy immediately ran towards us with outstretched arms. I knelt down to greet her and she threw herself into my arms with the biggest hug ever. I wrapped my arms around her and knew this just felt right. It was the best feeling and the best greeting I could ever have hoped for. After giving me a huge hug, Lucy then gave a big hug to my husband, who picked her up and carried her as she giggled all the way to the foster carers' flat.

The positive feelings buoyed both my husband and me as we headed into the start of our introductions with Lucy.

It didn't take us long to realise, however, that Lucy would greet absolutely any stranger in exactly the same loving and friendly way that she had greeted us at our first meeting, meaning her warm and welcoming embrace was not special, just for us and had no bearing on the future development of our relationship.

---

---

## Meeting Connor and Ben for the first time

Connor and Ben had seen photographs and watched a home movie of their new parents countless times. The boys were reported to be very excited to meet their new mummy and daddy.

When the first day of the introductions came, Connor and Ben misbehaved all morning resulting in the foster carers feeling stressed and Connor and Ben being in bad moods when they first met their new parents.

As the first meeting went ahead, the excited new parents were very disappointed to see that Connor and Ben appeared disinterested and resistant to any form of interaction they offered. The boys seemed to be in a bad mood with everything.

It wasn't the best first impression, and the adoptive parents left that first day already questioning whether they had made the right decision to adopt siblings. The second and third meetings were no better and the parents were getting more doubtful. It wasn't until the fourth meeting that Connor and Ben showed the delightful side that the parents had heard so much about from the foster carers and social workers. From that fourth meeting onwards the introduction period just got better and better and the relationship between the boys and their parents started to develop.

The introduction period was reported by the adoptive parents to be the most stressful part of the adoption process by far.

---

## Have ideas of what to do with your child during the introductions

You will probably go into your introduction period with a daily itinerary of timings that have been agreed between you, all relevant social workers and the foster carers. However, until you meet your child in their foster carers' home, you really won't know what there is to do there with your child. Foster carers can be so different: they have different approaches, different homes and different facilities. Hope for the best and prepare for the worst. Have a few books and simple games at the ready that you can do with your child during your visits. In my experience and from what I have heard from others, be prepared with some books and games suitable for a much younger child, as it is possible that your child won't be ready for books and toys for their own age group.

If you take books and toys to play with your child, take them away with you at the end of each visit. If you are travelling home at the end of every day, you should be slowly transferring your child's belongings from where they live now to their new home with you. If you are bringing toys and books with you and leave them behind, it is counterproductive to the efforts of transferring their belongings! Also, as your child will associate you with these new activities it might help them to look forward to your visit each day.

It can feel very awkward being in the foster carers' home with your child. The purpose of the introductions is that the parenting of your child should gradually transition from the foster carers to you as your child starts to grow accustomed to you. It is a very artificial process, awkward and emotional for all involved. Your child will probably be confused. The foster carer will be trying to pull away and give you some privacy with your child. You will be trying to step in to the parental role, but if this is the first time for you, you may feel unsure about your parenting capabilities; you may be conscious of not wanting to encroach on the foster carers' turf. Also it is possible that your foster carers will have different boundaries and guidelines within which they are parenting, with regards to food, sweets, treats, snacks, screen time, television time and behaviour that they consider acceptable.

## Anticipate the arrival of your child's belongings

Be aware that although you will lovingly and thoughtfully plan and prepare your child's bedroom and will possibly spend days and evenings dreaming of them in there, by the time they finally arrive the reality may look very different to the dream. Between completing their bedroom and your child moving in you will need to find a home for all of your child's belongings that accompany them from their foster carers!

---

### Where to put all the stuff?

At the end of each day during the introduction period, the foster carers were excellent at surreptitiously sending us away with bags of Lucy's clothes and toys for us to take home, with the intent that by the end of the introduction period, all of Lucy's belongings would have moved ahead of her to her new home.

Every day, we had bags of unfamiliar items including dozens of cuddly toys, plastic toys, masses of clothes and old books. None of these items were familiar to us, yet they kept flooding into our home. We didn't want them, but as they were part of Lucy neither did we want to reject them.

We were completely overwhelmed by the dozens of unfamiliar items that were not part of us, not chosen by us and didn't seem to belong in our home. Lucy's beautiful, clean, fresh new room was beginning to look second-hand, worn out and cluttered before she had even arrived. We felt emotionally exhausted with the introductions and overwhelmed with all the bags of extra possessions we hadn't fully anticipated. I felt myself start to panic as I was becoming too tired to think straight and didn't seem able to tackle the challenge of the accumulating clutter. I assumed that Lucy would need all of her familiar belongings around her. I didn't know what she would and wouldn't miss if it wasn't there. I was starting to feel guilty that I wasn't accepting her 100 per cent as I didn't want all of the clutter that came with her.

My mum was the voice of reason who made me see that actually what Lucy needed were a few items that were familiar in her new room so that it wasn't all alien to her, and all the rest could go into 'holding' until it became apparent whether there were specific items she missed, in which case they could be retrieved and the rest could be passed on. Also, as Lucy had kept her most treasured cuddly toys with her for her last night at the foster carers, there was no chance of us putting those away.

Once I had this new perspective, I chose the nicest toys and 'bagged' the rest. Needless to say, when Lucy did come, she was comforted to see some of her familiar toys in her new room and she was very excited and interested by everything that was new. She never asked for, or appeared to remember the many items we had 'bagged', so we must have chosen the right ones.

The same happened with her clothes. We received bags and bags of unfamiliar clothes that either seemed to be too small, were for the wrong season or were just not the type of clothes we would have chosen. Again I felt overwhelmed, and again my mum stepped in and helped me sort through the piles. In the end everything went to charity apart from a very few items. We had assumed that Lucy would come with appropriate clothes so hadn't been clothes shopping for her before the introduction period started, and once it had started we didn't have time!

When I had sorted through Lucy's clothes and realised I had practically nothing for her to wear I found myself experiencing a source of stress that I hadn't anticipated. This stress was starting to make me feel panicky and overwhelmed before Lucy had even moved in. Luckily a friend had lots of lovely Lucy-sized clothes that looked like new, and we managed to collect those on the very morning that Lucy was due to move in. I also made an emergency dash to buy underwear that would fit her. All was well. Lucy had a wardrobe with some lovely, seasonally appropriate clothes that fitted to see us through the first few months until we could actually go shopping with her ourselves.

Thinking back, I should have asked the foster carers to point out Lucy's favourite clothes and toys so that we would have known what we needed to keep. Also I should have bought some clothes in appropriate sizes, just before the introductions started, as I could easily have returned them if it turned out we didn't need them. Isn't hindsight wonderful?

---

Don't underestimate the mix of emotions that may threaten to overwhelm you in the first few days of meeting your child and them arriving into your home. In addition, the emotionally charged task of having to sort through your child's possessions and decide what to keep and what not to keep may be harder than you anticipate. The more of this you can get done before you arrive home with your child, the better. Clearly if you are adopting an older child, this introduces another dynamic, as they may well want to keep everything! On the other hand, it may be that your child comes to you with next to nothing so deciding what to keep might be less of an issue. Instead you may need to deal with feelings of sadness for your child that they are arriving with precious little.

## Carefully manage your child's transition from their current home to yours

It is important for you to be involved in the step-by-step plan of what will happen on the day you actually collect your child.

From what I had read, it is symbolically important for your child to be handed over to you by their foster carers rather than you taking your child from the foster carers. At some point most of the children in the care system have been taken from their parents. Now that they are settled with their foster carers, if you take your child from the foster carers you may trigger all the feelings previously experienced when they were taken last time – both their own emotions, and the ones they witnessed their parents experience.

If the foster carers hand the children to you, it symbolises that the transition is happening with their blessing. Although it might still cause your child some distress, it is hoped that this will be less than the distress they experienced the first time round. How much truth there is in this, I'm not sure, but it seemed to make sense so we made sure we had a say in the way the handover happened, to be the least stressful to Lucy.

The transition from the foster carers to you should be calm and swift, with the foster carers walking your child to you and saying goodbye, wishing them well and you helping your child get into your car or to continue the journey with you, however that is to happen. It is advisable to have a few snacks, books or toys with you as diversionary tactics to help them settle if they get upset.

---

### Collecting Lucy

It was the most exciting day. We left home early in the morning to arrive at the foster carers' home for 9am. The idea was that Lucy would get up and have breakfast, and spend a little time with her foster family as they said goodbye. The foster father would nip down with the rest of Lucy's belongings, of which there weren't many as we had already moved most of them into our home. Then the foster mother, along with Lucy's social worker would walk her down to our car, say their final goodbye, and we would help Lucy get into the car and away we would go.

The night before, we had put Lucy to bed and had explained that we would be coming to collect her in the morning. Lucy had seemed excited.

Initially, the morning went as planned. The foster father handed over the remainder of Lucy's belongings without her noticing, and the social worker and foster mother appeared on time and walked Lucy towards us and our car. As they got close, however, Lucy realised that something different was happening, something that she wasn't fully understanding. She was too young to understand what was really going on, but she seemed to understand that something significant was happening and that it centred on her. Lucy started sobbing, pulling away and trying to hide behind anything that she could, at one point she was clinging to a lamppost, screaming and crying and refusing to get in the car. It was an awful situation. Lucy was distraught and we felt awful. The foster mother was clearly upset and was choking back tears trying to be brave.

Finally we managed to get Lucy strapped into the car and she continued sobbing and screaming as we drove off. Luckily we had a big cuddly toy strapped into the middle seat, with me on the other side in the rear of the car, and within five minutes Lucy was happily playing with the cuddly toy, looking through the books we had that were now familiar to her and eating some snacks. She seemed happy and fine.

Halfway home we stopped at a service station on the motorway to use the facilities. Just as we got into the ladies' restroom Lucy was sick. I think she probably still had a bit of the stomach bug that had afflicted her earlier in the week but, as she had now been fine for a few days, I think this sickness episode was largely due to the trauma and shock of having been separated from her foster carers whom she loved. Even though we planned it to be as smooth as possible, it was still a shock to Lucy's system.

All in all, it wasn't the best transition, but by the time we arrived home, Lucy was happy and excited to be in her new home with her new bedroom and excited to play with her new big brother. The next few days were our honeymoon period.

---

After all of the build up to the matching panel and the excitement of meeting your child for the first time followed by the intensity of the introduction period culminating in the transition day, soon you will find yourself largely left alone by social services and expected to start this new chapter of your life with your new family.

In our experience, and in talking with other adoptive families it seems that many of us in hindsight would have welcomed more contact with the foster family and social workers in the early days following transition. The level of contact you actually need and want after your child has moved in may be different to what you anticipated. If you need more help and contact, do not hesitate to reach out at this crucial time.

## Plan your first few days

We all know that we are not at our most resourceful and patient when we are physically and emotionally tired. The more you can have planned for the first few days after your child arrives, in terms of activities, meals, snacks and routines, the better. You don't have to follow everything you have planned, but if you feel tired, overwhelmed or confused, you will have something to fall back on.

Arrange to have your cupboards stocked with food, the house tidy, ready for your new addition, and a clear diary. Keep friends and family at arm's length at least for the first week. You will know when the time is right to invite people in, but make sure to do it when you and your child are ready and not because you are being pressured by friends and family to meet your new arrival.

What your child needs in the early weeks is you. You may want to show your new child off, and invite people in to meet him or her, but for whose benefit it is really? Yours or your child's? It may be that you really need the extra support, to give you the strength to keep going, in which case it is ultimately for your child. But if all is well, then try to keep just your nuclear family around your adopted child for a few weeks as this will really help them get a head start on their attachment to you.

## Summary

★ As soon as the matching panel is over and you have a verbal approval, it is almost certain that the 'match' will go ahead and you will start the introductions with your child in the coming weeks.

★ Prepare both emotionally and practically for the introductions. It is difficult to know how your child will respond to you when you first meet them, but realise however they respond has little to no indication of how things will unfold in the fullness of time.

★ Practical preparations will make the introduction period a little easier. Plan to take some activities just in case you need them, and think about what you can do while you are in the foster carers' home and the surrounding area.

★ Think ahead about what to do with all of your child's belongings. Do you have room for everything? Do they need everything? Do you want them to keep everything? Do not underestimate how overwhelming it can be to receive boxes and bags of unfamiliar items, not knowing what to keep and what to let go.

- ★ Ask for the foster carers' help to identify your child's favourite items. Once you have your child's approximate sizes, buy some clothes for them – if you don't need them, most shops will let you return them for a full refund within a certain time frame.
- ★ Plan for the transition day and make sure that everyone knows their role at the crucial point of the handover.
- ★ Have food, snacks, games and activities prepared for the first week at least so that is one level of stress you will have removed.
- ★ If you feel you need more support or contact from the social workers and/or foster carers, reach out to them and secure the support you need.
- ★ Don't rush to introduce lots of family and friends to your child: focus on being together as a family and starting to bond as a family unit.

CHAPTER 15

# Carefully Integrate Your Child into Your Life

By the time your child arrives you will have given much thought to the potential challenges ahead, and how to build a relationship with your child that paves the way for a successful placement, a happy and settled child and a stable and rewarding family unit. You will have prepared your close friends and family to the best of your ability in anticipation of your child moving in.

Up until now all preparation will have been emotional, theoretical and based on educated best guesses. Once your child moves in, the situation becomes real. You will be actively managing interactions, encouraging relationships and facilitating bonding between your child and anyone significant, with the intent to fully integrate this precious child into your life.

The purpose of this chapter is to help you anticipate how the other significant people in your life may react to your child and how preparation and special consideration for them too, can help smooth the process of your family bonding with your child.

## Help existing children manage the reality of a new sibling

Expecting birth children and other existing adopted siblings to instinctively know how to interact with a new arrival to the family is a huge ask!

You might find it difficult learning the most effective ways to communicate and interact with your new child when they actually arrive – and you are a grown up! Imagine how challenging it may be for your birth children or other adopted children, who are now having to welcome another child into their home and their lives, and are being expected to 'play nicely' and 'share' and not least of all 'love' this new child.

Usually your adopted child will be one of the youngest if not the youngest in your house, so helping the older siblings learn how to communicate effectively with them will expedite the process of them learning to 'play nicely' and get along. Using positive reinforcement, encouragement and rewards can help children play well together.

If you do need to intervene in a heated situation, strive to calm the situation down, use empathic listening for all parties involved, enforce structure and a boundary if need be, and encourage all children to participate in figuring out what course of action they want to take next and how they want to play. Sometimes the children will want to play separately and do their own thing; at other times they may want to change the rules of the game they are playing and continue, or play a new game entirely.

## Make time for existing children

It is most important that you regularly create the space and time for your existing children to talk about how they are feeling, and for them to be allowed to express their frustrations without feeling judged or blamed. Your existing children will experience your new child differently to you and the more they can feel listened to by you and their frustrations understood by you, the better.

If particular problems arise that are causing any of your existing children frustration with your adopted child, work with them to come up with a solution that is effective from their perspective and that helps them continue to be patient and supportive as their new sibling settles and your family unit as a whole reshapes.

---

### Mend, replace and respect his space

After Lucy moved in, it was evident that the preparation we had done with our son was appropriate. However, it had been difficult for us and our son to anticipate the depth of the emotions he would feel in response to Lucy's behaviours.

Our son was particularly frustrated when Lucy was either not careful with his toys, or not considerate with something he was creating. He had been used to building a Lego model or similar and it still being there when he came back to it at a later time. He would also take good care of his books and toys. Lucy had not learned how to look after toys or to respect other people's property. This caused a lot of frustration early on for our son.

We were very open with our son and encouraged him to talk openly with us. His granny was also an excellent ally, as if there were emotions he didn't want to confide in us for any reason, he would share those with his granny.

My husband had a chat with our son at one point when our son was feeling particularly frustrated with Lucy. My husband was seeking to understand the causes of the frustration and what we could do to improve the situation.

As a result of the discussion it was agreed that anything Lucy broke we would mend and if this wasn't possible, we would replace it with a new one. We also agreed that our son's bedroom should be his own personal space to retreat to whenever he wanted some time on his own. If at any time he didn't want Lucy in his room, that was okay; we would never insist that he had to share his personal bedroom space with Lucy.

So we agreed to 'mend, replace and respect his space'. This gave our son the resilience to continue, and the permission to withdraw to his own space when he had had enough.

It worked very well, and to this day both children honour each other's bedroom space. They play in each other's rooms with permission, but when asked to leave they do so.

## Support your other children's emotional needs

Despite all of your excellent preparation with any existing children in your family, it will still be a challenge to fully anticipate the gamut of emotions they may experience when your adopted child moves into your home.

Prepare to support your existing children's emotional needs as well as your adopted child's. The worry, tension, frustration and stress involved if your existing children do not bond with your adopted child in creating the new family unit may put the adoptive placement at risk.

Do not underestimate the amount of your time and energy your new adopted child will need, and potentially, therefore, the shortfall in time and attention that your existing children may feel that they receive. So before your new child arrives, strive to safeguard some time to spend with your existing children on their own. You and your partner individually and together need to spend time with any existing children, making them feel special as well, and doing some of the activities that you used to do before your adopted child joined your family. As your family adapts to absorb the latest addition, and as your existing children have bonded with their new sibling, the need for this 'alone' time with you may reduce. From then on, as with other families it will be important for you to spend time with all of your children together and separately.

---

### Ensuring our son felt special too

When Lucy arrived we introduced some structure and routines for our son that helped him have the one-on-one time he needed with us, as well as making him feel special in his own right.

Bedtimes were staggered to ensure that Lucy always went to bed before our son, which enabled him to spend some time chilling out on his own without Lucy and also allowed us to spend some time with him one-on-one. While I put Lucy to bed, my husband would spend time with our son and vice versa.

As our son is three and a half years older than Lucy, the type of films he would like to watch would be much more grown up than those we would feel were appropriate for Lucy. So as a family we may watch a family film acceptable for young children, and after Lucy has gone to bed at the weekend we may watch a film appropriate for older children that our son could enjoy with us. He would consider this a privilege.

If Lucy eats sugary food, biscuits and sweets, it triggers some hyperactive behaviour, which it does not for our son. Therefore, as a matter of course we don't have sweets and chocolate available at home in front of Lucy. After Lucy has gone to bed at the weekend, however, one of our son's privileges is that he is allowed some sweets and chocolate that Lucy is not allowed.

These are not huge differences or privileges, but they mean a lot to our son. He doesn't get them because he is the birth child and she is adopted, but rather because he is slightly older. In a few years when Lucy is older these differences will even out, as they will be going to bed at the same time, enjoying similar level films and we hope that Lucy's response to the odd sugary treat may have normalised.

---

It may be that your existing children suddenly get more 'needy' of your time and attention in response to the new arrival. Try not to get frustrated by the extra demands this will put on you, instead recognise it as part of your existing child's process of testing the security of their attachment with you and your love for them. In time, when they feel reassured that you have enough love and nurturing to go round, this 'needy' behaviour should subside.

It may be that your existing children are curious how you feel about the new arrival, wanting to know if you love the new sibling, and whom you love most. This is natural and is your child seeking reassurance that they are still special in your life. Be honest in your response. If you do feel love for your new child straight away, explain that to your existing child, and explain how the love feels the same or different, or what quantity of love you feel. If you don't yet feel love for your new child, be honest about this too with your existing child. Explain that love grows over time and every day you love your new child more and soon you will love them as much as the existing child. You can explain that love feels different towards different children. It can be the same amount of love but feels different. It can feel different to love a girl from a boy, different to love an older to a younger child, different to love a mother or a father, brother or a sister. So the quantity of love can be the same but all love differs. If it feels exactly the same for you then explain that.

Your existing child may be trying to gauge how they should be feeling by asking you how you are feeling, so being sensitive and considered in your response is important.

## Quality time

Our son has always liked the physical sensation of feeling close and certainly enjoyed his hugs. However, when Lucy moved in his demand for hugs and cuddles shot up exponentially.

Any time Lucy came over for a hug, in the early weeks he would instantly want one too and would almost become quite panicky if he couldn't have one. We sensed it was really important not to push him away, but at the same time knew it was important to give Lucy the hugs she needed. We didn't get it right all of the time and sometimes there were tears from our son. But we went out of our way to be available to him at all times and to reassure him that we had enough love for both children.

Sometimes we would do tag-team hugging between my husband and me, swapping children and sharing hugs. We would create opportunities by sitting close watching a film, reading a book or some other similar activity. We spent a lot of time with our son at bedtime, one of us sitting close reading him stories. Our bedtime routine would often span two hours, ensuring that first Lucy and then our son got quality time with us. It certainly was a large investment of time, but one that has definitely paid off.

In the early months when Lucy was at home full time and our son was at school, making sure to spend time with our son when he got home was really important to us as well as him. Lucy loves playing in the bath so, a few times per week, we would let her have an early extended bath, which gave us a good uninterrupted 30–40 minutes with our son when he got home: some quality time when he could talk, share and feel listened to. Lucy loved this 'special' bath time, as she got to play with her toys, make up stories and generally have a whale of a time in the bath. In this way she did not feel left out of the one-on-one time we were having with our son.

## Communicate, communicate, communicate!

If you are adopting as a couple it is so very important to stay emotionally connected to your partner as you integrate a child into your lives. Communication is vital. Share how you are feeling, ask how your partner/spouse is feeling, seek to understand and not to judge. Being part of a strong open and honest unit as you go through the early challenges of settling a new child into your home will make the process easier.

Lack of communication, harbouring frustrations, appointing blame and not supporting each other will be a quick way to pile more stress onto a potentially vulnerable situation.

If you are a single adopter, make sure to stay very connected to your support network so that you feel their support as you integrate your child into your life.

## Anticipate your child's support needs

Once you have started the introduction period and especially after your child has moved in, you will quickly start to get an idea of what additional support they might need. Realise that there may be more to know about your child and/or their background from social services. Don't be afraid to ask questions, and to keep asking questions, until your queries are satisfied. If you notice anything during the introductions that you weren't aware of, you can already start exploring support needs.

---

### Access support early on

Bethany's parents noticed that Bethany wasn't making much sense verbally during their interactions. She was almost five years old and she babbled a lot, but most of what she said was unintelligible. She had a few short sentences that were difficult to understand and that was it. This delay had not been indicated to them at all as Bethany was meant to be meeting all her developmental milestones, which was evidently not the case. They were concerned, as they didn't know if this was due to her hearing, a speech impediment or developmental delay.

Before the introduction period had finished and before Bethany had moved in, they had already made contact with their local medical centre, registered Bethany and requested a health care worker to visit them in the week that Bethany moved in to help them get familiar with the local medical support services so that they could access them immediately.

Within a couple of weeks of Bethany moving in, she was already receiving the assessments she needed and her parents the support from their local health care worker that they required for Bethany.

The adoptive parents were proactive in making sure they started enquiring and accessing support as soon as they could, so that Bethany could receive support as soon as possible.

---

Outside your immediate family and close friends there will be other people significant to the success of the placement. Your support network will radiate out to include extended family members, acquaintances, colleagues, social services, health services, schools and other support services. The more thought you can give to these more remote relationships and what needs to be in place so that they can offer the support that you, your recently placed child and your family need, the better.

Once a child has been placed for adoption, if all seems to be going well you will quickly find that the focus of social services moves away from your family to one of their many other priorities. If there is a feeling that you will cope, it is highly unlikely that any additional resources are going to be offered.

There is normally a period of time between your child moving in and you becoming their legal parent. Once you have officially adopted your child and you are their legal parent, you lose any leverage to get any additional support. Once officially adopted, your child is then your responsibility and not the responsibility of social services and so you will have to fight for any additional resources you may need alongside any other adoptive or birth parents. While your child is still legally the responsibility of social services, even though they are living with you, you may find it easier to get them the support they need.

Ask your social worker to help you find out the different types of support that are available to your child and to you as a family. Different services are available in different localities, and I am sure the same is to be said of different counties and even different countries, if you are adopting outside of the UK. Do not be afraid of raising the possibility of needing extra support. Each borough should have some services to support you after you adopt your child, but it seems that these are not widely publicised as the resources are so tight. Some adoptive parents said that they felt as though they might be regarded as a failure if they raised the fact that they need more support. If you need help, ask for it. Ask what is available, explain how it will help you and your child and find out the process to go through to apply for it. Sometimes the wheels turn very, very slowly and need a lot of effort from you to turn them, but don't give up.

Join the discussion boards in the various online adoption forums and ask for the experience of other adoptive families. Much good advice is freely available through these boards. Post-adoption support should be more widely available for all adoptive parents, and it seems that this is now starting to be recognised, so there is never a better time than now to fight for what you need.

A higher than average proportion of adopted children have attention deficit hyperactivity disorder (ADHD) and attention deficit disorder (ADD) as well as varying forms of sensory processing disorder and attachment disorders. It may well be that through reading up on these you will know more that your local doctor and have more of an idea if your child is exhibiting traits associated with these disorders. As adoptive parents our learning never stops. We are the sponsors, advocates and cheerleaders for our children, and we should arm ourselves with information to make sure they stand the best chance of getting the support they need.

## Create opportunities for your child

If you already have children, you will probably be aware of all of the toddler groups, nurseries and activity groups for children in your area. If you are a new parent, however, you may not be so aware. Depending on where you live, some nurseries and activity clubs have waiting lists of a few years – yes years! Which means that expectant mums often put their child's name on the waiting list before the child is born. If you only have a few weeks' notice before your child arrives, depending on their age, you may find yourself in the position of not finding a vacancy at a suitable local nursery or any suitable activity clubs for your child.

This applies to just about everything you can think of: football, swimming, dance, gymnastics, rugby, cricket, horse-riding, art club, Rainbows, Brownies, Guides, Beavers, Cubs, Scouts, to name but a few. Depending on where you live, you may have to put your child's name down very early to get a place to join at the starting age for the club. I wanted my son to join Beavers, which is the feeder group to Cubs. I put his name down before his third birthday and was still on the waiting list when he turned six, which was the time he should have joined. So when I knew we were having a four-year-old girl placed with us for adoption and enquired about Rainbows, which is the feeder for Brownies, I was disappointed to find that Rainbows starts at age five and I should have put her name down when she was two. Clearly this would have been impossible as I didn't know she existed at that time!

---

### Take people into your confidence

I have discovered that if you take people into your confidence and explain the situation to them, most people like to help out.

Without going into any detail, I simply explained that my daughter had had an unfortunate start in life, which we were hoping to negate, but that I was finding all clubs closed to her due to the long waiting lists. I expressed the disappointment and frustration I felt on her behalf that she was continuing to be impacted even now that she was starting her new life with us.

The people who ran these clubs were very understanding and saw the part they could play in helping Lucy develop and move on. Lucy was fortunate enough to get a place at Rainbows, a place in a local gymnastics class, as well as a place at the nursery at which we thought she would best thrive. We explained our situation; these compassionate people wanted to help Lucy and offered her the next available place. The nursery even contacted Ofsted and with their permission created one extra space just for Lucy!

These clubs have definitely helped with Lucy's socialisation and integration, and she has grown and thrived.

---

Don't leave it too late to plan ahead and think of the clubs your child might enjoy. It is all part of socialising, expanding their experiences and developing. If you put your name on a list, you don't have to take the place when your name comes to the top, but if you are not on the list at all you may struggle to get your child into any of the activities they might want or need to help with their development.

## Help the teachers to help your child

It is normal to hope that your child will have no issues at nursery or school and will blend in without standing out. However, if your child is adopted, or is in the process of being adopted, there is little benefit to be had by hiding this fact from the people who will be nurturing them at nursery or school. Far better to take the school and your child's teacher into your confidence and ask for their support and understanding in helping your child develop. You don't need to share everything, but if there are challenges your child may have in certain situations or behaviours that they might exhibit at school, then sharing pertinent information along with strategies to manage behaviour or situations may help the teacher deal with situations in a way that reinforces the approaches you take at home. The more consistency that your child can experience, regardless of whether they are at home or at school, the better this will be for your child's adjustment, sense of well-being and therefore development.

Don't assume that your child's school or their particular teacher will be familiar with the potential challenges facing many children from the care system. To them your child may appear intelligent and 'together', but they will be unaware that this could be a thin surface veneer, unsupported by the layers upon layers of nurturing and development enjoyed by most children from stable homes. Your child may therefore not get the empathy and the consideration that they should from their school or teachers.

If you feel challenged at home by some behaviours and at a loss how to respond to your child when they come out with something unexpected, imagine how the unprepared teachers will feel! Far better to help them prepare by sharing your approaches.

During their time with you, your child will be developing in the most amazing ways. Their brain will be developing, and they will be making new connections and processing new and old experiences and memories. Occasionally your child may be processing an old memory or making a new connection that may stay with them as they go to school. On these occasions it is useful for their teacher to understand what is going on for them so that they can support them appropriately.

There will be times when something happens that you think may impact your child's behaviour negatively in the short term. In these cases, be brave and share your concerns, then the school can be ready to support your child. Not sharing information may lead the school to misinterpret your child's behaviour and think they are just being naughty and disruptive.

---

### Hindsight is 20-20

One day during her first half-term at school, in the hustle and bustle outside the school drop-off point, Lucy was accidently elbowed in the face by a dad who was bending down to help his daughter take off her coat. The elbow caught Lucy on her cheekbone and a big red welt immediately came up. Lucy didn't cry or complain; she just went quiet. I tried to explain to her hassled teacher as Lucy went in, that she had just been elbowed in the face and that it might impact her behaviour that day. I naively trusted that the teacher would look out for Lucy and be supportive of her throughout the day.

As I walked away from the school I hesitated and considered returning to the school and going to the school office to ask if I could have a quick word with Lucy's teacher. However, I didn't want to be perceived as a fussy mum; I knew the teacher would be busy first thing with registration; I was sure I was making a fuss out of nothing. Ultimately I convinced myself that all would be well and I shouldn't worry.

When I collected Lucy from school at the end of the day I was met by a disgruntled teacher, who told me crossly that Lucy had had her worst day ever. Apparently Lucy's behaviour had been resistant and challenging all day, which had resulted in her name card being placed on the 'cloud' (the place for difficult children). Eventually as the teacher couldn't change Lucy's behaviour, she had removed Lucy's merits, those she had previously earned for hard work and good behaviour!

I was upset for Lucy, and so frustrated and disappointed with the teacher. But mostly I was cross with myself for ignoring my intuition and assuming that the teacher would make allowances and offer the appropriate level of support. In hindsight, I should have gone to the school office and requested a few minutes with the teacher specifically to help make her aware of the change in behaviour that may result from Lucy being elbowed in the face.

I have never made that mistake again. If I feel something is appropriate, I act on it every time.

---

At school there will be lots of children in the class all demanding the teacher's attention. Your child's teacher will probably be grateful if you can help them quickly understand your child and share strategies with them that work for you at home. With the best will in the world, they can't give your child the level of attention you provide at home.

Your school or nursery may or may not have experience of 'looked after' or adopted children. Either way, you can choose to partner with the school, and help them learn about adopted children generally or the challenges such children may face. You can share what you have learned and read, recommending books and leaflets, even relevant courses for members of staff to attend so that they are better prepared to help nurture and develop your child. There are a number of organisations that run courses; regardless of which country you are in, if you search the internet for 'adoption courses' you will find the ones local to you.

## Instigate a home/school communication book

Ask for a 'home/school communication book'. Provide one if necessary. This is a plain notebook that should be kept in your child's school bag. The book goes to school with your child every day and comes home with them to you at the end of every day. It is a way for you and your child's teacher to share anything significant that occurs and to keep each other up to date, so that you and the school can both be aware of, prepared for and, therefore, anticipate situations that may arise.

I instigated a home/school communication book early on in Lucy's first term at school, and still use one today. The book stays in Lucy's school bag and goes back and forth between home and school every day. I write down anything significant that I think the teacher should be aware of that day, and the teacher writes me a few lines each day on anything significant from her perspective. I check the book every day when Lucy comes home and, if there is a comment from the teacher, I always sign to show that I have seen the comments, or I will reply if required. When I write anything in the book, I mark the page with a bright sticky note, so the teacher knows to open it and read it. I recognise that the teacher is busy so I don't expect her to check the book unless I indicate with a sticky note that I have written something in the book. When the teacher has read the comment, they remove the marker. There are days when the teacher is just too busy to read the book, in which case the marker stays in place and I know that they haven't seen it. If it is urgent I can then contact the teacher through the school office.

I am in the fortunate position now of having cultivated an excellent relationship with my daughter's school, and feel fully supported by them and each of her teachers in showing her consistency, anticipating situations that may cause challenges and assisting her to develop in the best way possible. In addition to the home/school communication book, I meet with Lucy's teacher every few weeks to discuss Lucy's progress and what strategies we can try between us to help her make progress in certain situations. This excellent relationship didn't happen by chance. It took time and patience, and has been an iterative process of communication, understanding and cultivation of a mutual respect. I know the teachers are busy. Lucy is but one of 30 children in her class.

The importance of cultivating a proactive and trusting relationship with your child's nursery or school in support of your child cannot be overstated. In order for your child to be fully supported at home and at school, both you and your child's teacher(s) must recognise that your child's unconventional early start in life may give rise to additional considerations and create a need for deeper understanding at school.

---

### Poor home/school relationships

I know of a highly informed, forward thinking adoptive father who wanted to share information with his son's school. Unfortunately, the school in their naivety refused to recognise that his son may have been any different or have had any challenges as a result of his background. Even in the face of psychological and educational assessments that concluded severe learning delay and ongoing processing challenges, the teachers refused to engage in a conversation with the father. Ultimately their denial to recognise the special circumstances resulted in them interacting with the child in a way that the parents considered to be psychologically damaging to their son, and they removed him from the school.

At the other end of the spectrum, I spoke to a teacher with an adopted child in her class. The school and teachers are very aware of the potential challenges experienced by adopted children and want to tailor their interactions to help this child thrive. In this case, however, it is the parents of this adopted child who are in denial about what challenges their child may have at school. The child is clearly presenting with issues over food, possessiveness and aggression, but the uninformed parents in their desperation to have a 'normal' child refuse to acknowledge these challenges or connect this with their child's unfortunate start in life. Unchecked and unsupported, this child is not making progress, and it is felt that this, unfortunately, is largely down to the adoptive parents' denial that their child is any different to the other children in the class.

---

As an adoptive parent there will be many situations outside of your control, but you can choose to fully educate yourself about the potential impact and challenges that your child may face at school. There are books and courses galore through which you can educate yourself. If you are prepared, you can build relationships with your child's school and teachers to help them educate themselves better as well.

## Anticipate potentially challenging topics at school

There may be topics and projects at school that are fun and engaging to most children, but could present challenges or stir up memories and emotions for your child. Mother's Day or Father's Day, for example, may be a challenge emotionally for your child; drawing a family tree; bringing in a baby photo

– all may present challenges for different reasons. School trips may present a safety challenge: if your child is one with poor attachment and poor stranger awareness, the school will have to be made aware to keep a tight hold of your child's hand! Open communications and good relations with your child's school and teachers will enable you to work together to anticipate situations and handle them in a way that your child can be fully involved and benefit from the participation. For example, on Mother's Day or Father's Day make it okay for the children in the class to make multiple cards for different people if that is what they want to do; on class trips arrange for your child to be in a smaller group with an experienced teacher with whom your child is familiar; instead of 'baby' photos (which many adopted children do not have) the teacher could ask children to bring in their 'favourite photo of when you were young'.

Partner with your child's teacher to anticipate class projects and how they may need to be presented or reshaped slightly to embrace and accommodate rather than unintentionally highlight or alienate your child.

## Remember to live your life!

Parenting can be exhausting, and arguably more so, at least in the initial weeks and months, if you are learning to parent an adopted child.

Getting out of the house itself can be a challenge, especially if your child is feeling vulnerable in their attachment to you. Even if they seem settled it is quite natural for them to have little bubbles of insecurity here and there. Anticipate early on what you may be able to do or arrange that will allow you to have time away from home without causing your child any distress. You will need time off in those early months, and it is never too soon to think about how you might achieve it.

## Managing insecurities

There were times in the first two years with Lucy when she would seem really settled, yet vulnerable at the same time. There are plenty of instances when all seemed fine but then she would have a big insecurity wobble in my absence.

One time when I was at work, Lucy had been with us over a year and seemed really settled. A usual occurrence, my husband was with Lucy one day during the school holidays and for no apparent reason Lucy started to feel really insecure. Every hour my husband called me as Lucy was sobbing and was convinced I wasn't coming home. I'd speak to her, and reassure her, she would seem okay and then I would get another phone call a little later and we would repeat the process. Needless to say I got home as soon as I could from work that day.

Although Lucy was used to what time my husband would get home after work, occasionally, she would get really tearful towards the end of the day, as she missed her daddy and wanted him to come home. She found it hard to measure time, and would work herself into a state convincing herself he wasn't coming. He wouldn't even be late – but Lucy would feel much happier and settled when everyone was home.

During Lucy's reception year at school, having been very settled for the first two terms, Lucy started to get really anxious and tearful at school as she missed us, her new family. She would apparently become inconsolable, with the teachers not really knowing what to do. To help with this, we sent in a picture of our family of four that included Lucy, to school, and she was allowed to get it out and look at it whenever she wanted, but especially if she was feeling tearful. This insecurity while at school lasted for about a month and then disappeared as quickly as it had come.

Getting out in the evenings was a challenge for us after Lucy arrived. Although we didn't try it in the first couple of months, when we did it was very unsettling for her. Once I realised this,

I let Lucy know that I had a favourite cuddly toy, and I would let her see me with it hugging it, and she knew I kept it on my bed. It was mine, it was special, she was not allowed to play with it. When I felt that she coveted it enough, I hinted that she might be allowed to take it to bed with her if I ever went out for the evening, but that it was special and it would be her job to cuddle it and look after it properly until I got home. Lucy quickly agreed and actually wanted us to go out!

The first time we tried the cuddly toy substitute, we went out for half an hour, then returned home and Lucy handed the cuddly toy back (after all she wasn't allowed it when I was in the house, it was my special toy!). The next time we went for an hour, and Lucy had fallen asleep in bed soon after we left, so I retrieved the toy in the morning. Going out after that was never a challenge, as long as Lucy has the toy she is happy. Lucy has been with us over three years now, and she still looks forward to having the toy when we go out.

---

Adopting a child can be a hugely rewarding experience for you and for them. Moving from an unsettled and potentially rocky start to a place when your child is fully integrated in your life and your family unit is growing stronger, thriving and thoroughly enjoying life together is a wonderful place to be.

It is so important to be there fully for your child, but you won't be able to do that unless you are there fully for yourself as well. Do plan ahead and think of how you may be able to get out of the house for the odd evening with your partner, spouse or friends. Getting a good dose of normality into your life occasionally will help keep you strong in times when you are feeling challenged.

## Summary

- ★ There are certain factors that have to be in place in order for an adoption placement to thrive. One of the factors is that all other children in the house bond with the new coming child. Expecting existing children to love, share and play nicely with a child who is causing them frustration, is a big ask. Make time to help existing children anticipate and learn how to interact with the new arrival. Help existing children feel as special as the new arrival. Encourage the existing children to voice any frustrations they have to you, so that you can help mitigate these. Far better a frustration shared and resolved than a frustration harboured.
- ★ It may be difficult for existing children to share their parental time with a new sibling, so make extra efforts at least in the early weeks to spend chunks of time with your other children so that they can still enjoy the one-on-one time with you, without having to share you with the new addition to the family.
- ★ Communicate, communicate, communicate with your partner, spouse and/or support network. Share thoughts and feelings, don't suppress them.
- ★ As soon as you get a sense of what additional support your child may need, start asking for it. Resources are spread thinly, and once social services perceive that your child is settled, they may naturally focus their attention elsewhere. This is not a criticism of social services; it is simply a necessity and is understandable. It is your responsibility to fight for your child and get them the support that they need.
- ★ Once your child is integrated within your family, you will want to broaden their circles and get them involved in appropriate toddler or children's activity clubs, nursery or school or whatever is appropriate for them. Depending on

where you live, there may be long waiting lists. If you are prepared to share your situation at a high level, you may feel people want to help you and your child by creating a space at the top or near the top of the list so that your child can join that club or activity sooner.

★ Your adopted child is special: they will probably have challenges that other children who have been nurtured from birth do not have, so it is vital that you co-create a good system of communication with the clubs, nursery or school that your child attends. Consistency in approach for your child whether they are at home, nursery or school will help them progress more quickly than if they have to learn to respond to different expectations at different places.

★ Recognise that your life is going to change, and that there are conscious, practical efforts you can make to quickly incorporate the elements of normality back into your life. Don't leave things to chance: the more you can anticipate and prepare with your child, the quicker you will be able to wrap into your life the elements of normality that otherwise may take longer to reappear.

# FINAL WORDS

I wish you well on your adoption journey. If we'd have known what we know now at the beginning of our adoption journey, as a family we would definitely have been better prepared for the ride and would have suffered less stress, anxiety and frustration along the way.

Those adopters who had been on the journey themselves, and had come out of the other side as a solid family unit didn't tell us of the emotional challenges, and those who had not survived the journey were not always available or able to broach the subject.

I have no doubt that some adopters will find the process of assimilating another family's child into their lives a breeze. There will be others, however, like us, that will find the emotions generated by the journey more of a challenge; they may question their motivations and sanity, and will find the process much harder. It is to these people that I reach out and encourage anticipation, preparation and an assumption that the journey may well be more emotionally taxing than you imagine. If you experience challenging emotions, recognise them as part of the process. Be confident that if you are diligent in your approach, fully nurturing your child and parenting to the best of your ability, you will see many positive changes in your child, and both your child and your family can go on to flourish.

Whatever your adoption situation, keep a journal of the small changes you start to notice as well as those that are more significant. When you read back over your notes, this journal will remind you of just how far you and your child have come. You won't necessarily notice the progress week on week, but when you reflect back on the breakthroughs they will be huge, and they will spur you on and give you fortitude to continue.

It was a rocky road for us that has now levelled out into a smooth path. Life is good. Lucy is a happy, funny, well mannered, well behaved, engaging, bright little girl, who fits in well with her peer group, has lots of friends, is doing well at school and is a very highly valued and popular member of her class community as well as our extended family. She is a complete delight and we love her as if she were our own birth child. This is a million miles from where we were and how we felt in the early weeks and months following her placement with us. Yes, we still have challenges but *every* parent has challenges of some description with their children, and many parents face far bigger challenges with their birth children than many adoptive parents face with their adoptive children.

We are not naive. We are fully aware that we may have challenges ahead as Lucy grows up and goes through different developmental stages. We need to keep reading, listening to others, learning and anticipating what may be in store for us as a family, as Lucy's unfortunate start in life may continue to have an impact at different points in her life. We are confident, however, as a result of the parenting approach we have taken, as a family unit we will be best placed to navigate these challenges together.

---

### A treasured memory

After Lucy had been with us about eight months her behaviour was settling and her speech was improving. At bedtime one evening Lucy gave me a huge hug and said, 'I really miss you,

Mummy', to which I replied, a little confused, 'But I'm right here, Lucy'. Lucy looked at me and explained, 'But Mummy, I miss you before, when I there with other mummies'. To which I responded, 'Oh Lucy, I missed you then as well'. To which Lucy simply acknowledged, 'I know Mummy, I could hear you crying'.

I think this was Lucy's way of expressing that she realised she was finally in a home with a family that wanted her, loved her and cared for her. These were feelings that she had deserved all along, and although she didn't know the extent of what she was missing before, she really understood it now.

---

We are frequently asked, if we knew then what we know now, would we go through the whole adoption process again, with all of its challenges and emotional turmoil? With hand on heart, knowing what we know, our answer is an emphatic 'in a heartbeat'.

If you would like more help or resources, please visit www.sophieashtonadoption.co.uk

# GLOSSARY

All terms below, I have explained with an interpretation relevant to this book. Some terms can apply to adults as well, but for the purpose and focus of this book I refer to children in my explanation.

**Adoption day**: In the capacity of this book is used to describe the day that the court rules adoptive parents now have legal responsibility for the child placed in their care.

**Adoption matching panel**: A proposed match between a child and adoptive parents will be presented to an adoption matching panel that will consist of a number of people in roles such as: a medical adviser, legal adviser, a local councillor, experienced social workers, people independent of social services and a minute taker.

**Adoption order**: This is the order made by the court that gives parental responsibility for a child to the adopter(s).

**Attachment**: The close feeling of connection that children develop towards those people that care for them.

**Attachment disorder**: A condition in which children have difficulty forming lasting relationships.

**Attention deficit disorder (ADD)/attention deficit hyperactivity disorder (ADHD)**: A well-recognised neuro-developmental condition that combines elements of inattentiveness, hyperactivity and impulsiveness. Children with these symptoms often have a short attention span, are easily distracted, restless, fidget constantly and are impulsive in nature.

**Disruption**: When a child who is placed with a family for adoption is handed back into the care system.

**Dysregulation**: Emotional dysregulation or becoming 'dysregulated' is a term frequently used in the adoption world to explain the emotional state of a child when their emotional response to a situation is poorly modulated and does not fall within the conventionally acceptable range of emotional responses to a situation. Children may appear quite calm in some situations and then react in an out-of-control, random, exaggerated way in other situations, often displaying behaviours much younger or older than their years.

**Emotional age**: The presenting age of an individual as determined by their stage of emotional development. Emotional age may be older or younger than their actual age measured by time since birth.

**Fight, flight or freeze**: This is the body's response that is triggered when we feel a strong emotion like fear. It enables us to react with appropriate actions, to run away, to fight or sometimes to freeze to be a less visible target. The adrenal glands release adrenalin to fuel the response.

**Introductions/introduction period**: The intense period of time that you spend initially meeting with your child, getting to know them and transitioning the parenting from their foster carers to you. The introduction period culminates with your child moving into your home.

**Hypervigilance**: This is an enhanced state of sensory sensitivity exhibited by children who through prior experience are conditioned to detect threats. This enhanced sensitive state is often accompanied by an exaggerated behavioural response to situations. The child may be ultrasensitive to movement in their peripheral vision, or alarmed by sounds that do not cause concern to others.

**Life-story work**: This is any intervention that you can do with your child that helps them learn more about their past, present and future, and helps them to develop their identity.

**Matching panel**: The panel of people that approves the match between you and the child you wish to adopt.

**Metaphor**: A description that helps bring the meaning of a concept to life by transferring the meaning and association with something familiar to something less familiar.

**Sensory overload**: When one or more of our senses experience overstimulation from the environment. The potential for sensory overload is measured by the child's capacity to cope with sensory stimulation rather than the quantity of environmental triggers.

**Sensory processing disorder**: A condition where the brain has problems receiving and responding to information that comes in through the senses, resulting in children under- or overreacting to certain sensory stimulation.

**Time out**: An educational and parenting technique recommended by some developmental psychologists as an effective form of child discipline. Its benefits and drawbacks are widely debated on the internet and written about by many parenting experts.

# BIBLIOGRAPHY


Adoption UK (2012) *Education Now*. London: Adoption UK.

Archer, C. (1999) *First Steps in Parenting the Child Who Hurts – Tiddlers and Toddlers*. London: Jessica Kingsley Publishers (original work published in 1997).

Argent, H. (2010) *Adopting a Brother or Sister – A Guide for Young Children*. London: British Association for Adoption and Fostering (BAAF).

Argent, H. (2014) *Related by Adoption – A Handbook for Grandparents and Other Relatives*. London: British Association for Adoption and Fostering (BAAF).

Bagnall, S. (2008) *The Teazle's Baby Bunny*. London: British Association for Adoption and Fostering (BAAF).

Biddulph S. (2013) *Raising Girls – Helping your Daughter to Grow up Wise, Warm and Strong*. London: HarperThorsons.

Biddulph, S. (2015) *Raising Boys – Why Boys are Different and How to Help them Become Happy and Well Balanced Men*. London: HarperThorsons (original work published in 1998).

Cairns, K. (2002) *Attachment, Trauma and Resilience – Therapeutic Caring for Children*. London: British Association for Adoption and Fostering (BAAF).

Donovan, S. (2013) *No Matter What – An Adoptive Family's Story of Hope, Love and Healing*. London: Jessica Kingsley Publishers.

Faber, A. and Mazlish, E. (2012) *How to Talk: Siblings Without Rivalry – Help your Children Live Together so You Can Live too*. London: Piccadilly Press (original work published in 1987).

Faber, A. and Mazlish, E. (2013) *How to Talk So Kids Will Listen and Listen So Kids Will Talk*. New York: Avon Books Inc. (original work published in 1982).

Fahlberg, V. (2012) *A Child's Journey Through Placement*. London: British Association for Adoption and Fostering (BAAF) (original work published in 1991).

Foster, C. (2008) *Big Steps for Little People – Parenting Your Adopted Child*. London: Jessica Kingsley Publishers.

Foxton, J. (2001) *Nutmeg Gets Adopted*. London: British Association for Adoption and Fostering (BAAF).

Hughes, D.A. (2009) *Attachment Focused Parenting – Effective Strategies to Care for Children*. New York: W.W. Norton & Company Inc.

Kasza, K. (2003) *A Mother for Chocco*. London: Puffin Books (original work published in 1996).

Kubler-Ross, E. (2009) *On Death and Dying – 40th Anniversary Edition*. London: Routledge (original work published in 1969).

Livingstone, T. (2005) *Child of Our Time – How to Achieve the Best for your Child from Conception to 5 years*. London: Random House Group Ltd.

Lord, J. (2013) *Adopting a Child – A Guide for People Interested in Adoption*. London: British Association for Adoption and Fostering (BAAF) (original work published in 2002).

Morris, A. (1999) *The Adoption Experience – Families Who Give Children a Second Chance*. London: Jessica Kingsley Publishers.

Owen, N. (2001) *The Magic of Metaphor – 77 Stories for Teachers, Trainers and Thinkers*. Bancyfelin: Crown House Publishing Company.

Pauc, R. (2006) *Is That My Child – Exploding the Myths of Dyspraxia, Dyslexia, Tourette's Syndrome of Childhood, ADD, ADHD and OCD*. London: Virgin Books Ltd.

Post, B.B. (2009) *The Great Behaviour Breakdown*. Palmyra, VA: Post Institute & Associates.

Rees, J. (2009) *Life Story Books for Adopted Children – A Family Friendly Approach*. London: Jessica Kingsley Publishers.

Salter, A.N. (2013) *The Adopter's Handbook – Information, Resources and Services for Adoptive Parents*. London: British Association for Adoption and Fostering (BAAF) (original work published in 2002).

Statham, B. (2007) *What's Really in Your Basket?* Chichester: Summersdale.

Stone, D., Patton, B. and Heen, S. (2000) *Difficult Conversations – How to Discuss What Matters Most*. London: Penguin Books (original work published in 1999).

Tynan, B. (2008) *Make Your Child Brilliant – Uncovering your Child's Hidden Gifts*. London: Quadrille Publishing Ltd.

Wilson, P. (1999) *The Big Book of Calm: Over 100 Successful Techniques for Relaxing Mind and Body*. London: Penguin Group.